Tweets for every occasion

(Ok, Xeets?)

By Isabelle Carrington

Created in part with the help of Qyx AI Book Creator.

Table of Contents

Introduction

Let's face it, we've all been there. Staring at that blinking cursor on Twitter (or X, as it's now fashionably called), fingers hovering over the keyboard, mind drawing a complete blank. You want to say *something* – be it witty, profound, or just plain informative – but the perfect 280 characters seem to be hiding in some remote corner of the internet, refusing to be summoned.

That's where this book comes in.

Whether you're a seasoned Twitter veteran or a newbie just starting to explore the platform, "Tweets for Every Occasion" is your guide to crafting engaging and effective tweets for literally any situation life throws your way. From celebrating life's big moments to ranting (politely, of course) about your pet peeves, we've got you covered.

This isn't just another dry social media guide filled with jargon and complicated algorithms. We're keeping it light, fun, and practical. Think of it as your friendly Twitter companion, offering a helping hand and a hearty chuckle whenever you need it.

Inside, you'll find chapters dedicated to a wide range of topics:

- **Need to congratulate a friend on their new job?** Chapter 1 on celebrating life's milestones has got your back.

- **Want to express your undying love for your favorite sports team (without resorting to ALL CAPS)?** Chapter 2 on cheering your team on will show you how.

- **Feeling inspired by a breathtaking sunset?** Chapter 8 on connecting with nature will help you capture that feeling in a tweet.

- **Just finished reading an amazing book and want to share your thoughts?** Chapter 11 on bookworm tweets is your go-to guide.

- **And yes, we even tackle the tricky world of politics and current events** (with a focus on respectful dialogue, of course) in Chapters 3 and 17.

Each chapter is packed with tweet examples, tips, and tricks to spark your creativity and help you find your unique Twitter voice. We'll also delve into the finer points of the platform, like mastering the art of the hashtag (Chapter 23) and building your personal brand (Chapter 20).

So, whether you're aiming to become the next Twitter influencer or simply want to share your thoughts and connect with others, this book is your roadmap to navigating the exciting world of 280 characters.

Get ready to ditch the writer's block and unleash your inner Twitter superstar. The world is waiting to hear what you have to say!

Note:

This book was created in part with the help of Qyx AI Book Creator by QyxAI.com.

CHAPTER ONE: Celebrating Life's Milestones

Life is a series of moments, big and small, that shape who we are and where we're going. And what better way to share those moments with the world than through a well-crafted tweet? From graduations and weddings to new jobs and personal achievements, Twitter (or X) provides a platform to celebrate these milestones with friends, family, and followers.

This chapter will equip you with a treasure chest of tweet ideas for life's biggest and most exciting moments. We'll explore various milestones, offering examples and tips to help you craft tweets that are both heartfelt and engaging.

Graduations: Caps Off to a New Beginning

Graduation marks the culmination of years of hard work, late-night study sessions, and perhaps a few too many caffeine-fueled all-nighters. It's a time to celebrate accomplishments and look forward to the future. Here are some tweet ideas to capture the spirit of this special occasion:

For the Graduate:

- "Officially a graduate! So excited to start this next chapter. #ClassOf2024 #GraduationDay"

- "Couldn't have done it without the support of my amazing family and friends. Thank you for everything! #Graditude #DiplomaInHand"

- "Feeling a mix of excitement and nostalgia as I say goodbye to college. Here's to new adventures! #GraduationCeremony #NextChapter"

- "Time to trade in textbooks for paychecks (hopefully!). #JobHunting #GraduateLife"

- "To my fellow graduates: Let's go change the world! #Commencement #FutureIsBright"

For Friends and Family:

- "So proud of my [son/daughter/friend/sibling] on their graduation! Wishing you all the best in your future endeavors. #ProudParent #GraduationDay"

- "Congratulations [graduate's name]! Your hard work and dedication have paid off. #ClassOf2024 #SoProud"

- "Can't believe how fast time flies. It seems like just yesterday we were dropping you off for your first day of school. Congratulations on graduating! #Graduation #TimeFlies"

- "Cheers to the graduate! May your future be filled with success and happiness. #GraduationCelebration #Cheers"

Pro-Tip: Include relevant hashtags like #Graduation, #ClassOf[Year], and the name of your school or university to increase the visibility of your tweets.

Weddings: Tying the Knot and Tweeting About It

Weddings are joyous celebrations of love and commitment, filled with laughter, happy tears, and maybe a little bit of dancing (or a lot, depending on the crowd!). Whether you're the happy couple, a member of the wedding party, or a guest, Twitter is a great way to share the love and excitement of the big day.

For the Happy Couple:

- "We did it! Officially Mr. and Mrs. [Last Name]. Thank you to everyone who made our wedding day so special. #JustMarried #WeddingDay"

- "Today was a dream come true. So lucky to have found my soulmate. #HappilyEverAfter #WeddingBliss"

- "Starting our forever together. Can't wait to see what adventures lie ahead. #MrAndMrs #Newlyweds"

- "Dancing the night away with the love of my life. #WeddingReception #BestDayEver"

For the Wedding Party and Guests:

- "Wishing the happy couple a lifetime of love and happiness! #WeddingDay #BeautifulCeremony"

- "So honored to be a part of [couple's names] special day. #Bridesmaid #Groomsman #WeddingFun"

- "What a beautiful wedding! The love between these two is truly inspiring. #LoveIsInTheAir #WeddingVibes"

- "Celebrating the new Mr. and Mrs. [Last Name]! May your journey together be filled with joy and laughter. #WeddingToast #CheersToTheHappyCouple"

Pro-Tip: If the couple has a wedding hashtag, be sure to include it in your tweets. This helps to gather all the wedding-related posts in one place, creating a fun and memorable online keepsake.

New Jobs and Career Milestones: Tweeting Your Professional Wins

Landing a new job, getting a promotion, or achieving a significant career milestone is definitely tweet-worthy! Sharing your professional successes on Twitter can help you build your professional network, connect with colleagues, and inspire others.

For the New Hire/Promotee:

- "Excited to announce that I've joined [Company Name] as their new [Job Title]! Looking forward to this new chapter in my career. #NewJob #CareerGoals"

- "Thrilled to have been promoted to [New Position] at [Company Name]! Grateful for the opportunity to grow and learn. #CareerGrowth #Promotion"

- "After months of hard work, I finally achieved [Career Milestone]! Feeling proud and motivated to keep pushing forward. #AchievementUnlocked #CareerSuccess"

- "Ready to take on new challenges and make a difference in my new role at [Company Name]. #LetsDoThis #CareerJourney"

For Colleagues and Friends:

- "Congratulations to [Name] on their new job at [Company Name]! You're going to be amazing! #NewBeginnings #CareerMove"

- "So proud of [Name] for getting that well-deserved promotion! You've worked hard and earned it. #Congratulations #CareerMilestones"

- "Wishing [Name] all the best in their new role as [Job Title]! Excited to see what you accomplish. #GoGetEm #CareerSuccess"

Pro-Tip: When tweeting about your career, consider using relevant industry hashtags and mentioning your company's Twitter handle. This can help increase the visibility of your tweets and connect you with other professionals in your field.

Personal Achievements: Sharing Your Wins, Big and Small

Life's milestones aren't limited to graduations, weddings, and career advancements. Personal achievements, no matter how big or small, deserve to be celebrated! Whether you've finally finished that marathon you've been training for, learned a new language, or overcome a personal challenge, Twitter can be a great place to share your accomplishments and inspire others.

Examples:

- "Just finished my first marathon! It was tough, but so worth it. Feeling proud and accomplished. #MarathonRunner #FitnessGoals"

- "Finally fluent in Spanish! Hola mundo! #LanguageLearning #AchievementUnlocked"

- "Overcame my fear of public speaking and gave a presentation today. One step outside my comfort zone! #PersonalGrowth #ChallengeAccepted"

- "Reached my weight loss goal! Hard work and dedication pay off. #FitnessJourney #HealthyLifestyle"

- "Learned how to play the guitar! My fingers may be sore, but my heart is full. #NewSkills #MusicLover"

Pro-Tip: Be authentic and share your journey. People connect with real stories and experiences. Don't be afraid to share your struggles and how you overcame them. Your vulnerability can inspire others to pursue their own goals.

Celebrating Others: Spreading Joy and Showing Support

Celebrating the milestones of others is just as important as celebrating your own. When someone you know achieves something special, take a moment to acknowledge their accomplishments on Twitter. It's a simple gesture that can mean a lot.

Examples:

- "Huge congrats to my friend [Name] on winning the [Award/Competition]! So well-deserved! #ProudFriend #YouRock"

- "Sending a shout-out to my amazing coworker [Name] on their work anniversary! Thank you for your dedication and hard work. #WorkAnniversary #Teamwork"

- "So proud of my [son/daughter/sibling/friend] for [Achievement]! You're an inspiration! #ProudParent #AmazingKid"

- "Congratulations to [Name] on [Milestone]! Wishing you all the best in this new chapter. #Cheers #YouGotThis"

Pro-Tip: Personalize your tweets to make them more meaningful. Instead of just saying "Congratulations," mention something specific about the person's achievement or why you're proud of them.

A Few Final Tips for Tweeting Life's Milestones

- **Keep it concise:** Twitter's character limit encourages brevity. Get straight to the point and convey your message effectively.

- **Use visuals:** Adding a photo or video to your tweet can make it more engaging and memorable.

- **Tag relevant people:** If you're tweeting about someone else's milestone, be sure to tag them in your tweet.

- **Engage with replies and comments:** Respond to people who congratulate you or comment on your tweet. It's a great way to show your appreciation and build connections.

- **Be mindful of privacy:** Not everyone wants their personal life broadcast on social media. Before tweeting about someone else's milestone, make sure they're comfortable with you sharing it publicly.

Life's milestones are precious moments that deserve to be celebrated and shared. By following the tips and examples in this chapter, you can craft tweets that capture the joy and excitement of these occasions, connecting with others and spreading positivity along the way. So, go forth and tweet your heart out!

CHAPTER TWO: Cheering on Your Team

Sports. They unite us, they divide us, they make us scream at our televisions like lunatics. And in the age of social media, they provide a constant source of conversation, debate, and, let's be honest, some pretty epic Twitter (or X) meltdowns.

Whether you're a die-hard fan who paints their face in team colors or a casual observer who enjoys the occasional game, this chapter will help you navigate the world of sports-related tweets. We'll explore different ways to express your fandom, celebrate victories, commiserate over losses, and engage in friendly (or not-so-friendly) banter with fellow fans.

Pre-Game Hype: Building the Excitement

The anticipation leading up to a big game is almost as exciting as the game itself. Twitter is the perfect platform to build the hype, share your predictions, and connect with other fans who are just as pumped as you are.

Tweet Examples:

- "Is it game day yet?! Can't wait to see [Your Team] dominate the field/court/ice tonight! #GameDay #LetsGo[TeamName]"

- "Feeling confident about a [Your Team] victory tonight. [Opponent] better be prepared! #Prediction #[TeamName]GonnaWin"

- "Game day rituals: Jersey on, snacks ready, lucky socks in place. Let's do this! #SuperstitiousButNotSuperstitious #GameDayPrep"

- "Anyone else nervous/excited for tonight's game? Let's hear your predictions in the comments! #[TeamName]vs[Opponent] #GameDayChat"

- "Tailgating with the crew before the big game! Let's get this party started! #TailgateParty #[TeamName]Fans"

Pro-Tip: Use relevant hashtags to increase the visibility of your tweets and join the conversation with other fans. Team hashtags, game-specific hashtags, and general sports hashtags (e.g., #NFL, #NBA, #MLB) are all great options.

During the Game: Live-Tweeting the Action

As the game unfolds, Twitter becomes a virtual stadium filled with fans sharing their thoughts, reactions, and play-by-play commentary. Live-tweeting is a fun way to engage with other fans in real-time and experience the game together, even if you're miles apart.

Tweet Examples (Positive):

- "YES! [Player Name] with the clutch shot/goal/touchdown! [Your Team] is on fire! #Go[TeamName] #AmazingPlay"

- "That was an incredible save/block/tackle! [Player Name] is a beast! #DefenseWinsChampionships #[TeamName]Strong"

- "The crowd is going wild! The energy in the stadium is electric! #GameDayVibes #[TeamName]Nation"

- "Loving the teamwork and hustle from [Your Team] tonight. They're playing like a well-oiled machine! #TeamEffort #[TeamName]Pride"

- "Can't believe how close this game is! Every possession matters! #NailBiter #[TeamName]vs[Opponent]"

Tweet Examples (Negative):

- "Come on, refs! That was a terrible call! #BadCall #GetItTogether"

- "[Player Name], what was that?! You gotta make that play! #Frustrating #StepItUp"

- "We need to get our offense/defense going. This is not the [Your Team] I know! #WakeUpCall #LetsGo[TeamName]"

- "Can't believe we're losing to [Opponent]. This is not how I wanted to spend my [Day of the Week]. #Disappointing #[TeamName]NeedsToRally"

- "I need a drink. #StressfulGame #[TeamName]PleaseDontLose"

Pro-Tip: Be mindful of spoilers. If you're watching a game on delay, be aware that your live tweets might spoil the outcome for others. Consider using a spoiler warning hashtag (e.g., #SpoilerAlert) if you're tweeting about a key play or the final score.

Post-Game Reactions: Celebrating Victories and Handling Defeats

The final whistle blows, the game is over, and the emotions are running high. Whether your team emerged victorious or suffered a heartbreaking loss, Twitter is the place to share your post-game thoughts and connect with other fans who are experiencing the same rollercoaster of emotions.

Tweet Examples (Victory):

- "YES! [Your Team] wins! What an amazing game! So proud of our team! #Victory #[TeamName]Champions"

- "[Player Name] was the MVP tonight! Incredible performance! #GameChanger #[TeamName]Hero"

- "That was a hard-fought win! [Your Team] showed grit and determination. #NeverGiveUp #[TeamName]Strong"

- "Celebrating with my fellow [Team Name] fans! Tonight's a good night! #VictoryParty #[TeamName]Nation"

- "Can't wait for the next game! Let's keep this winning streak going! #[TeamName]OnFire #NextGame"

Tweet Examples (Defeat):

- "Tough loss for [Your Team] tonight. We'll get 'em next time! #NeverGiveUp #[TeamName]Strong"

- "Disappointed with the outcome, but proud of the effort. We'll learn from this and come back stronger. #BounceBack #[TeamName]Pride"

- "It's okay to be sad, [Team Name] fans. We'll have our day. #Heartbreak #ButWeStillLoveYou"

- "On to the next one. We'll be back. #WeBelieve #[TeamName]Forever"

- "At least the [Food/Beverage] was good. #SilverLinings #[TeamName]FanProblems"

Pro-Tip: Win or lose, be respectful of other teams and their fans. Avoid gloating or making derogatory comments. Remember that it's just a game, and sportsmanship is important.

Player Appreciation: Showing Love for Your Favorite Athletes

Every team has its star players, the ones who make your jaw drop with their skills and inspire you with their dedication. Twitter is a great way to show your appreciation for these athletes and let them know how much you admire their talent.

Tweet Examples:

- "[Player Name] is an absolute legend! Best [Position] in the game! #GOAT #[TeamName]MVP"

- "So impressed with [Player Name]'s work ethic and dedication. A true role model for young athletes. #Inspiration #[TeamName]Pride"

- "Thank you, [Player Name], for everything you do for our team! We're lucky to have you! #FanLove #[TeamName]Forever"

- "Can't wait to see what [Player Name] does next! The future is bright! #RisingStar #[TeamName]Future"

- "Sending positive vibes to [Player Name] as they recover from their injury. Get well soon! #WeMissYou #[TeamName]Family"

Pro-Tip: If you're tagging a player in your tweet, make sure you're using their correct Twitter handle. Also, be mindful of their privacy and avoid sending overly personal or intrusive messages.

Engaging in Friendly Banter: The Art of the Twitter Trash Talk

Sports rivalries are part of what makes the games so exciting. And Twitter provides the perfect platform for engaging in some friendly (or not-so-friendly) banter with fans of opposing teams. But remember, there's a fine line between playful trash talk and crossing the line into disrespect.

Tweet Examples (Friendly Banter):

- "Sorry, [Opponent] fans, but [Your Team] is just too good tonight! #TooEasy #[TeamName]Domination"

- "Looks like [Opponent] forgot how to play [Sport]. Maybe they should try a different sport? #JustSaying #[TeamName]Rules"

- "I'm not saying [Opponent] is bad, but... they're pretty bad. #SorryNotSorry #[TeamName]IsBetter"

- "I'm starting to feel bad for [Opponent] fans. They must be used to losing by now. #Ouch #[TeamName]WinsAgain"

- "Hey [Opponent] fans, don't worry, there's always next year! #Maybe #[TeamName]IsTooStrong"

Tweet Examples (Crossing the Line):

- "[Opponent] fans are all a bunch of [Insult]. They don't even deserve to be called fans. #ToxicFandom #NoRespect"

- "I hope [Player Name] gets injured. They're the only reason [Opponent] is even in this game. #DirtyPlayer #DeservesToLose"

- "[Opponent] is the worst team in the league. They should just disband. #TheySuck #WasteOfSpace"

- "I can't believe anyone would root for [Opponent]. They're a disgrace to the sport. #Shameful #[TeamName]IsTheOnlyRealTeam"

Pro-Tip: Always err on the side of caution when engaging in trash talk. Avoid personal insults, derogatory language, and anything that could be considered hateful or discriminatory. Remember that sports are meant to be fun, and healthy competition is part of the game.

Sharing Memes and GIFs: Adding Humor to the Conversation

The internet is a treasure trove of sports-related memes and GIFs, and Twitter is the perfect place to share them with your fellow fans. A well-timed meme or GIF can perfectly capture the emotions of a game, add humor to the conversation, and make your tweets more engaging.

Examples:

- **Share a meme celebrating a big win:** Find a meme that depicts your team's dominance or your opponent's despair.

- **Share a GIF of a funny moment from the game:** Capture a hilarious play, a coach's reaction, or a fan's antics.

- **Use a meme to express your frustration after a loss:** Find a meme that captures the feeling of disappointment or anger.

- **Share a GIF of your favorite player celebrating:** Show your appreciation for your team's star athletes.

- **Create your own meme or GIF:** If you're feeling creative, use a meme generator or GIF maker to create your own unique content.

Pro-Tip: Make sure the memes and GIFs you share are relevant to the conversation and appropriate for your audience. Avoid anything that could be considered offensive or harmful.

Following Sports News and Commentary: Staying Up-to-Date

Twitter is a great source for breaking news, analysis, and commentary from sports journalists, experts, and insiders. By following reputable sources, you can stay up-to-date on the latest happenings in the sports world and engage in informed discussions with other fans.

Examples of Accounts to Follow:

- **Official league accounts:** (e.g., @NFL, @NBA, @MLB)

- **Team accounts:** (e.g., @Yankees, @Lakers, @Patriots)

- **Sports news outlets:** (e.g., @ESPN, @BleacherReport, @TheAthletic)

- **Sports journalists and commentators:** (e.g., @AdamSchefter, @WojESPN, @JeffPassan)

- **Sports bloggers and podcasters:** (e.g., @BillSimmons, @ZachLowe_NBA, @KenRosenthalMLB)

Pro-Tip: Be critical of the information you see on Twitter. Not everything you read is accurate or unbiased. Verify information from multiple sources before sharing it with others.

Using Twitter to Connect with Fellow Fans: Building Your Sports Community

Twitter can be a great way to connect with other fans who share your passion for your favorite team or sport. By following other fans, engaging in conversations, and participating in Twitter chats, you can build a vibrant online community and share your love of the game with like-minded individuals.

Examples of How to Connect:

- **Follow other fans:** Search for fans of your team or sport and follow them.

- **Participate in Twitter chats:** Many sports teams and media outlets host regular Twitter chats where fans can discuss the latest news and happenings.

- **Join fan groups and communities:** Search for Twitter groups and communities dedicated to your team or sport.

- **Engage in conversations:** Reply to tweets from other fans, share your thoughts and opinions, and participate in debates.

- **Use relevant hashtags:** Hashtags can help you connect with other fans who are talking about the same topics.

Pro-Tip: Be respectful and courteous to other fans, even if you disagree with their opinions. Remember that everyone is entitled to their own perspective, and healthy debate is part of what makes sports fandom so engaging.

A Few Final Tips for Tweeting About Sports

- **Be passionate but respectful:** Show your love for your team, but don't let it turn into negativity or disrespect towards others.

- **Use humor wisely:** Memes and GIFs can be a great way to add humor to your tweets, but make sure they're appropriate and relevant.

- **Don't be afraid to share your opinions:** Twitter is a platform for sharing your thoughts and engaging in discussions. But remember to be respectful of others' views, even if you disagree.

- **Use relevant hashtags:** Hashtags can help you connect with other fans and increase the visibility of your tweets.

- **Engage with other fans:** Reply to tweets, participate in chats, and join fan communities to build your sports network on Twitter.

Sports are a powerful force that can bring people together and create lasting memories. By following the tips and examples in this chapter, you can use Twitter to enhance your sports fandom, connect with other fans, and share your passion for the game with the world. So, go forth and tweet your heart out – your team is counting on you!

CHAPTER THREE: Navigating the World of Politics (Respectfully)

Politics. It's a topic that can spark passionate debates, ignite strong opinions, and, let's face it, sometimes lead to heated arguments (both online and offline). In the realm of Twitter (or X), where brevity reigns supreme and opinions fly fast and furious, navigating the political landscape can be a tricky endeavor.

This chapter aims to equip you with the tools and strategies to engage in political discussions on Twitter in a way that is both informative and respectful. We'll explore various aspects of political tweeting, from expressing your own views to engaging with those who hold opposing beliefs, all while maintaining a civil and productive tone.

Why Engage in Political Discussions on Twitter?

In today's interconnected world, social media platforms like Twitter have become important avenues for public discourse. Engaging in political discussions on Twitter can offer several benefits:

- **Raising awareness:** You can use Twitter to share information about important political issues, candidates, and policies, helping to educate and inform your followers.

- **Promoting civic engagement:** Twitter can be a powerful tool for encouraging people to participate in the political process, whether it's by voting, contacting their elected officials, or attending rallies and protests.

- **Holding elected officials accountable:** Twitter provides a platform for holding politicians and government agencies accountable for their actions and decisions.

- **Connecting with like-minded individuals:** You can use Twitter to connect with other people who share your political views and build a community of support.

- **Engaging in respectful debate:** While it can be challenging, Twitter can also be a space for engaging in constructive dialogue with people who hold different political perspectives.

Expressing Your Political Views: Finding Your Voice

Sharing your political views on Twitter can be a powerful way to make your voice heard and contribute to the public conversation. However, it's important to do so in a way that is thoughtful, respectful, and informative.

Tips for Expressing Your Political Views:

- **Be informed:** Before tweeting about a political issue, take the time to educate yourself on the topic. Read articles from reputable sources, research different perspectives, and consider the nuances of the issue.

- **Be clear and concise:** Twitter's character limit encourages brevity. Get straight to the point and express your views in a clear and concise manner.

- **Be respectful:** Even when disagreeing with others, maintain a respectful tone. Avoid personal attacks, name-calling, and inflammatory language.

- **Provide evidence:** Support your claims with evidence from credible sources. Link to articles, studies, or data that back up your points.

- **Use hashtags strategically:** Hashtags can help increase the visibility of your tweets and connect you with others who are interested in the same topics. Use relevant political hashtags (e.g., #Elections2024, #ClimateChange, #Healthcare) to reach a wider audience.

- **Be open to feedback:** Not everyone will agree with your views. Be prepared to engage in constructive dialogue with those who hold different perspectives.

Examples of Tweets Expressing Political Views:

- "I believe that access to affordable healthcare is a fundamental human right. We need to expand healthcare coverage to ensure that everyone has the care they need. #HealthcareForAll #MedicareForAll"

- "Climate change is a real and urgent threat to our planet. We need to take bold action to reduce greenhouse gas emissions and transition to a clean energy economy. #ClimateActionNow #GreenNewDeal"

- "I'm concerned about the rise of political extremism and the spread of misinformation. We need to promote critical thinking and media literacy to combat these threats to our democracy. #ProtectDemocracy #FightMisinformation"

- "I'm voting for [Candidate Name] because I believe they have the experience and vision to lead our country forward. They will fight for working families and protect our environment. #Vote[CandidateName] #Election2024"

- "I'm disappointed by the recent decision by the Supreme Court to overturn Roe v. Wade. We need to protect a woman's right to choose. #ReproductiveRightsAreHumanRights #MyBodyMyChoice"

Engaging with Opposing Views: Promoting Respectful Dialogue

One of the biggest challenges of engaging in political discussions on Twitter is encountering people who hold opposing views. It can be tempting to dismiss or attack those who disagree with you, but this rarely leads to productive dialogue. Instead, strive to engage with opposing views in a respectful and open-minded manner.

Tips for Engaging with Opposing Views:

- **Listen actively:** Before responding to someone who disagrees with you, take the time to understand their perspective. Read their tweet carefully and try to see the issue from their point of view.

- **Ask clarifying questions:** If you're unsure about someone's position, ask them to clarify their views. This can help avoid misunderstandings and promote a more productive conversation.

- **Find common ground:** Even when you disagree on fundamental issues, there may be areas of common ground that you can identify. Focusing on these shared values can help build bridges and foster mutual understanding.

- **Challenge ideas, not people:** When responding to opposing views, focus on challenging the ideas presented, rather than attacking the person who holds them. Avoid personal insults, name-calling, and ad hominem attacks.

- **Be willing to change your mind:** Entering a conversation with the assumption that you're always right is not conducive to productive dialogue. Be open to the possibility that you might learn something new or change your mind based on the evidence and arguments presented.

- **Know when to disengage:** Not all conversations are worth having. If you find yourself in a discussion that is becoming unproductive or disrespectful, it's okay to disengage. You don't have to engage with everyone who disagrees with you.

Examples of Tweets Engaging with Opposing Views:

- "I understand your concerns about the economic impact of [Policy], but I believe that the social benefits outweigh the costs. Studies have shown that [Policy] would reduce poverty and improve public health. #[PolicyDebate]"

- "I disagree with your assertion that [Candidate] is a socialist. Their policies are actually more aligned with [Ideology]. Here's an article that explains their platform in more detail: [Link to Article] #[CandidateName]"

- "I appreciate your willingness to engage in this discussion, even though we disagree on this issue. I think it's important to have these conversations so that we can better understand each other's perspectives. #CivilDiscourse #PoliticalDebate"

- "I'm not sure I understand your point about [Issue]. Could you please clarify what you mean by [Specific Point]? I'm open to hearing your perspective. #SeekingUnderstanding #OpenDialogue"

- "I've enjoyed this conversation, but I think we've reached a point where we're just repeating ourselves. I respect your right to hold a different opinion, but I don't think we're going to change each other's minds on this issue. #AgreeToDisagree #EndofDiscussion"

Dealing with Political Trolls and Bots: Staying Above the Fray

Unfortunately, the political landscape on Twitter can be a breeding ground for trolls and bots that aim to disrupt conversations, spread misinformation, and sow discord. It's important to be aware of these tactics and to develop strategies for dealing with them effectively.

Identifying Political Trolls and Bots:

- **Suspicious usernames:** Trolls and bots often have generic or nonsensical usernames.

- **Lack of personal information:** Their profiles may lack personal details or have very little activity.

- **Repetitive or automated tweets:** They may tweet the same message repeatedly or use automated tools to generate tweets.

- **Inflammatory language:** They may use inflammatory language, personal attacks, and insults to provoke a reaction.

- **Suspicious links:** They may share links to fake news websites or other dubious sources.

Strategies for Dealing with Political Trolls and Bots:

- **Don't feed the trolls:** Responding to trolls often only encourages them. Ignoring them is often the best course of action.

- **Report and block:** If a troll is harassing you or spreading misinformation, you can report their account to Twitter and block them from interacting with you.

- **Mute or unfollow:** If you find yourself constantly encountering trolls or bots, you can mute or unfollow them to avoid seeing their tweets.

- **Use Twitter's advanced search features:** You can use Twitter's advanced search features to filter out tweets from accounts that you don't want to see.

- **Focus on building a positive community:** Surround yourself with like-minded individuals who are committed to respectful dialogue and productive conversation.

Examples of Tweets Dealing with Political Trolls and Bots:

- "I'm not going to engage with this account because it appears to be a bot. I encourage everyone to be cautious about interacting with accounts that spread misinformation and engage in harmful behavior. #BotAlert #FightMisinformation"

- "This tweet is full of hateful and divisive language. I'm reporting this account to Twitter and blocking it. There's no place for this kind of behavior on this platform. #NoHateSpeech #ReportAndBlock"

- "I'm muting this account because it's constantly tweeting irrelevant and inflammatory content. I'm only interested in engaging with accounts that are committed to respectful dialogue. #MuteButton #FocusOnPositivity"

- "I'm unfollowing this account because it's been sharing fake news and conspiracy theories. I only want to follow accounts that provide accurate and reliable information. #Unfollow #FactCheck"

- "I'm focusing on building a positive and supportive community on Twitter. I encourage everyone to follow accounts that promote respectful dialogue, share accurate information, and engage in constructive conversations. #PositiveVibes #TwitterCommunity"

Promoting Political Participation: Encouraging Civic Engagement

Twitter can be a powerful tool for promoting political participation and encouraging civic engagement. You can use the platform to share information about upcoming elections, voter registration deadlines, candidate forums, and other opportunities to get involved in the political process.

Tips for Promoting Political Participation:

- **Share voter registration information:** Remind your followers about voter registration deadlines and provide links to online registration resources.

- **Promote candidate forums and debates:** Share information about upcoming candidate forums and debates so that your followers can learn more about the candidates and their positions on the issues.

- **Encourage people to vote:** On Election Day, remind your followers to vote and share information about polling locations and hours.

- **Share information about important political issues:** Educate your followers about the issues that are at stake in the election and encourage them to research the candidates' positions on these topics.

- **Highlight the importance of civic engagement:** Remind your followers that their voices matter and that they can make a difference by participating in the political process.

Examples of Tweets Promoting Political Participation:

- "The deadline to register to vote in the upcoming election is [Date]. Make sure you're registered so that you can have your voice heard! Here's a link to register online: [Link to Voter Registration Website] #RegisterToVote #Vote2024"

- "There's a candidate forum for the [Office] election happening on [Date] at [Time] at [Location]. This is a great opportunity to learn more about the candidates and their positions on the issues. #CandidateForum #[Office]Election"

- "It's Election Day! Don't forget to vote! Polls are open from [Time] to [Time]. Find your polling location here: [Link to Polling Location Finder] #Vote #ElectionDay"

- "The upcoming election will have a significant impact on [Issue]. Make sure you're informed about the candidates' positions on this important topic before you cast your vote. #ResearchTheCandidates #[Issue]Matters"

- "Your voice matters! Participating in the political process is essential to a healthy democracy. Make sure you're registered to vote, stay informed about the issues, and make your voice heard! #CivicEngagement #DemocracyInAction"

Using Twitter for Political Advocacy: Supporting Causes You Care About

Twitter can be an effective platform for advocating for political causes that you care about. You can use the platform to raise awareness, mobilize support, and put pressure on decision-makers.

Tips for Using Twitter for Political Advocacy:

- **Identify your goals:** What are you trying to achieve with your advocacy efforts? Are you trying to raise awareness about an issue, change a policy, or elect a particular candidate?

- **Target your audience:** Who are you trying to reach with your message? Are you trying to persuade undecided voters, mobilize supporters, or pressure elected officials?

- **Craft a compelling message:** Your message should be clear, concise, and persuasive. Use strong language, compelling visuals, and personal stories to connect with your audience.

- **Use hashtags strategically:** Hashtags can help increase the visibility of your tweets and connect you with others who are advocating for the same cause.

- **Engage with influencers and organizations:** Connect with influencers, organizations, and other advocates who are working on the same issue. Retweet their content, amplify their message, and collaborate on campaigns.

- **Track your progress:** Monitor the reach and engagement of your tweets to see how your advocacy efforts are performing.

Examples of Tweets Using Twitter for Political Advocacy:

- "We need to demand that our elected officials take action to address the gun violence epidemic in our country. Contact your representatives and demand common-sense gun safety legislation. #GunSafetyNow #EnoughIsEnough"

- "The [Proposed Policy] would harm our environment and threaten our public health. We need to stop this policy from being implemented. Sign this petition to voice your opposition: [Link to Petition] #Stop[ProposedPolicy] #ProtectOurEnvironment"

- "We need to elect more women to office. Women's voices are essential to a just and equitable society. Support women candidates in the upcoming election. #ElectWomen #WomensRepresentationMatters"

- "We need to stand in solidarity with the people of [Country/Region] who are fighting for their freedom and democracy. Here's how you can support their struggle: [Link to Resources] #StandWith[Country/Region] #DemocracyForAll"

- "We need to hold [Company/Organization] accountable for their harmful practices. Boycott their products and services and demand that they change their policies. #Boycott[Company/Organization] #CorporateAccountability"

Navigating the Political Landscape on Twitter: A Few Final Thoughts

Engaging in political discussions on Twitter can be a rewarding but challenging experience. It's important to be informed, respectful, and strategic in your approach. By following the tips and examples in this chapter, you can use Twitter to express your views, engage with others, promote political participation, and advocate for the causes you care about, all while maintaining a civil and productive tone.

Remember that Twitter is just one platform for political engagement. It's important to supplement your online activism with offline action, such as voting, contacting your elected officials, and participating in protests and rallies.

The political landscape is constantly evolving, and the way we engage in political discussions on Twitter will continue to change as well. It's important to stay informed about the latest trends and best practices for using Twitter for political engagement.

By using Twitter thoughtfully and responsibly, you can contribute to a more informed, engaged, and democratic society.

CHAPTER FOUR: Expressing Gratitude and Appreciation

In our fast-paced, often chaotic world, it's easy to get caught up in the daily grind and forget to express gratitude for the people and things that make our lives better. But taking a moment to acknowledge and appreciate the good in our lives can have a profound impact on our well-being and our relationships with others.

And what better way to spread a little gratitude than through a heartfelt tweet?

This chapter will explore the art of expressing gratitude and appreciation on Twitter (or X). We'll delve into different ways to say "thank you," acknowledge acts of kindness, celebrate the people who inspire us, and cultivate a culture of appreciation in our online interactions.

The Power of Gratitude: Why It Matters

Before we dive into the specifics of crafting gratitude-filled tweets, let's take a moment to reflect on why expressing gratitude is so important. Research has shown that gratitude has numerous benefits for both our mental and physical health:

- **Increased happiness and well-being:** People who regularly practice gratitude tend to be happier and more satisfied with their lives.

- **Reduced stress and anxiety:** Focusing on the positive aspects of our lives can help to reduce stress and anxiety levels.

- **Improved relationships:** Expressing gratitude to others can strengthen our relationships and foster a sense of connection.

- **Enhanced resilience:** Gratitude can help us to cope with challenges and setbacks more effectively.

- **Increased physical health:** Studies have shown that gratitude can improve sleep quality, boost the immune system, and even reduce the risk of chronic diseases.

By expressing gratitude on Twitter, we can not only reap these benefits for ourselves but also inspire others to cultivate a more grateful mindset.

Saying Thank You: Simple Gestures of Appreciation

Sometimes, the simplest expressions of gratitude can have the biggest impact. A heartfelt "thank you" can go a long way in showing someone that you appreciate their efforts, their kindness, or their support.

Tweet Examples:

- "Just wanted to say a huge thank you to [Name] for their help with [Task/Project]. I really appreciate your time and effort! #Grateful #ThankYou"

- "Thank you to everyone who wished me a happy birthday yesterday! I felt so loved and appreciated. #BirthdayGratitude #ThankYouForTheWishes"

- "I'm so grateful for the support of my amazing followers! Your kind words and encouragement mean the world to me. #ThankYouFollowers #YoureTheBest"

- "Thank you to [Company/Organization] for their excellent customer service. They went above and beyond to resolve my issue. #CustomerServiceRocks #Appreciation"

- "Thank you to the healthcare workers, first responders, and essential workers who are keeping us safe and healthy during these challenging times. We appreciate your dedication and sacrifice. #ThankYouHeroes #EssentialWorkers"

Pro-Tip: When expressing gratitude, be specific about what you're thankful for. Instead of just saying "thank you," mention the specific action or quality that you appreciate. This makes your message more personal and meaningful.

Acknowledging Acts of Kindness: Spreading Positivity

When someone goes out of their way to do something kind for you, take a moment to acknowledge their generosity and express your appreciation on Twitter. This not only shows the person that you value their kindness but also inspires others to spread positivity and goodwill.

Tweet Examples:

- "A huge shout-out to [Name] for their random act of kindness today! They paid for my coffee when I forgot my wallet. The world needs more people like you! #KindnessMatters #PayItForward"

- "I'm so grateful for my neighbor, [Name], who shoveled my driveway after the snowstorm. It was such a thoughtful gesture! #NeighborlyLove #GoodDeeds"

- "Thank you to the stranger who helped me carry my groceries to my car. Your kindness made my day! #HelpingHand #SmallActsBigImpact"

- "I'm so touched by the outpouring of support I've received from my online community after sharing my story. Your kind words and encouragement have helped me through a difficult time. #CommunityLove #GratefulForSupport"

- "Thank you to [Company/Organization] for donating to [Charity/Cause]. Your generosity will make a difference in

the lives of many people. #GivingBack
#CorporateSocialResponsibility"

Pro-Tip: Consider tagging the person or organization you're thanking in your tweet, especially if it's a public act of kindness. This gives them recognition and allows others to see their good deed.

Celebrating the People Who Inspire Us: Expressing Admiration

We all have people in our lives who inspire us with their talent, their kindness, their courage, or their achievements. Take a moment to celebrate these individuals on Twitter and express your gratitude for the positive impact they have on your life.

Tweet Examples:

- "I'm so inspired by [Name]'s dedication to [Cause/Passion]. They're making a real difference in the world! #RoleModel #Inspiration"

- "Thank you to [Teacher/Mentor/Coach] for believing in me and helping me to reach my potential. I wouldn't be where I am today without your guidance and support. #GratefulForMentors #LifeChangers"

- "I'm in awe of [Artist/Musician/Writer]'s talent. Their work is truly inspiring and brings so much joy to my life. #CreativeGenius #ArtLover"

- "I'm so grateful for the friendship of [Name]. They're always there for me, no matter what. True friends are a treasure! #FriendshipGoals #Blessed"

- "I'm inspired by [Athlete/Activist/Leader]'s courage and determination. They're a role model for us all. #NeverGiveUp #MakingADifference"

Pro-Tip: When celebrating someone who inspires you, be specific about what qualities or achievements you admire. This makes your message more personal and meaningful.

Cultivating a Culture of Appreciation: Spreading Gratitude Online

Expressing gratitude on Twitter isn't just about individual acts of appreciation. It's also about cultivating a culture of appreciation in our online interactions. By making gratitude a regular part of our Twitter presence, we can create a more positive and supportive online environment.

Tips for Cultivating a Culture of Appreciation:

- **Start a gratitude thread:** Encourage your followers to share what they're grateful for by starting a gratitude thread. You can ask a specific question, such as "What are you most grateful for today?" or "Who are you most grateful for in your life?"

- **Share gratitude quotes and memes:** Spread positivity by sharing inspiring quotes and memes about gratitude.

- **Retweet and amplify messages of gratitude:** When you see someone expressing gratitude on Twitter, retweet their message to help spread their positive vibes.

- **Participate in gratitude challenges:** Many online communities host gratitude challenges, where participants commit to expressing gratitude daily for a certain period of time.

- **Make gratitude a part of your daily Twitter routine:** Take a few minutes each day to tweet about something you're grateful for. It could be something big or small, personal or professional.

Examples of Tweets Cultivating a Culture of Appreciation:

- "Let's start a gratitude thread! What are you most grateful for today? #GratitudeChallenge #SpreadPositivity"

- ""Gratitude makes sense of our past, brings peace for today, and creates a vision for tomorrow." - Melody Beattie #GratitudeQuote #Inspiration"

- "Retweet if you're grateful for something today! Let's spread some positivity on Twitter. #GratefulHeart #ThankfulThursday"

- "I'm participating in the #30DaysOfGratitude challenge. Join me in expressing gratitude daily for the next 30 days! #GratitudePractice #Mindfulness"

- "Today, I'm grateful for the sunshine, the laughter of my children, and the support of my friends and family. What are you grateful for? #DailyGratitude #CountYourBlessings"

Expressing Gratitude in Different Contexts: Tailoring Your Message

The way you express gratitude on Twitter will vary depending on the context and the recipient of your message. Here are a few examples of how to tailor your message for different situations:

Expressing Gratitude to a Customer:

- "Thank you for your recent purchase from [Your Business]! We appreciate your support and hope you enjoy your new [Product/Service]. #CustomerAppreciation #ThankYouForYourBusiness"

- "We're so grateful for your positive feedback on [Product/Service]! We strive to provide the best possible experience for our customers. #CustomerSatisfaction #HappyCustomers"

- "Thank you for being a loyal customer of [Your Business]! We appreciate your continued support and look forward to serving you in the future. #CustomerLoyalty #ThankYouForYourSupport"

Expressing Gratitude to a Colleague:

- "I just wanted to say thank you to [Colleague's Name] for their help with the [Project/Task]. I really appreciate your willingness to go the extra mile. #TeamworkMakesTheDreamWork #GratefulForColleagues"

- "I'm so lucky to work with such a talented and supportive team. Thank you to all my colleagues for making every day a joy. #WorkFamily #Appreciation"

- "Congratulations to [Colleague's Name] on their promotion! You deserve it! Thank you for your hard work and dedication. #CareerSuccess #CelebratingColleagues"

Expressing Gratitude to a Friend or Family Member:

- "I'm so grateful for your friendship, [Friend's Name]. You're always there for me, through thick and thin. #TrueFriend #Blessed"

- "Thank you, [Family Member's Name], for always believing in me and supporting my dreams. I love you! #FamilyLove #UnconditionalSupport"

- "I'm so lucky to have you in my life, [Significant Other's Name]. Thank you for everything you do. #LoveOfMyLife #GratefulHeart"

Expressing Gratitude to a Mentor or Teacher:

- "Thank you, [Mentor/Teacher's Name], for your guidance and wisdom. You've had a profound impact on my life. #GratefulForMentors #LifeChangers"

- "I'm so grateful for the opportunity to have learned from you, [Mentor/Teacher's Name]. Your teachings have shaped who I am today. #EducationMatters #InspirationalTeachers"

- "I'll never forget the lessons you taught me, [Mentor/Teacher's Name]. Thank you for your patience, your encouragement, and your belief in me. #Mentorship #MakingADifference"

A Few Final Tips for Expressing Gratitude on Twitter

- **Be sincere and authentic:** Your expressions of gratitude should come from the heart. Don't just tweet about gratitude because you think you should. Tweet about it because you genuinely feel it.

- **Keep it concise and to the point:** Twitter's character limit encourages brevity. Get straight to the point and express your gratitude in a clear and concise manner.

- **Use visuals:** Adding a photo or video to your tweet can make it more engaging and memorable. For example, you could share a photo of yourself with the person you're thanking or a photo that represents what you're grateful for.

- **Use relevant hashtags:** Hashtags can help increase the visibility of your tweets and connect you with others who are expressing gratitude. Some popular gratitude hashtags include #Gratitude, #Thankful, #Grateful, #Appreciation, and #Blessed.

- **Make it a regular practice:** The more you practice gratitude, the more natural it will become. Try to express gratitude on Twitter at least once a week, or even once a day.

By incorporating these tips into your Twitter routine, you can make expressing gratitude a natural and meaningful part of your online presence. You'll not only brighten the day of those you thank but also cultivate a more positive and appreciative mindset for yourself and your followers.

CHAPTER FIVE: Sharing Your Creative Side

We all have a creative spark within us, whether it's a passion for writing, painting, photography, music, or any other form of artistic expression. And in today's digital age, platforms like Twitter (or X) provide incredible avenues for sharing our creative endeavors with the world.

This chapter is dedicated to unleashing your inner artist and using Twitter to showcase your creative talents. We'll explore various ways to share your work, connect with fellow creatives, find inspiration, and build a supportive online community that celebrates the power of art and imagination.

Showcasing Your Visual Art: Painting, Drawing, and Photography

If you're a visual artist, Twitter can be a fantastic platform for sharing your creations with a wider audience. Whether you're a painter, a drawer, a photographer, or a digital artist, you can use Twitter to showcase your work, gain feedback, and connect with potential buyers or collaborators.

Tips for Sharing Visual Art on Twitter:

- **Use high-quality images:** Twitter is a visual platform, so it's important to use high-resolution images that showcase your work in the best possible light.

- **Optimize images for Twitter:** Twitter has specific image size and format requirements. Make sure your images are optimized for the platform to ensure they display correctly.

- **Use descriptive captions:** Write captions that provide context for your artwork, such as the title, the medium, the inspiration behind the piece, or the story you're trying to tell.

- **Use relevant hashtags:** Hashtags can help increase the visibility of your tweets and connect you with other artists and art enthusiasts. Some popular art hashtags include #art, #artist, #painting, #drawing, #photography, #digitalart, #illustration, and #creative.

- **Engage with other artists:** Follow other artists on Twitter, comment on their work, and participate in art-related conversations. Building a community of support and inspiration is essential for any creative endeavor.

- **Promote your website or online store:** If you have a website or online store where you sell your artwork, be sure to include a link in your Twitter bio and in your tweets.

- **Participate in art challenges:** Many online communities host art challenges, where participants create artwork based on a specific theme or prompt. Participating in these challenges can be a great way to push your creative boundaries and connect with other artists.

Examples of Tweets Showcasing Visual Art:

- **Painter:** "Just finished this new oil painting, titled 'Sunset Serenade.' Inspired by the vibrant colors of the evening sky. #oilpainting #landscapepainting #art #artist"

- **Drawer:** "Here's a quick sketch I did today of a majestic lion. Practicing my animal drawing skills. #drawing #sketch #lion #wildlifeart #artist"

- **Photographer:** "Captured this stunning shot of the Milky Way last night. The beauty of the night sky never ceases to amaze me. #photography #astrophotography #milkyway #nightsky #artist"

- **Digital Artist:** "Created this surreal digital artwork using Photoshop. Exploring the themes of dreams and imagination. #digitalart #surrealism #photoshop #art #artist"

- **Illustrator:** "Here's a new illustration I created for a children's book. Bringing the story to life through vibrant colors and whimsical characters. #illustration #childrensbook #art #artist"

Sharing Your Writing: Poetry, Prose, and Blogging

Twitter can be a great platform for writers to share their work, connect with readers, and build a following. Whether you're a poet, a novelist, a blogger, or a screenwriter, you can use Twitter to showcase your writing skills and engage with the literary community.

Tips for Sharing Your Writing on Twitter:

- **Share excerpts from your work:** Tweet short excerpts from your poems, stories, blog posts, or scripts to give readers a taste of your writing style.

- **Use strong visuals:** Pair your writing excerpts with eye-catching images or videos to make your tweets more engaging.

- **Use relevant hashtags:** Hashtags can help increase the visibility of your tweets and connect you with other writers and readers. Some popular writing hashtags include #writing, #writer, #poetry, #prose, #blogging, #amwriting, #writerslife, and #creativewriting.

- **Engage with other writers:** Follow other writers on Twitter, comment on their work, and participate in writing-related conversations. Building a community of support and inspiration is essential for any writer.

- **Promote your website or blog:** If you have a website or blog where you publish your writing, be sure to include a link in your Twitter bio and in your tweets.

- **Participate in writing challenges:** Many online communities host writing challenges, such as NaNoWriMo (National Novel Writing Month) or #vss365 (Very Short Story 365). Participating in these challenges can be a great way to motivate yourself to write and connect with other writers.

Examples of Tweets Sharing Writing:

- **Poet:** "Here's a new poem I wrote about the beauty of nature. 'The whispering wind, the rustling leaves, a symphony of nature's sleeves.' #poetry #naturepoetry #poem #writer"

- **Novelist:** "Sharing a sneak peek from my upcoming novel, 'The Secret of the Lost City.' 'The adventurer's heart pounded as he stepped into the ancient ruins...' #novel #fiction #amwriting #writer"

- **Blogger:** "Just published a new blog post about the benefits of mindfulness meditation. 'Find your inner peace through the practice of mindful awareness.' #blogging #mindfulness #meditation #writer"

- **Screenwriter:** "Working on a new screenplay about a group of friends who embark on a road trip adventure. 'The open road beckoned, promising freedom and unexpected twists.' #screenwriting #script #adventure #writer"

Sharing Your Music: Songs, Instrumentals, and Performances

Musicians can leverage Twitter to share their musical creations, connect with fans, and promote their work. Whether you're a singer, a songwriter, an instrumentalist, or a music producer, you can use Twitter to showcase your musical talent and build a following.

Tips for Sharing Your Music on Twitter:

- **Share snippets of your songs or instrumentals:** Tweet short audio or video clips of your music to give listeners a taste of your sound.

- **Use high-quality audio and video:** Ensure that the audio and video you share are of high quality to provide the best listening experience for your audience.

- **Use descriptive captions:** Provide context for your music, such as the song title, the genre, the inspiration behind the piece, or the story you're trying to tell.

- **Use relevant hashtags:** Hashtags can help increase the visibility of your tweets and connect you with other musicians and music lovers. Some popular music hashtags include #music, #musician, #singer, #songwriter, #instrumentalist, #musicproducer, #indiemusic, #rockmusic, #pop music, and #hiphop.

- **Engage with other musicians and fans:** Follow other musicians and music lovers on Twitter, comment on their work, and participate in music-related conversations.

- **Promote your music on streaming platforms:** If your music is available on streaming platforms like Spotify, Apple Music, or YouTube Music, be sure to include links in your Twitter bio and in your tweets.

- **Live-tweet your performances:** If you're performing live, use Twitter to share updates, photos, and videos from your performance. Engage with your audience in real-time and create a buzz around your show.

Examples of Tweets Sharing Music:

- **Singer/Songwriter:** "Just finished recording a new song called 'Lost in the Stars.' It's a heartfelt ballad about longing and hope. #singersongwriter #ballad #music #musician"

- **Instrumentalist:** "Here's a short guitar instrumental I composed. Inspired by the beauty of nature and the power of music. #guitarist #instrumental #music #musician"

- **Music Producer:** "Working on a new electronic music track. Experimenting with different sounds and textures to create a unique sonic experience. #musicproducer #electronicmusic #music #musician"

- **Band:** "We're playing a live show at [Venue] on [Date]. Come join us for a night of great music! #liveshow #music #band #musician"

Sharing Your Other Creative Pursuits: Crafting, Cooking, and More

Twitter is not just limited to traditional art forms. You can also use the platform to share your other creative passions, such as crafting, cooking, baking, DIY projects, fashion design, and more. Whatever your creative outlet, there's an audience on Twitter who will appreciate your talent and enthusiasm.

Tips for Sharing Other Creative Pursuits on Twitter:

- **Share photos and videos of your creations:** Showcase your finished products, your creative process, or behind-the-scenes glimpses of your work.

- **Use descriptive captions:** Provide context for your creations, such as the materials you used, the techniques you employed, the inspiration behind your work, or the story you're trying to tell.

- **Use relevant hashtags:** Hashtags can help increase the visibility of your tweets and connect you with others who share your creative interests. Some popular hashtags for various creative pursuits include #crafting, #DIY, #cooking, #baking, #fashion, #photography, #design, and #handmade.

- **Engage with other creatives:** Follow other creatives on Twitter, comment on their work, and participate in conversations related to your shared interests.

- **Promote your website or online store:** If you have a website or online store where you sell your creations, be sure to include a link in your Twitter bio and in your tweets.

- **Participate in creative challenges:** Many online communities host creative challenges related to various hobbies and interests. Participating in these challenges can be a great way to spark your creativity and connect with other enthusiasts.

Examples of Tweets Sharing Other Creative Pursuits:

- **Crafting:** "Just finished knitting this cozy scarf for the winter. Perfect for staying warm and stylish. #knitting #scarf #handmade #craft"

- **Cooking:** "Made a delicious homemade pasta dish tonight. The aroma filled the whole house! #cooking #pasta #foodie #homemade"

- **Baking:** "Baked a batch of chocolate chip cookies. They're warm, gooey, and irresistible! #baking #cookies #chocolatechip #sweettooth"

- **DIY Projects:** "Built a new bookshelf for my living room. It was a fun and rewarding project! #DIY #bookshelf #woodworking #homeimprovement"

- **Fashion Design:** "Designed a new dress for an upcoming fashion show. Inspired by the elegance of vintage fashion. #fashiondesign #dress #vintage #style"

Finding Inspiration and Connecting with Fellow Creatives

Twitter can be a wellspring of inspiration for creatives. By following other artists, writers, musicians, and creators, you can discover new ideas, techniques, and perspectives that can fuel your own creative endeavors.

Tips for Finding Inspiration and Connecting with Fellow Creatives on Twitter:

- **Follow hashtags related to your creative interests:** Search for hashtags related to your creative passions and follow them to see what other people are creating and sharing.

- **Join Twitter chats related to your creative field:** Many online communities host Twitter chats where creatives can connect, share ideas, and discuss industry trends.

- **Participate in creative challenges and prompts:** Engage in online challenges and prompts that spark your creativity and encourage you to try new things.

- **Follow influencers and thought leaders in your creative field:** Stay up-to-date on the latest trends and insights by following leading figures in your creative industry.

- **Connect with local creatives in your area:** Use Twitter to find and connect with other creatives in your local community. You can attend events, workshops, or meetups to build relationships and collaborate on projects.

Examples of Tweets Finding Inspiration and Connecting with Fellow Creatives:

- "Looking for some #writinginspiration today. What are your favorite writing prompts or exercises? #writerslife #amwriting"

- "Excited to join the #ArtChat tonight! Looking forward to connecting with other artists and discussing our creative processes. #artist #artcommunity"

- "Participating in the #30DayPhotoChallenge this month. It's a great way to push my photography skills and explore new creative avenues. #photography #photochallenge"

- "Just discovered a new #musician on Twitter who's making amazing music. Their sound is so unique and inspiring! #musiclover #indiemusic"

- "Attending a local #craftfair this weekend. Looking forward to meeting other talented crafters and supporting handmade businesses. #crafts #handmade #community"

Building a Supportive Online Community: Celebrating Creativity Together

One of the most rewarding aspects of sharing your creative side on Twitter is the opportunity to build a supportive online community. By connecting with other creatives, sharing your work, and offering encouragement and feedback, you can create a space where creativity is celebrated and nurtured.

Tips for Building a Supportive Online Community on Twitter:

- **Be generous with your likes, retweets, and comments:** Show your support for other creatives by liking, retweeting, and commenting on their work. A little encouragement can go a long way.

- **Offer constructive feedback:** If someone asks for feedback on their work, be willing to offer your thoughts and insights in a respectful and helpful way.

- **Celebrate the successes of others:** When a fellow creative achieves a milestone, such as publishing a book, releasing an album, or exhibiting their artwork, take a moment to congratulate them and share their success with your followers.

- **Collaborate on projects:** Look for opportunities to collaborate with other creatives on projects that align with your shared interests.

- **Organize online or in-person events:** Host Twitter chats, online workshops, or in-person meetups to connect with other creatives and build a sense of community.

Examples of Tweets Building a Supportive Online Community:

- "Just discovered this amazing #artist on Twitter. Their work is so beautiful and inspiring! Give them a follow! #artcommunity #supportartists"

- "Congratulations to [Writer's Name] on publishing their first novel! So proud of your accomplishment! #writingcommunity #writerslife #booklaunch"

- "Offering free #feedback on #poetry today. If you'd like me to read and critique your poem, please share it in the comments! #poetrycommunity #writershelpingwriters"

- "Excited to be collaborating with [Musician's Name] on a new song! Stay tuned for updates! #musiccollaboration #musician #musiccommunity"

- "Hosting a #TwitterChat for #crafters next week. Join us to discuss our favorite crafting techniques and projects! #craftcommunity #handmade #DIY"

Promoting Your Creative Work: Building an Audience and Finding Opportunities

While Twitter is a great platform for sharing your creative work and connecting with other creatives, it can also be a valuable tool for promoting your work and finding new opportunities.

Tips for Promoting Your Creative Work on Twitter:

- **Use a professional profile picture and bio:** Make a good first impression by using a professional profile picture and writing a compelling bio that highlights your creative skills and experience.

- **Share your work consistently:** The more you share your work on Twitter, the more visibility you'll gain. Aim to tweet regularly, whether it's daily, a few times a week, or weekly, depending on your schedule and creative output.

- **Engage with your audience:** Respond to comments and questions, participate in conversations, and build relationships with your followers.

- **Run contests and giveaways:** Generate excitement and attract new followers by running contests and giveaways related to your creative work.

- **Collaborate with influencers and brands:** Partner with influencers and brands in your creative field to promote your work to a wider audience.

- **Use Twitter Ads:** If you have a budget for marketing, consider using Twitter Ads to target your creative work to specific demographics and interests.

Examples of Tweets Promoting Your Creative Work:

- "I'm a #freelance #writer specializing in #blogging and #contentmarketing. Check out my portfolio: [Link to Portfolio] #writerslife #hiring"

- "My new #photography #prints are now available for purchase on my website: [Link to Website] Limited edition prints, signed and numbered. #artforsale #artist"

- "I'm offering #music #production services for #singers and #songwriters. Contact me to discuss your project: [Email Address] #musician #musicproducer"

- "Enter to win a free #handmade #scarf from my Etsy shop! Just retweet this tweet and follow me to enter. #giveaway #crafting #etsyseller"

- "Excited to be partnering with [Brand Name] to promote my new #cookbook! Check out their website for a special discount code: [Link to Website] #foodie #cooking #recipe"

Protecting Your Creative Work: Copyright and Attribution

It's important to be mindful of copyright and attribution when sharing your creative work on Twitter. Here are a few tips to protect your intellectual property:

- **Watermark your images and videos:** Adding a watermark to your visual content can help to deter unauthorized use.

- **Include copyright notices in your captions:** State that your work is copyrighted and reserve all rights.

- **Register your work with the Copyright Office:** For added protection, consider registering your work with the U.S. Copyright Office.

- **Use Creative Commons licenses:** If you're comfortable with others using your work under certain conditions, you can use a Creative Commons license to specify how your work can be shared and attributed.

- **Be cautious about sharing unfinished work:** If you're sharing unfinished work, be aware that it may be copied or used without your permission.

Examples of Tweets Protecting Your Creative Work:

- "Sharing a new #painting I'm working on. Please note that this artwork is copyrighted and all rights are reserved. #art #artist #copyright"

- "This #photograph is licensed under a Creative Commons Attribution-NonCommercial-NoDerivs 3.0 Unported License. You are free to share this image, but you must give attribution and you cannot use it for commercial purposes or create derivative works. #photography #creativecommons"

- "I'm excited to share a sneak peek of my upcoming #novel. Please respect my copyright and do not reproduce or distribute this excerpt without my permission. #writing #writer #copyright"

A Few Final Tips for Sharing Your Creative Side on Twitter

- **Be authentic and true to your style:** Don't try to be someone you're not. Let your unique personality and creative voice shine through in your tweets.

- **Don't be afraid to experiment:** Twitter is a great platform for trying new things and pushing your creative boundaries. Don't be afraid to experiment with different formats, styles, and techniques.

- **Be patient and persistent:** Building a following and gaining recognition for your creative work takes time and effort. Don't get discouraged if you don't see results overnight. Keep creating, keep sharing, and keep connecting with other creatives.

- **Have fun!** Sharing your creative side on Twitter should be an enjoyable experience. Embrace the process, connect with others who share your passion, and celebrate the power of art and imagination.

CHAPTER SIX: Finding Humor in Everyday Life

Life can be a whirlwind of responsibilities, deadlines, and unexpected curveballs. But amidst the chaos, there's always room for a little laughter. Humor is the spice of life, the antidote to stress, and the universal language that connects us all.

And what better platform for sharing a chuckle than Twitter (or X)?

This chapter is all about finding the funny in the mundane, the absurd, and the downright bizarre moments that make up our daily lives. We'll explore various ways to inject humor into your tweets, from crafting witty observations to sharing relatable anecdotes and mastering the art of the meme. Get ready to unleash your inner comedian and spread some laughter across the Twitterverse.

Observational Humor: Finding the Funny in the Mundane

The world around us is a constant source of comedic material, just waiting to be discovered. Observational humor involves noticing the quirks, absurdities, and contradictions of everyday life and sharing them in a way that makes others laugh.

Tips for Crafting Observational Humor:

- **Pay attention to your surroundings:** Be mindful of the things you see, hear, and experience throughout your day. Look for the unexpected, the ironic, and the humorous in the mundane.

- **Find the relatable:** Focus on observations that others can relate to. The more universal the experience, the more likely it is to resonate with your audience.

- **Keep it concise:** Twitter's character limit encourages brevity. Get straight to the point and deliver your punchline effectively.

- **Use exaggeration and hyperbole:** Amplify the humor by exaggerating or overstating the situation or observation.

- **Don't be afraid to be self-deprecating:** Sometimes, the funniest observations are the ones that poke fun at ourselves. Sharing your own relatable flaws or mishaps can be incredibly endearing and humorous.

Examples of Tweets Using Observational Humor:

- "My superpower is finding the one open checkout lane at the grocery store that has the slowest cashier. #GroceryStoreStruggles #AlwaysPickTheWrongLine"

- "I'm convinced that socks have a secret portal to another dimension. They disappear in the laundry and never return. #SockMonster #WhereDoSocksGo"

- "The awkward moment when you wave back at someone who wasn't actually waving at you. #SocialAwkwardness #InvisibleFriends"

- "My brain in the morning: 'I need coffee.' My brain 5 minutes later: 'I need more coffee.' #CoffeeAddict #CaffeineFix"

- "I'm so good at procrastinating that I procrastinate on procrastinating. #ProcrastinationLevelExpert #NeverDoTodayWhatYouCanPutOffIndefinitely"

Anecdotal Humor: Sharing Your Funny Stories

Everyone has a collection of funny stories, those embarrassing, awkward, or unexpected moments that make you cringe and laugh at the same time. Sharing these anecdotes on Twitter can be a great way to connect with others, entertain your followers, and remind everyone that we all have our share of hilarious mishaps.

Tips for Sharing Anecdotal Humor:

- **Choose relatable stories:** Select stories that others can relate to, whether it's a childhood memory, a dating disaster, or a workplace blunder.

- **Set the scene:** Provide enough context for your story so that your audience can understand the situation and the humor.

- **Build suspense:** Create anticipation for the punchline by gradually revealing the details of the story.

- **Use dialogue and vivid descriptions:** Bring your story to life by incorporating dialogue and using descriptive language that paints a picture in the reader's mind.

- **End with a strong punchline:** The punchline is the culmination of your story. Make it memorable and impactful.

Examples of Tweets Sharing Anecdotal Humor:

- "When I was a kid, I thought the Olympics were held on Mount Olympus and that the athletes were all Greek gods. #ChildhoodMisconceptions #MythologicalMixUp"

- "Went on a blind date last night. He spent the entire meal talking about his ex-girlfriend. I'm pretty sure I'm now a certified therapist. #DatingDisasters #WorstDateEver"

- "Accidentally replied 'I love you too' to a work email from my boss. I'm currently updating my resume. #WorkplaceBlunder #EmailFail"

- "Tried to impress my crush by showing off my dance moves. Ended up tripping and spilling my drink all over them. Smooth operator, right here. #AwkwardMoments #EpicFail"

- "My dog ate my homework. Literally. I'm not sure how to explain that to my teacher. #DogShaming #CanineCulprit"

Self-Deprecating Humor: Laughing at Yourself

Self-deprecating humor involves making fun of your own flaws, quirks, or mistakes. It's a disarming and endearing form of humor that can make you more relatable and approachable. When used effectively, self-deprecating humor can be incredibly funny and can help you to connect with others on a deeper level.

Tips for Using Self-Deprecating Humor:

- **Be genuine:** Your self-deprecating humor should be authentic and reflect your true personality. Don't try to be someone you're not.

- **Don't overdo it:** While self-deprecating humor can be funny, don't overdo it. Too much self-deprecation can make you appear insecure or lacking in confidence.

- **Focus on relatable flaws:** Choose flaws or mistakes that others can relate to. This makes your humor more universal and appealing.

- **Avoid sensitive topics:** Steer clear of self-deprecating humor that touches on sensitive topics, such as mental health, physical appearance, or traumatic experiences.

- **Use it sparingly:** Self-deprecating humor is most effective when used sparingly. It can lose its impact if you use it too frequently.

Examples of Tweets Using Self-Deprecating Humor:

- "I'm so clumsy that I could trip over a flat surface. #GracefulLikeABabyGiraffe #CoordinationSkillsOfASloth"

- "My fashion sense can best be described as 'I tried.' #FashionDisaster #WhatWasIThinking"

- "I'm not sure what's worse: my singing voice or my dance moves. It's a toss-up. #ToneDeaf #TwoLeftFeet"

- "I'm so bad at cooking that I could burn water. #KitchenNightmare #CulinaryChallenged"

- "My brain has two settings: 'on' and 'squirrel!' #EasilyDistracted #AttentionSpanOfAGnat"

Topical Humor: Finding the Funny in Current Events

Current events, both big and small, can provide fodder for humorous tweets. Whether it's a political gaffe, a celebrity mishap, or a viral trend, you can use Twitter to share your witty take on the latest happenings and make your followers laugh.

Tips for Using Topical Humor:

- **Stay informed:** Keep up with current events by reading news articles, following social media trends, and paying attention to what people are talking about.

- **Find the humorous angle:** Look for the ironic, the absurd, or the unexpected in current events.

- **Be timely:** Topical humor is most effective when it's timely. Tweet about current events while they're still relevant and fresh in people's minds.

- **Be respectful:** While it's okay to poke fun at current events, be mindful of sensitive topics and avoid making jokes that could be offensive or hurtful.

- **Use relevant hashtags:** Use hashtags related to the current event to increase the visibility of your tweets and join the conversation.

Examples of Tweets Using Topical Humor:

- "[Politician's Name] said they were going to 'drain the swamp.' Turns out, they brought their own inflatable pool. #PoliticalHumor #DrainingTheSwamp"

- "[Celebrity's Name] wore a dress made entirely of meat to the awards show. I'm not sure if it's fashion or a barbecue. #CelebrityFashion #MeatDress"

- "The new viral trend is people balancing brooms on their fingers. I can barely balance my checkbook. #ViralTrends #BroomChallenge"

- "Scientists have discovered a new planet that's made entirely of chocolate. I'm packing my bags. #SpaceExploration #ChocolatePlanet"

- "The stock market is going crazy. I'm investing in ramen noodles and duct tape. #Economy #RamenNoodleEconomy"

Wordplay and Puns: Tickling Your Followers' Funny Bones

Wordplay and puns are classic forms of humor that can be incredibly effective on Twitter. A clever pun or a witty play on words can make your followers chuckle and appreciate your linguistic creativity.

Tips for Using Wordplay and Puns:

- **Be original:** Try to come up with your own puns and wordplay, rather than relying on tired clichés.

- **Keep it concise:** Puns are often most effective when they're short and to the point.

- **Use relevant hashtags:** Use hashtags related to the topic of your pun or wordplay to increase the visibility of your tweets.

- **Don't be afraid to be silly:** Puns are inherently silly, so embrace the absurdity and have fun with it.

- **Don't overuse them:** While puns can be funny, don't overuse them. Too many puns can become tiresome.

Examples of Tweets Using Wordplay and Puns:

- "I'm reading a book about anti-gravity. It's impossible to put down. #Punny #BookLover"

- "I used to hate facial hair, but then it grew on me. #PunIntended #BeardLover"

- "Why don't scientists trust atoms? Because they make up everything! #SciencePuns #NerdHumor"

- "I'm so bad at puns that I should be arrested for a-salt and battery. #PunPolice #SorryNotSorry"

- "What do you call a lazy kangaroo? Pouch potato! #AnimalPuns #DadJokes"

Using Emojis and GIFs: Adding Visual Humor

Emojis and GIFs can be powerful tools for adding visual humor to your tweets. A well-placed emoji can convey a range of emotions, from sarcasm to excitement to amusement. And a funny GIF can perfectly capture the mood of a situation or add a humorous twist to your message.

Tips for Using Emojis and GIFs:

- **Use emojis sparingly:** Too many emojis can be overwhelming and distracting. Choose emojis that enhance your message and add to the humor.

- **Choose relevant GIFs:** Select GIFs that are relevant to the topic of your tweet and that convey the emotion or humor you're trying to express.

- **Use high-quality GIFs:** Avoid using low-resolution or grainy GIFs, as they can detract from the overall quality of your tweet.

- **Be mindful of cultural context:** Some emojis and GIFs can have different meanings in different cultures. Be aware of the potential for misinterpretation.

- **Don't overuse them:** While emojis and GIFs can be fun, don't overuse them. Too many emojis or GIFs can make your tweets appear cluttered and unprofessional.

Examples of Tweets Using Emojis and GIFs:

- "Just spilled coffee all over my keyboard. This is my life. ☐♀☐ #CoffeeFail #MondayMood"

- "My dog when I try to take his picture: 🐶 #DogShaming #PhotogenicPup"

- "Trying to adult today: ☐ #AdultingIsHard #NeedANap"

- "When someone tells me I need to exercise more: 🍟 #FitnessGoals #MaybeTomorrow"

- "My reaction when I finally finish a difficult task: 🎉 #AchievementUnlocked #NailedIt"

Mastering the Art of the Meme: Sharing Viral Humor

Memes have become a ubiquitous part of internet culture, and Twitter is a prime platform for sharing these viral nuggets of humor. A well-chosen meme can perfectly capture the zeitgeist, express a shared experience, or simply make people laugh.

Tips for Using Memes:

- **Stay up-to-date on meme trends:** Pay attention to the latest meme trends and use them to your advantage.

- **Choose relevant memes:** Select memes that are relevant to the topic of your tweet and that resonate with your audience.

- **Use high-quality memes:** Avoid using low-resolution or poorly formatted memes.

- **Give credit where credit is due:** If you're using a meme that someone else created, be sure to give them credit.

- **Don't overuse them:** While memes can be funny, don't overuse them. Too many memes can make your tweets appear unoriginal and spammy.

Examples of Tweets Using Memes:

- **Drakeposting Meme:** "Me trying to decide what to have for dinner: [Drakeposting meme with Drake looking disgusted at one option and approving of the other]" #DinnerDecisions #FoodieProblems"

- **Distracted Boyfriend Meme:** "Me trying to be productive: [Distracted Boyfriend meme with the boyfriend representing productivity and the girlfriend representing distractions]" #Procrastination #FocusFail"

- **Woman Yelling at a Cat Meme:** "Me trying to explain to my dog why he can't eat my food: [Woman Yelling at a

Cat meme with the woman representing you and the cat representing your dog]" #DogShaming #FoodThief"

- **Success Kid Meme:** "Me finally figuring out how to use the new coffee machine: [Success Kid meme]" #AdultingWin #CoffeeConqueror"

- **Change My Mind Meme:** "Pineapple belongs on pizza. Change my mind. [Change My Mind meme]" #PizzaDebate #PineappleOnPizza"

Engaging in Humorous Twitter Conversations: Banter and Witty Replies

Twitter is not just a platform for broadcasting your own humorous content. It's also a great place to engage in witty banter and humorous conversations with other users.

Tips for Engaging in Humorous Twitter Conversations:

- **Be quick-witted:** Twitter conversations move fast, so be prepared to come up with witty replies on the spot.

- **Use humor appropriately:** Not every conversation is appropriate for humor. Be mindful of the context and the tone of the conversation before cracking a joke.

- **Don't be afraid to be self-deprecating:** Self-deprecating humor can be a great way to disarm others and make yourself more relatable.

- **Avoid controversial topics:** Steer clear of humor that could be offensive or hurtful to others.

- **Know when to disengage:** Not every conversation is worth continuing. If a conversation becomes unproductive or disrespectful, it's okay to disengage.

Examples of Humorous Twitter Conversations:

User 1: "Just spilled coffee all over my new shirt. This is why I can't have nice things."

User 2: "Don't worry, it just adds a little extra flavor. ☕ #CoffeeStainFashion"

User 1: "I'm so bad at cooking that I could burn water."

User 2: "Challenge accepted! I'll bring the fire extinguisher. 🔥 #CulinaryCompetition"

User 1: "My dog ate my homework. Literally."

User 2: "Did you try explaining to your teacher that your dog is a very hungry scholar? 📚 #DogAteMyHomeworkExcuse"

Humor and Brand Building: Using Humor to Connect with Your Audience

If you're using Twitter for business or brand building, humor can be a powerful tool for connecting with your audience and making your brand more memorable.

Tips for Using Humor for Brand Building:

- **Know your audience:** Understand your target audience's sense of humor before incorporating humor into your brand's Twitter presence.

- **Be consistent with your brand's voice:** Ensure that the humor you use is aligned with your brand's overall voice and personality.

- **Use humor sparingly:** Too much humor can detract from your brand's message and make you appear unprofessional.

- **Avoid controversial or offensive humor:** Steer clear of humor that could alienate or offend your target audience.

- **Monitor your results:** Track the engagement and reach of your humorous tweets to see what resonates with your audience.

Examples of Brands Using Humor on Twitter:

Wendy's: Wendy's is known for its sassy and humorous Twitter presence. They often engage in playful banter with other brands and customers, using witty comebacks and memes to build their brand personality.

MoonPie: MoonPie's Twitter account is a masterclass in absurdist humor. They often tweet nonsensical and humorous content that has nothing to do with their product, but that has helped them to build a loyal and engaged following.

Netflix: Netflix uses humor to promote its shows and movies, often sharing relatable memes and GIFs that connect with their audience's interests and pop culture knowledge.

A Few Final Tips for Finding Humor on Twitter

- **Don't be afraid to be silly:** Humor is often about embracing the absurd and the unexpected. Don't be afraid to let your silly side show.

- **Be mindful of your audience:** Not everyone has the same sense of humor. Be aware of your audience's sensibilities and avoid humor that could be offensive or hurtful.

- **Don't take yourself too seriously:** Life is too short to be serious all the time. Use humor to lighten the mood and connect with others.

- **Practice makes perfect:** The more you practice finding and sharing humor on Twitter, the better you'll become at it. Experiment with different styles of humor and see what resonates with your audience.

- **Have fun!** Humor is contagious. When you're having fun, your followers will too.

By following these tips and examples, you can use Twitter to share your unique sense of humor, connect with others who appreciate a good laugh, and make the Twitterverse a little bit brighter and more enjoyable for everyone. So go forth, unleash your inner comedian, and spread some laughter across the digital landscape.

CHAPTER SEVEN: Spreading Positivity and Inspiration

In the often chaotic and negativity-laden world of social media, it's easy to get swept up in the drama, the cynicism, and the endless stream of bad news. But amidst the noise, there's a growing movement of individuals who are using their platforms to spread positivity, inspire hope, and make the online world a more uplifting and encouraging space.

This chapter is dedicated to harnessing the power of Twitter (or X) to be a force for good. We'll explore various ways to share inspiring messages, celebrate acts of kindness, promote positive self-talk, offer support and encouragement to others, and cultivate a culture of optimism and resilience in the digital sphere. Get ready to unleash your inner cheerleader and become a beacon of light in the Twitterverse.

Sharing Inspiring Quotes and Messages: Uplifting Your Followers

One of the simplest yet most effective ways to spread positivity on Twitter is by sharing inspiring quotes and messages. A well-chosen quote can offer a fresh perspective, provide a much-needed dose of encouragement, or simply remind your followers of the good in the world.

Tips for Sharing Inspiring Quotes and Messages:

- **Choose quotes that resonate with you:** Select quotes that speak to your values, your beliefs, or your personal experiences. The more authentic your message, the more impactful it will be.

- **Keep it concise:** Twitter's character limit encourages brevity. Choose quotes that are short and to the point, but that still pack a punch.

- **Use strong visuals:** Pair your quotes with eye-catching images or videos to make your tweets more engaging and shareable.

- **Use relevant hashtags:** Hashtags can help increase the visibility of your tweets and connect you with others who are interested in positivity and inspiration. Some popular hashtags include #inspiration, #motivation, #positivity, #quotes, #wisdom, #kindness, and #hope.

- **Give credit to the source:** If you're sharing a quote from a specific person or book, be sure to give credit to the source.

- **Share your own reflections:** Along with the quote, consider sharing your own thoughts or reflections on what the quote means to you or how it applies to your life.

Examples of Tweets Sharing Inspiring Quotes and Messages:

- ""The only way to do great work is to love what you do." - Steve Jobs #Inspiration #Motivation #FollowYourPassion"

- ""Believe you can and you're halfway there." - Theodore Roosevelt #BelieveInYourself #YouGotThis #PositiveVibes"

- ""The future belongs to those who believe in the beauty of their dreams." - Eleanor Roosevelt #DreamBig #NeverGiveUp #Hope"

- ""The best and most beautiful things in the world cannot be seen or even touched - they must be felt with the heart." - Helen Keller #Kindness #Compassion #Love"

- ""Challenges are what make life interesting. Overcoming them is what makes life meaningful." - Joshua Marine #Resilience #GrowthMindset #NeverGiveUp"

Celebrating Acts of Kindness: Highlighting the Good in the World

In a world that often focuses on negativity and conflict, it's important to take the time to celebrate the acts of kindness and compassion that are happening all around us. By highlighting these positive stories on Twitter, we can inspire others to spread goodwill and make the world a better place.

Tips for Celebrating Acts of Kindness on Twitter:

- **Share your own experiences:** If you witness an act of kindness, share your story on Twitter. Describe what happened and how it made you feel.

- **Retweet and amplify positive stories:** When you see others sharing stories of kindness, retweet their messages to help spread the positivity.

- **Use relevant hashtags:** Hashtags can help increase the visibility of your tweets and connect you with others who are interested in celebrating acts of kindness. Some popular hashtags include #kindness, #compassion, #gooddeeds, #payitforward, #randomactsofkindness, and #makeadifference.

- **Start a kindness challenge:** Encourage your followers to participate in a kindness challenge, such as performing a random act of kindness each day for a week or a month.

- **Support organizations that promote kindness:** Share information about organizations that are dedicated to spreading kindness and compassion, such as the Random Acts of Kindness Foundation or the World Kindness Movement.

Examples of Tweets Celebrating Acts of Kindness:

- "Just saw a stranger help an elderly woman cross the street. It was a small act of kindness, but it made my heart smile. #KindnessMatters #PayItForward"

- "Retweet if you've done a random act of kindness today! Let's spread some positivity in the world. #GoodDeeds #MakeADifference"

- "I'm participating in the #KindnessChallenge this week. My goal is to perform one random act of kindness each day. Join me! #SpreadKindness #Compassion"

- "Check out the Random Acts of Kindness Foundation (@RAKFoundation) for inspiring stories and resources on how to spread kindness. #RAK #KindnessMovement"

- "Today, I'm celebrating the healthcare workers, teachers, and essential workers who are making a positive impact on our communities every day. Thank you for your dedication and compassion. #ThankYouHeroes #MakingADifference"

Promoting Positive Self-Talk: Building Confidence and Resilience

The way we talk to ourselves can have a profound impact on our self-esteem, our motivation, and our overall well-being. Negative self-talk can erode our confidence and make us more susceptible to stress and anxiety. Positive self-talk, on the other hand, can boost our self-esteem, help us to overcome challenges, and build resilience in the face of adversity.

Tips for Promoting Positive Self-Talk on Twitter:

- **Share affirmations and positive self-talk mantras:** Tweet affirmations and positive self-talk statements that you find helpful or inspiring.

- **Challenge negative thoughts:** When you notice yourself engaging in negative self-talk, challenge those thoughts and replace them with more positive and realistic ones.

- **Share your own experiences with positive self-talk:** If you've found positive self-talk to be beneficial in your own life, share your story on Twitter. This can help to inspire others to try it themselves.

- **Use relevant hashtags:** Hashtags can help increase the visibility of your tweets and connect you with others who are interested in positive self-talk and mental health. Some popular hashtags include #positiveselftalk, #selflove, #selfcare, #mentalhealth, #mindfulness, and #resilience.

- **Follow accounts that promote positive self-talk:** There are many Twitter accounts that share inspiring messages, affirmations, and tips for cultivating a positive mindset. Following these accounts can provide you with a regular dose of encouragement and support.

Examples of Tweets Promoting Positive Self-Talk:

- ""I am strong. I am capable. I am worthy." Repeat these affirmations daily to boost your self-esteem. #PositiveSelfTalk #SelfLove"

- "Challenge your negative thoughts. Are they really true? Are they helpful? Replace them with more positive and realistic thoughts. #Mindfulness #MentalHealth"

- "Positive self-talk has been a game-changer for me. It's helped me to overcome challenges, build confidence, and cultivate a more positive mindset. Give it a try! #SelfCare #Resilience"

- "Follow @PositiveVibesOnly for daily doses of inspiration and positive self-talk tips. #Motivation #Positivity"

- "Remember that you are not your thoughts. You have the power to choose your thoughts and create a more positive inner dialogue. #Mindfulness #SelfAwareness"

Offering Support and Encouragement to Others: Spreading Kindness and Empathy

One of the most powerful ways to spread positivity on Twitter is by offering support and encouragement to others. A kind word, a gesture of empathy, or a simple message of hope can make a world of difference to someone who is struggling.

Tips for Offering Support and Encouragement on Twitter:

- **Listen actively:** Pay attention to what others are sharing on Twitter. If someone is expressing sadness, frustration, or anxiety, take the time to listen to their story.

- **Offer words of encouragement:** Let people know that you care and that they're not alone. Share messages of hope, resilience, and strength.

- **Validate their feelings:** Acknowledge their emotions and let them know that it's okay to feel the way they do.

- **Offer practical help:** If someone is struggling with a specific problem, offer practical help or resources if you're able to.

- **Be mindful of your boundaries:** While it's important to be supportive, it's also important to be mindful of your own boundaries. You don't have to be everyone's therapist or savior. If you're feeling overwhelmed, it's okay to take a step back.

Examples of Tweets Offering Support and Encouragement:

- "If you're feeling down today, remember that you're not alone. There are people who care about you and want to help. Don't be afraid to reach out for support. #MentalHealthMatters #YouAreNotAlone"

- "Sending love and strength to everyone who is going through a tough time right now. You are stronger than you think. Keep fighting. #Resilience #Hope"

- "I know it's hard to stay positive when things are difficult, but try to focus on the good things in your life, no matter how small they may seem. Gratitude can be a powerful antidote to negativity. #Positivity #Gratitude"

- "If you're struggling with anxiety, here are some resources that might be helpful: [Link to Resources] #AnxietySupport #MentalHealth"

- "Remember that it's okay to ask for help. There's no shame in admitting that you need support. Reach out to a friend, family member, or mental health professional. #YouAreNotAlone #SeekHelp"

Cultivating a Culture of Optimism and Resilience: Building a Positive Online Community

Spreading positivity on Twitter isn't just about individual acts of kindness and encouragement. It's also about cultivating a culture of optimism and resilience within the online community. By promoting positive values, celebrating successes, and supporting each other through challenges, we can create a more uplifting and empowering online environment.

Tips for Cultivating a Culture of Optimism and Resilience on Twitter:

- **Focus on solutions, not problems:** When discussing challenges or issues, try to focus on solutions and positive actions that can be taken.

- **Celebrate successes, both big and small:** Acknowledge and celebrate the achievements of yourself and others, no matter how small they may seem.

- **Practice gratitude:** Share what you're grateful for on a regular basis. Gratitude can help to shift your focus from negativity to positivity.

- **Promote forgiveness and compassion:** Encourage forgiveness, both for yourself and for others. Compassion and understanding can help to heal wounds and build bridges.

- **Challenge negativity and cynicism:** When you encounter negativity or cynicism on Twitter, don't be afraid to challenge it. Offer a different perspective or share a message of hope.

Examples of Tweets Cultivating a Culture of Optimism and Resilience:

- "Instead of focusing on what's wrong with the world, let's focus on what we can do to make it a better place. Small acts of kindness and compassion can have a ripple effect. #MakeADifference #PositiveChange"

- "Congratulations to everyone who achieved a goal this week, no matter how big or small! Celebrate your successes and keep striving for your dreams. #AchievementUnlocked #NeverGiveUp"

- "Today, I'm grateful for the sunshine, the laughter of my children, and the support of my friends and family. What are you grateful for? #Gratitude #CountYourBlessings"

- "Forgiveness is a powerful act of self-care and healing. Let go of resentment and anger and embrace compassion and understanding. #Forgiveness #Compassion"

- "Negativity and cynicism are contagious. Let's choose to spread positivity, hope, and encouragement instead. #ChoosePositivity #BeTheChange"

Spreading Positivity Through Visuals: Images, GIFs, and Videos

Visual content can be incredibly effective in conveying emotions and inspiring positive feelings. Use images, GIFs, and videos to enhance your positive messages and make them more engaging and shareable.

Tips for Using Visuals to Spread Positivity:

- **Choose uplifting and inspiring images:** Select images that evoke feelings of joy, hope, peace, or gratitude. Nature scenes, images of happy people, or inspiring quotes overlaid on beautiful backgrounds can all be effective.

- **Use GIFs to express positive emotions:** GIFs can be a great way to convey emotions like excitement, happiness, or encouragement. Find GIFs that celebrate successes, express gratitude, or offer support.

- **Create short videos with positive messages:** Consider creating short videos with inspiring messages, affirmations, or stories of kindness. You can use video editing tools to add music, text overlays, and other effects to make your videos more engaging.

- **Share motivational or funny animal videos:** Animal videos often have a way of brightening people's days. Share videos of cute animals doing funny or heartwarming things to spread some smiles.

- **Use relevant hashtags:** Use hashtags related to the theme of your visuals to increase the visibility of your tweets. For example, you could use hashtags like #naturephotography,

#inspirationalquotes, #positivevibes, #cuteanimals, or #motivationalvideos.

Examples of Tweets Using Visuals to Spread Positivity:

- **Image:** "A beautiful sunset to remind you that even after the darkest of days, there's always a new beginning. #Sunset #Hope #NewBeginnings" (accompanied by a stunning image of a sunset)

- **GIF:** "When you finally achieve that goal you've been working towards! 🎉 #Success #Celebration #YouDidIt" (accompanied by a GIF of someone celebrating)

- **Video:** "A short video with affirmations to start your day with positivity and self-love. You are worthy. You are capable. You are loved. #PositiveAffirmations #SelfLove #Motivation" (accompanied by a short video with inspiring music and text overlays)

- **Animal Video:** "This adorable puppy learning to walk will melt your heart! 🐶 #CuteAnimals #PuppyLove #PositiveVibes" (accompanied by a video of a puppy taking its first steps)

Using Twitter's Features to Spread Positivity: Polls, Threads, and Lists

Twitter offers various features that you can use to enhance your positive messaging and engage with your audience in creative ways.

Tips for Using Twitter's Features to Spread Positivity:

- **Create polls to spark positive discussions:** Use Twitter polls to ask questions related to positivity, gratitude, kindness, or personal growth. For example, you could ask, "What are you most grateful for today?" or "What's your favorite way to spread kindness?"

- **Use threads to share longer stories or insights:** If you have a longer story of kindness, an inspiring experience, or a series of tips for cultivating positivity, consider using a Twitter thread to share your message in a more organized and engaging way.

- **Create Twitter lists to curate positive content:** Create Twitter lists of accounts that share positive and inspiring content. You can then share these lists with your followers to help them discover new sources of positivity.

- **Use Twitter Moments to highlight positive stories:** Twitter Moments allow you to curate a collection of tweets around a specific theme. You could create a Moment that highlights stories of kindness, inspiring quotes, or positive news from around the world.

- **Participate in positive Twitter chats:** Many online communities host Twitter chats focused on positivity, personal growth, and mental health. Participating in these chats can be a great way to connect with like-minded individuals and share inspiring ideas.

Examples of Tweets Using Twitter's Features to Spread Positivity:

- **Poll:** "What's your favorite way to spread kindness? A) Random acts of kindness B) Volunteering C) Offering words of encouragement D) Other (please specify in the comments) #Kindness #Positivity #Poll"

- **Thread:** "I want to share a story about a random act of kindness that I experienced today... (continues in a thread with multiple tweets telling the story) #KindnessMatters #PayItForward #Thread"

- **List:** "I've created a Twitter list of accounts that share positive and inspiring content. Check it out for your daily dose of good vibes! #Positivity #Inspiration #TwitterList"

- **Moment:** "I've curated a Twitter Moment that highlights stories of kindness from around the world. Let's celebrate the good in humanity! #KindnessMatters #MakeADifference #TwitterMoment"

- **Chat:** "Excited to join the #PositivityChat tonight at 8pm EST! Let's discuss how to cultivate a more positive mindset and spread optimism in our communities. #PositiveVibes #PersonalGrowth #TwitterChat"

Spreading Positivity in Your Professional Life: Workplace Culture and Leadership

Positivity and inspiration aren't just limited to your personal life. You can also use Twitter to spread positivity in your professional life, whether you're an employee, a manager, or a business owner.

Tips for Spreading Positivity in Your Professional Life on Twitter:

- **Share articles and resources on positive leadership:** If you're in a leadership position, share articles and resources that promote positive leadership styles, employee engagement, and a healthy workplace culture.

- **Recognize and celebrate employee achievements:** Use Twitter to publicly acknowledge and celebrate the accomplishments of your employees or colleagues. This can boost morale and foster a sense of appreciation.

- **Share positive news about your company or industry:** Highlight the good things that are happening in your company or industry. This can help to build a positive brand image and attract talent.

- **Offer support and encouragement to colleagues:** If a colleague is going through a tough time, offer words of support and encouragement on Twitter. This can help to build a sense of camaraderie and teamwork.

- **Promote a culture of learning and growth:** Share articles, resources, and insights that promote continuous learning and professional development. This can help to create a more engaged and motivated workforce.

Examples of Tweets Spreading Positivity in Your Professional Life:

- **Leadership:** "Just read a great article on the benefits of servant leadership. Highly recommend it for anyone in a leadership position. #Leadership #ServantLeadership #EmployeeEngagement"

- **Employee Recognition:** "Want to give a shout-out to [Employee's Name] for their outstanding work on the [Project]. Your dedication and hard work are greatly appreciated! #EmployeeAppreciation #TeamworkMakesTheDreamWork"

- **Company News:** "Excited to announce that [Your Company] has been recognized as one of the best places to work in [Industry]! Proud to be part of such a positive and supportive team. #BestPlacesToWork #CompanyCulture #PositiveWorkplace"

- **Colleague Support:** "Sending positive vibes to [Colleague's Name] as they navigate a challenging project. You got this! We're here to support you. #Teamwork #SupportYourColleagues #Resilience"

- **Learning and Growth:** "Just finished a great online course on [Skill]. Highly recommend it for anyone looking to expand their knowledge and skills. #ContinuousLearning #ProfessionalDevelopment #GrowthMindset"

Measuring the Impact of Your Positivity: Tracking Engagement and Feedback

While it's not always easy to quantify the impact of positivity, there are ways to track the engagement and feedback on your positive tweets to get a sense of how your messages are being received.

Tips for Measuring the Impact of Your Positivity:

- **Track your likes, retweets, and replies:** Monitor the number of likes, retweets, and replies you receive on your positive tweets. This can give you an indication of how many people are engaging with your content.

- **Use Twitter Analytics to track your reach and impressions:** Twitter Analytics provides insights into the reach and impressions of your tweets, as well as the demographics of your audience. This can help you to understand who is seeing your messages and how they're responding.

- **Ask for feedback from your followers:** Consider asking your followers for feedback on your positive tweets. You could create a poll asking them how your messages make them feel or ask them to share their own stories of positivity in the comments.

- **Pay attention to the sentiment of the replies and comments:** Read the replies and comments on your positive tweets to gauge the overall sentiment. Are people responding positively to your messages? Are they sharing their own stories of inspiration or kindness?

- **Don't get discouraged by negativity:** Not everyone will respond positively to your messages. There will always be some negativity or cynicism on social media. Don't let this discourage you from continuing to spread positivity.

Examples of Tweets Measuring the Impact of Your Positivity:

- "I'm curious to know how my positive tweets make you feel. Please take a moment to vote in this poll: A) Inspired B) Uplifted C) Encouraged D) Other (please specify in the comments) #Positivity #Feedback"

- "I'm using Twitter Analytics to track the reach and engagement of my positive tweets. It's interesting to see who is seeing my messages and how they're responding. #TwitterAnalytics #DataDrivenPositivity"

- "I'm so grateful for the positive feedback I've received on my tweets about kindness and gratitude. It's inspiring to see how many people are committed to making the world a better place. #KindnessMatters #SpreadPositivity"

- "I've noticed that my tweets about positive self-talk have been getting a lot of engagement lately. It's encouraging to see that so many people are interested in cultivating a more positive mindset. #PositiveSelfTalk #MentalHealth"

- "I'm not going to let the negativity of a few trolls discourage me from spreading positivity on Twitter. I believe that kindness and optimism are more powerful than hate and cynicism. #ChoosePositivity #BeTheChange"

A Few Final Tips for Spreading Positivity and Inspiration on Twitter

- **Be authentic and genuine:** Your positive messages should come from the heart. Don't try to be someone you're not. Let your unique personality and values shine through in your tweets.

- **Be consistent:** The more you share positive and inspiring content, the more impact you'll have. Make it a regular part of your Twitter routine.

- **Engage with others:** Don't just broadcast your own messages. Engage with other users, respond to comments, and participate in conversations.

- **Use a variety of formats:** Mix up your content with quotes, stories, images, GIFs, videos, polls, and threads to keep your audience engaged.

- **Don't be afraid to be vulnerable:** Sharing your own struggles and triumphs can make you more relatable and inspire others to overcome their own challenges.

- **Celebrate the good in the world:** Focus on the positive aspects of life and share stories of kindness, hope, and resilience.

- **Be the change you want to see:** Use your Twitter platform to be a force for good in the world. Spread positivity, inspire hope, and make a difference in the lives of others.

By following these tips and examples, you can use Twitter to become a beacon of light in the digital world. You'll not only brighten the day of your followers but also cultivate a more positive and inspiring online environment for everyone.

CHAPTER EIGHT: Connecting with Nature and the Outdoors

In our increasingly digital world, it's easy to get caught up in the hustle and bustle of everyday life and lose touch with the natural world around us. But nature has a profound power to soothe our souls, inspire awe, and remind us of the beauty and wonder that exists beyond our screens.

Twitter (or X), despite its digital nature, can be a surprisingly effective platform for connecting with nature and the outdoors. It allows us to share our experiences in nature, appreciate the beauty of the natural world through stunning photos and videos, learn from experts and enthusiasts, and advocate for environmental protection and conservation.

This chapter will explore how you can use Twitter to deepen your connection with nature, share your outdoor adventures, and inspire others to appreciate and protect our planet.

Sharing Your Nature Experiences: From Backyard Wonders to Mountaintop Views

Whether you're an avid hiker, a casual birdwatcher, or simply someone who enjoys a quiet walk in the park, Twitter provides a space to share your nature experiences with the world.

Tweet Examples:

- **Backyard Nature:** "Spotted a hummingbird flitting around my flowers this morning. Such a tiny but mighty creature! #Hummingbird #BackyardNature #NaturePhotography"

- **Urban Nature:** "Took a stroll through the city park today and was amazed by the resilience of nature amidst the concrete jungle. #UrbanNature #GreenSpaces #CityLife"

- **Hiking Adventures:** "Conquered [Mountain/Trail Name] today! The views were breathtaking and the sense of accomplishment was incredible. #Hiking #Adventure #NatureLover"

- **Camping Trip:** "Spending the weekend camping under the stars. There's nothing quite like disconnecting from technology and reconnecting with nature. #Camping #NatureEscape #Stargazing"

- **Beach Day:** "Enjoying the sun, sand, and surf at the beach today. The ocean has a way of washing away all your worries. #BeachLife #OceanLover #NatureTherapy"

Pro-Tip: Enhance your tweets by including photos or videos of your nature experiences. A stunning sunset, a close-up of a wildflower, or a video of a rushing river can transport your followers to the scene and evoke a sense of wonder.

Appreciating the Beauty of Nature: Showcasing Stunning Photography and Videography

Twitter is a visual platform, making it ideal for sharing the beauty of nature through stunning photography and videography. Whether you're a professional photographer or an amateur enthusiast, you can use Twitter to showcase your nature-inspired captures and inspire others to appreciate the wonders of the natural world.

Tweet Examples:

- **Landscape Photography:** "Captured this breathtaking view of the mountains at sunrise. Nature's artistry at its finest. #LandscapePhotography #Sunrise #NatureIsArt"

- **Wildlife Photography:** "Spotted a majestic bald eagle soaring through the sky today. Such a powerful and awe-inspiring creature. #WildlifePhotography #BaldEagle #NaturePhotography"

- **Macro Photography:** "Got up close and personal with this delicate wildflower. The intricate details of nature are truly amazing. #MacroPhotography #Wildflowers #NatureDetails"

- **Time-Lapse Videography:** "Created a time-lapse video of the clouds rolling over the mountains. Nature's constant motion is mesmerizing. #TimeLapse #Clouds #NatureVideo"

- **Underwater Videography:** "Exploring the vibrant coral reefs and diverse marine life of the ocean. A hidden world of beauty and wonder. #UnderwaterVideography #CoralReef #OceanLife"

Pro-Tip: Use relevant hashtags to increase the visibility of your nature photography and videography tweets. Hashtags like #NaturePhotography, #WildlifePhotography, #LandscapePhotography, #NatureVideo, #OutdoorPhotography, and #NatureLovers can help connect you with a wider audience.

Learning About Nature: Following Experts, Enthusiasts, and Organizations

Twitter is a valuable resource for learning about nature and the outdoors. By following experts, enthusiasts, and organizations in the field, you can gain insights into various aspects of the natural world, from wildlife biology and conservation to environmental science and sustainable living.

Examples of Accounts to Follow:

- **Scientists and Researchers:** Follow scientists and researchers who specialize in fields like ecology, biology, or environmental science to learn about their latest discoveries and research findings.

- **Nature Photographers and Videographers:** Follow talented nature photographers and videographers to admire their work and learn about their techniques and perspectives.

- **Conservation Organizations:** Follow organizations like the World Wildlife Fund (@WWF), the Nature Conservancy (@nature_org), or the Sierra Club (@SierraClub) to stay informed about conservation efforts and environmental issues.

- **Outdoor Enthusiasts and Bloggers:** Follow outdoor enthusiasts and bloggers who share their adventures, tips, and insights on hiking, camping, kayaking, and other outdoor activities.

- **National Parks and Nature Reserves:** Follow the Twitter accounts of your favorite national parks or nature reserves to stay updated on park news, events, and conservation efforts.

Pro-Tip: Engage with the accounts you follow by asking questions, sharing your thoughts, and participating in discussions. Twitter provides a unique opportunity to interact directly with experts and enthusiasts in the field of nature and the outdoors.

Identifying Plants and Animals: Using Twitter for Citizen Science

Twitter can be a valuable tool for identifying plants and animals you encounter in nature. By sharing photos and descriptions of your observations, you can tap into the collective knowledge of the Twitter community and get help with identification.

Tweet Examples:

- **Plant Identification:** "Found this beautiful wildflower on my hike today. Can anyone help me identify it? #PlantID #Wildflowers #NatureLover" (Include a clear photo of the flower)

- **Bird Identification:** "Heard a bird singing a beautiful song in my backyard this morning. Any ideas what species it might be? #BirdID #Birdsong #BackyardBirds" (Include a description of the bird's appearance and song)

- **Insect Identification:** "Spotted this interesting insect on my garden plants. Can anyone tell me what it is? #InsectID #GardenPests #NatureCuriosity" (Include a close-up photo of the insect)

- **Animal Tracks:** "Found these animal tracks on the trail today. Any guesses what animal made them? #AnimalTracks #WildlifeTracking #NatureMystery" (Include a clear photo of the tracks)

Pro-Tip: Use relevant hashtags like #PlantID, #BirdID, #InsectID, #WildlifeID, and #CitizenScience to increase the chances of getting help with identification from experts and enthusiasts in the Twitter community. You can also tag specific organizations or individuals who specialize in plant or animal identification.

Sharing Nature-Inspired Quotes and Poetry: Expressing Awe and Wonder

Nature has been a source of inspiration for poets, writers, and artists for centuries. Share your favorite nature-inspired quotes and poetry on Twitter to express your awe and wonder at the natural world and evoke similar feelings in your followers.

Tweet Examples:

- **Quote:** ""In every walk with nature, one receives far more than he seeks." - John Muir #NatureQuotes #Inspiration #NatureLover"

- **Poetry:** "The woods are lovely, dark and deep, / But I have promises to keep, / And miles to go before I sleep, / And miles to go before I sleep." - Robert Frost #Poetry #NaturePoetry #Woods"

- **Quote:** ""Adopt the pace of nature: her secret is patience." - Ralph Waldo Emerson #NatureWisdom #Patience #SlowLiving"

- **Poetry:** "I wandered lonely as a cloud / That floats on high o'er vales and hills, / When all at once I saw a crowd, / A host, of golden daffodils" - William Wordsworth #Daffodils #NatureBeauty #Poetry"

- **Quote:** ""The Earth has music for those who listen." - William Shakespeare #NatureSounds #ListenToNature #Mindfulness"

Pro-Tip: Pair your quotes and poetry with visually appealing images or videos that enhance the message and create a sense of tranquility or wonder. You can also use Twitter's threading feature to share longer poems or passages.

Promoting Environmental Awareness: Raising Your Voice for Conservation

Twitter can be a powerful tool for raising awareness about environmental issues and advocating for conservation efforts. Use your platform to share information about environmental challenges, promote sustainable practices, and encourage others to take action to protect our planet.

Tweet Examples:

- **Climate Change:** "Climate change is real and it's happening now. We need to take urgent action to reduce greenhouse gas emissions and transition to a clean energy future. #ClimateAction #ClimateChangeIsReal #SaveOurPlanet"

- **Plastic Pollution:** "Plastic pollution is devastating our oceans and harming marine life. Reduce your plastic consumption by using reusable bags, bottles, and straws. #PlasticFreeLiving #ReducePlastic #SaveOurOceans"

- **Deforestation:** "Deforestation is destroying our forests and threatening biodiversity. Support sustainable forestry practices and choose products made from recycled materials. #SaveOurForests #Deforestation #ProtectBiodiversity"

- **Water Conservation:** "Water is a precious resource. Conserve water by taking shorter showers, fixing leaks, and using drought-tolerant landscaping. #WaterConservation #SaveWater #ProtectOurWater"

- **Endangered Species:** "Many species are facing extinction due to habitat loss, poaching, and climate change. Support conservation efforts to protect endangered species and their habitats. #EndangeredSpecies #WildlifeConservation #ProtectOurPlanet"

Pro-Tip: Use relevant hashtags to increase the reach of your environmental awareness tweets. Hashtags like #ClimateAction, #PlasticFreeLiving, #SaveOurForests, #WaterConservation, #EndangeredSpecies, #EnvironmentalJustice, and #Sustainability can help connect you with others who are passionate about protecting the environment.

Sharing Tips for Sustainable Living: Inspiring Eco-Friendly Choices

Promote sustainable living practices on Twitter by sharing tips and resources that encourage others to make eco-friendly choices in their daily lives.

Tweet Examples:

- **Energy Efficiency:** "Reduce your energy consumption by switching to LED light bulbs, unplugging electronics when not in use, and using energy-efficient appliances. #EnergyEfficiency #SaveEnergy #GreenLiving"

- **Sustainable Transportation:** "Choose sustainable transportation options like walking, biking, or taking public transit whenever possible. Reduce your carbon footprint and improve your health. #SustainableTransportation #BikeMore #WalkMore"

- **Reduce, Reuse, Recycle:** "Embrace the three Rs: Reduce your consumption, reuse items whenever possible, and recycle properly. #ReduceReuseRecycle #ZeroWaste #WasteReduction"

- **Eco-Friendly Products:** "Choose eco-friendly products made from sustainable materials, such as bamboo, organic cotton, or recycled plastic. #EcoFriendlyProducts #SustainableShopping #GreenConsumer"

- **Composting:** "Compost your food scraps and yard waste to reduce landfill waste and create nutrient-rich soil for your garden. #Composting #FoodWaste #Gardening"

Pro-Tip: Share links to articles, websites, or organizations that provide more in-depth information about sustainable living practices. You can also share your own personal experiences with eco-friendly choices and encourage others to try them.

Participating in Nature-Related Challenges and Events: Connecting with the Community

Engage with the online nature community by participating in nature-related challenges and events on Twitter.

Examples of Challenges and Events:

- **#NaturePhotoChallenge:** Participate in photography challenges that focus on specific nature themes, such as landscapes, wildlife, or macro photography.

- **#BirdwatchingChallenge:** Join birdwatching challenges that encourage you to identify and document different bird species in your area.

- **#HikingChallenge:** Participate in hiking challenges that motivate you to explore new trails or achieve certain mileage goals.

- **#NatureJournalingChallenge:** Engage in nature journaling challenges that encourage you to observe and document the natural world through writing and drawing.

- **Virtual Nature Events:** Participate in virtual nature events, such as webinars, live streams, or Q&A sessions with experts in the field of nature and the outdoors.

Pro-Tip: Use relevant hashtags to find and participate in nature-related challenges and events on Twitter. You can also follow organizations and individuals who host these events to stay informed about upcoming opportunities.

Using Twitter to Advocate for Outdoor Access and Recreation

Advocate for policies and initiatives that promote outdoor access and recreation on Twitter. Share information about the benefits of spending time in nature, support organizations that are working to protect public lands, and encourage your followers to contact their elected officials to advocate for policies that support outdoor recreation.

Tweet Examples:

- **Benefits of Nature:** "Spending time in nature has numerous benefits for our physical and mental health. It reduces stress, improves mood, and boosts creativity. #NatureTherapy #GetOutdoors #MentalHealth"

- **Public Lands Protection:** "Our public lands are a national treasure. Support organizations like the Wilderness Society (@wilderness) that are working to protect these lands for future generations. #PublicLands #ProtectOurWild #Conservation"

- **Outdoor Recreation:** "Outdoor recreation is essential for our well-being and our economy. Support policies that promote access to parks, trails, and other outdoor spaces. #OutdoorRecreation #RecreationEconomy #GetOutside"

- **Environmental Justice:** "Everyone deserves access to clean air, clean water, and green spaces. Advocate for environmental justice policies that ensure equitable access to nature for all communities. #EnvironmentalJustice #GreenSpacesForAll #Equity"

- **Contact Your Elected Officials:** "Contact your elected officials to urge them to support policies that protect our environment and promote outdoor access and recreation. Your voice matters! #AdvocateForNature #CivicEngagement #MakeADifference"

Pro-Tip: Share links to petitions, advocacy campaigns, or contact information for elected officials to make it easy for your followers to take action. You can also use Twitter's polling feature to gauge your followers' opinions on outdoor recreation and environmental issues.

Using Twitter to Plan Your Outdoor Adventures: Finding Inspiration and Resources

Twitter can be a valuable resource for planning your next outdoor adventure. Use the platform to find inspiration, discover new destinations, research trails and campsites, and connect with other outdoor enthusiasts who can offer tips and advice.

Tweet Examples:

- **Destination Inspiration:** "Looking for inspiration for my next hiking trip. Any recommendations for scenic trails with stunning views? #HikingInspiration #TrailRecommendations #AdventureTime"

- **Campsite Research:** "Planning a camping trip to [Park/Region]. Any recommendations for campgrounds with beautiful scenery and good amenities? #CampingTips #CampgroundReviews #OutdoorAdventure"

- **Gear Recommendations:** "Need a new pair of hiking boots for my upcoming trip. Any recommendations for comfortable and durable boots that can handle rugged terrain? #HikingGear #GearReviews #OutdoorEssentials"

- **Trail Advice:** "Planning to hike the [Trail Name] next month. Any tips or advice from experienced hikers who have completed this trail? #TrailTips #HikingAdvice #OutdoorCommunity"

- **Connecting with Hikers:** "Looking to connect with other hikers in the [City/Region] area. Anyone interested in joining me for a hike on the [Trail Name] next weekend? #HikingBuddies #OutdoorEnthusiasts #GroupHike"

Pro-Tip: Use relevant hashtags to connect with other outdoor enthusiasts and find information about specific destinations, trails, or activities. You can also use Twitter's search function to find tweets and accounts that are relevant to your interests.

Sharing Your Outdoor Adventures with Friends and Family: Creating Lasting Memories

Use Twitter to share your outdoor adventures with friends and family, allowing them to experience the beauty of nature and the thrill of your explorations vicariously.

Tweet Examples:

- **Family Hike:** "Took the kids on a hike in the woods today. They loved exploring the trails and discovering all the wonders of nature. #FamilyFun #NatureWalk #MakingMemories"

- **Weekend Camping Trip:** "Spent the weekend camping with friends. We roasted marshmallows around the campfire, told stories under the stars, and made memories that will last a lifetime. #CampingTrip #FriendshipGoals #NatureEscape"

- **Kayaking Adventure:** "Went kayaking on the lake today. The water was calm and the scenery was stunning. A perfect day to reconnect with nature and enjoy the company of friends. #Kayaking #OutdoorAdventure #NatureLover"

- **Backpacking Trip:** "Just finished an epic backpacking trip through the mountains. The views were breathtaking, the challenges were rewarding, and the memories are unforgettable. #Backpacking #AdventureTime #NatureExploration"

- **Sharing Photos and Videos:** "Sharing some photos and videos from my recent hiking trip to [Destination]. The scenery was incredible and the experience was truly unforgettable. #HikingAdventure #TravelPhotography #NatureBeauty"

Pro-Tip: Tag your friends and family members in your tweets and encourage them to share their own outdoor adventures as well. You can also create a shared hashtag for your group's adventures to easily collect and relive your memories.

A Few Final Tips for Connecting with Nature and the Outdoors on Twitter

- **Be authentic and passionate:** Share your genuine love for nature and the outdoors in your tweets. Your enthusiasm will be contagious and inspire others to connect with nature as well.

- **Use high-quality visuals:** Twitter is a visual platform, so make sure your photos and videos are clear, well-composed, and visually appealing.

- **Use relevant hashtags:** Hashtags are essential for increasing the visibility of your tweets and connecting with a wider audience. Research relevant hashtags and use them strategically.

- **Engage with others:** Don't just broadcast your own content. Engage with other users, ask questions, share your thoughts, and participate in discussions.

- **Be respectful of nature:** When sharing your outdoor adventures, be mindful of the environment and practice Leave No Trace principles.

- **Inspire others to get outdoors:** Encourage your followers to explore the natural world around them, whether it's a local park, a nearby hiking trail, or a far-flung wilderness area.

- **Have fun!** Connecting with nature should be an enjoyable experience. Let your passion shine through in your tweets and inspire others to discover the joy and wonder of the outdoors.

By following these tips and examples, you can use Twitter to deepen your connection with nature, share your outdoor adventures, and inspire others to appreciate and protect our planet. So go forth, explore the natural world, and share your experiences with the Twitter community!

CHAPTER NINE: Foodie Tweets: Sharing Your Culinary Adventures

They say that the way to a person's heart is through their stomach. And in the world of Twitter (or X), the way to your followers' hearts (and retweets) is through their feed – specifically, a feed filled with mouthwatering food photos, witty culinary commentary, and engaging foodie discussions.

Whether you're a seasoned chef, a passionate home cook, or simply someone who appreciates a good meal, this chapter will equip you with the tools and inspiration to transform your Twitter presence into a delectable feast for the senses. We'll explore various ways to share your culinary adventures, from restaurant reviews and recipe recommendations to cooking tips and tricks and the art of the perfect food photo. Get ready to tantalize your followers' taste buds and become a culinary influencer in the Twitterverse.

Restaurant Reviews: Sharing Your Dining Experiences

Dining out is a social experience, and Twitter provides the perfect platform to share your restaurant adventures with your followers. Whether you're raving about a new culinary discovery, offering constructive criticism, or simply documenting your foodie escapades, your restaurant reviews can be a valuable resource for fellow food enthusiasts.

Tips for Crafting Engaging Restaurant Reviews:

- **Be specific and descriptive:** Instead of simply saying "The food was good," describe the specific dishes you tried, the flavors, the textures, and the presentation. Use vivid language that paints a picture in the reader's mind.

- **Highlight the standout dishes:** If there were particular dishes that you loved (or disliked), be sure to mention them by name. This can help your followers make informed decisions about what to order if they visit the restaurant.

- **Mention the ambiance and service:** The overall dining experience is not just about the food. Describe the ambiance of the restaurant, the level of service, and any other notable aspects of your visit.

- **Include photos of your food:** A picture is worth a thousand words, especially when it comes to food. Include high-quality photos of the dishes you tried to make your review more visually appealing.

- **Use relevant hashtags:** Hashtags can help increase the visibility of your review and connect you with other foodies in your area. Use hashtags like #restaurantreview, #foodreview, #[CityName]restaurants, #[CuisineType], and #foodie.

- **Be honest and objective:** While it's important to be positive and encouraging, it's also important to be honest and objective in your review. If you had a negative experience, don't be afraid to share it constructively.

- **Tag the restaurant (if they have a Twitter account):** Tagging the restaurant in your review can alert them to your feedback and potentially lead to a response or interaction.

Examples of Engaging Restaurant Reviews:

- **Positive Review:** "Just had an incredible meal at [Restaurant Name]! The [Dish Name] was a standout – perfectly cooked and bursting with flavor. The ambiance was cozy and the service was impeccable. Highly recommend! #RestaurantReview #[CityName]Eats #Foodie" (Include a photo of the dish)

- **Mixed Review:** "Had a decent meal at [Restaurant Name] last night. The [Dish Name] was delicious, but the [Dish Name] was a bit disappointing. The service was friendly, but the atmosphere was a little loud. Overall, it was a mixed experience. #FoodReview #[CuisineType] #HonestReview"

- **Negative Review:** "Unfortunately, I had a disappointing experience at [Restaurant Name]. The food was bland and overcooked, and the service was slow and inattentive. I wouldn't recommend it. #RestaurantReview #[CityName]Restaurants #NotImpressed"

- **Specific Dish Highlight:** "The [Dish Name] at [Restaurant Name] is a must-try! It's a culinary masterpiece – a perfect blend of flavors and textures. I'm still dreaming about it! #FoodieFinds #[CuisineType] #BestDishEver" (Include a close-up photo of the dish)

- **Ambiance and Service Focus:** "Loved the ambiance at [Restaurant Name]. It's the perfect spot for a romantic date night or a special occasion. The service was attentive and the staff was knowledgeable about the menu. #DateNight #FineDining #[CityName]Restaurants"

Recipe Recommendations: Sharing Your Culinary Favorites

If you're a passionate home cook or baker, Twitter provides a fantastic platform to share your favorite recipes with your followers. Whether it's a family recipe passed down through generations, a new culinary creation you're proud of, or a recipe you discovered online that you can't wait to try, your recommendations can inspire others to get in the kitchen and create their own culinary masterpieces.

Tips for Sharing Recipe Recommendations:

- **Provide a brief overview of the recipe:** Describe the dish, the key ingredients, and the level of difficulty. This can help your followers decide if the recipe is something they'd be interested in trying.

- **Share the source of the recipe:** If you're sharing a recipe from a cookbook, a website, or a blog, be sure to provide a link or citation. This gives credit to the original creator and allows your followers to access the full recipe.

- **Include photos of the finished dish:** Visuals are essential for making your recipe recommendations more appealing. Include high-quality photos of the finished dish to entice your followers to give it a try.

- **Use relevant hashtags:** Hashtags can help increase the visibility of your tweets and connect you with other food enthusiasts who are interested in similar recipes. Use hashtags like #recipe, #recipeshare, #homecooking, #baking, #[CuisineType], #[DishName], and #foodie.

- **Offer your own tips or modifications:** If you've made any modifications to the original recipe or have any tips for making it easier or more flavorful, be sure to share them with your followers.

- **Engage with followers who try the recipe:** Encourage your followers to share their experiences if they try the recipe. Respond to comments and questions and offer support and encouragement.

Examples of Recipe Recommendations:

- **Family Recipe:** "Sharing my grandma's famous chocolate chip cookie recipe today! It's been a family favorite for generations. #FamilyRecipe #ChocolateChipCookies #Baking" (Include a photo of the cookies and a link to the recipe)

- **New Culinary Creation:** "Just created a delicious new pasta dish with roasted vegetables and a creamy pesto sauce. It's healthy, flavorful, and easy to make. #HomeCooking #PastaRecipe #Vegetarian" (Include a photo of the dish and a link to the recipe)

- **Online Recipe Discovery:** "Found this amazing recipe for [Dish Name] on [Website/Blog]. Can't wait to try it! #RecipeInspiration #[CuisineType] #FoodieFinds" (Include a photo of the dish from the website/blog and a link to the recipe)

- **Recipe Modification:** "I made a few modifications to this [Dish Name] recipe, and it turned out even better than the original! I added [Ingredient] and [Ingredient] for extra flavor. #RecipeHack #HomeCooking #FoodieTips"

- **Follower Engagement:** "Has anyone tried the [Dish Name] recipe I shared last week? I'd love to hear your feedback! #RecipeReview #HomeCooking #FoodieCommunity"

Cooking Tips and Tricks: Sharing Your Culinary Expertise

If you've spent some time in the kitchen, you've probably picked up a few cooking tips and tricks along the way. Whether it's a time-saving technique, a flavor-enhancing secret, or a clever kitchen hack, sharing your culinary expertise on Twitter can be a valuable resource for fellow food enthusiasts.

Tips for Sharing Cooking Tips and Tricks:

- **Be clear and concise:** Get straight to the point and explain your tip or trick in a way that's easy to understand. Use bullet points or numbered lists for clarity.

- **Use visuals if helpful:** If your tip or trick involves a specific technique or process, consider including a photo or video to demonstrate it.

- **Focus on practical and actionable advice:** Share tips and tricks that your followers can easily implement in their own kitchens.

- **Use relevant hashtags:** Hashtags can help increase the visibility of your tweets and connect you with other food enthusiasts who are interested in similar cooking tips. Use hashtags like #cookingtips, #kitchentips, #foodhacks, #culinaryskills, #[CuisineType], and #foodie.

- **Engage with followers who try your tips:** Encourage your followers to share their experiences if they try your tips. Respond to comments and questions and offer support and encouragement.

Examples of Cooking Tips and Tricks:

- **Time-Saving Tip:** "Save time chopping vegetables by using a food processor. It's a game-changer for busy weeknight meals! #CookingTips #KitchenHacks #TimeSaver"

- **Flavor-Enhancing Secret:** "Add a pinch of salt to your chocolate chip cookie dough to enhance the sweetness and create a more complex flavor profile. #BakingTips #ChocolateChipCookies #FoodieSecrets"

- **Kitchen Hack:** "Prevent your cutting board from slipping by placing a damp towel underneath it. It's a simple trick that makes a big difference! #KitchenSafety #CookingHacks #CulinarySkills"

- **Technique Demonstration:** "Here's a quick video tutorial on how to perfectly dice an onion. It's a basic skill that every cook should master. #CookingTechniques

#KnifeSkills #CulinaryBasics" (Include a short video demonstrating the technique)

- **Follower Engagement:** "Has anyone tried my tip for [Cooking Technique]? I'd love to hear your feedback! #CookingTips #KitchenExperiments #FoodieCommunity"

Documenting Your Cooking Journey: Sharing Your Culinary Experiments

Cooking can be a journey of discovery, experimentation, and sometimes, even a few kitchen mishaps. Sharing your cooking journey on Twitter can be a fun and engaging way to connect with other food enthusiasts, learn from each other's experiences, and celebrate the joys (and occasional frustrations) of creating culinary magic.

Tips for Documenting Your Cooking Journey:

- **Share photos and videos of your cooking process:** Take your followers behind the scenes and show them what you're cooking, the ingredients you're using, and the steps you're taking.

- **Share your successes (and failures):** Cooking isn't always perfect. Don't be afraid to share your kitchen failures as well as your successes. It makes you more relatable and can be a source of humor and learning for others.

- **Ask for advice and suggestions:** If you're trying a new recipe or technique, don't hesitate to ask your followers for advice or suggestions. The Twitter community can be a valuable resource for culinary inspiration and troubleshooting.

- **Use relevant hashtags:** Hashtags can help increase the visibility of your tweets and connect you with other food enthusiasts who are interested in similar cooking experiences. Use hashtags like #cookingjourney,

#kitcheneexperiments, #foodieadventures, #homecooking, #baking, and #[CuisineType].

- **Engage with followers who are on a similar journey:** Connect with other food enthusiasts who are documenting their cooking journeys on Twitter. Share your experiences, offer encouragement, and learn from each other's successes and failures.

Examples of Tweets Documenting Your Cooking Journey:

- **Cooking Process:** "Trying a new recipe for [Dish Name] tonight. Wish me luck! □ #CookingJourney #KitchenAdventure #[CuisineType]" (Include a photo of the ingredients or the recipe)

- **Kitchen Success:** "Nailed it! My [Dish Name] turned out perfectly! So proud of myself. 🌀 #CookingWin #HomeCooking #FoodiePride" (Include a photo of the finished dish)

- **Kitchen Failure:** "Well, that didn't go as planned. My [Dish Name] is a bit of a disaster. 😊 Back to the drawing board! #KitchenFail #CookingLessons #NeverGiveUp" (Include a humorous photo of the failed dish)

- **Asking for Advice:** "I'm attempting to make [Dish Name] for the first time. Any tips or advice from experienced cooks? #CookingHelp #RecipeSOS #FoodieCommunity"

- **Connecting with Others:** "Loving all the #CookingJourney posts on Twitter! It's so inspiring to see what others are creating in the kitchen. Let's connect and share our experiences! #FoodieFriends #HomeCooking"

The Art of the Food Photo: Capturing Culinary Masterpieces

In the visually-driven world of Twitter, a well-composed and aesthetically pleasing food photo can make all the difference in capturing your followers' attention and enticing them to engage with your culinary content.

Tips for Taking Mouthwatering Food Photos:

- **Use natural lighting:** Natural light is your best friend when it comes to food photography. Avoid using harsh artificial light, which can create unappetizing shadows and distort colors.

- **Choose a clean and simple background:** A cluttered or distracting background can detract from the beauty of your food. Opt for a clean and simple background that allows your dish to be the star of the show.

- **Focus on the details:** Capture the intricate details of your dish, such as the textures, the colors, and the garnishes. A close-up shot can be incredibly effective in showcasing the beauty of your culinary creation.

- **Style your food thoughtfully:** A little bit of food styling can go a long way. Arrange your dish in an aesthetically pleasing way, add garnishes or props to enhance the visual appeal, and consider using contrasting colors and textures to create a more dynamic composition.

- **Use editing tools sparingly:** While editing tools can be helpful for adjusting brightness, contrast, and saturation, avoid over-editing your photos. You want your food to look natural and appetizing.

Examples of Tweets Showcasing Food Photography:

- **Natural Lighting:** "Enjoying a delicious brunch in the sunshine. The natural light makes the food look even more appetizing! #BrunchGoals #FoodPhotography

#NaturalLight" (Include a photo of your brunch with natural light streaming in)

- **Simple Background:** "Baked a batch of fresh sourdough bread. The crust is perfectly golden brown and the aroma is divine. #SourdoughBread #Baking #FoodPhotography" (Include a photo of the bread on a simple wooden cutting board)

- **Detail Shot:** "The intricate details of this sushi roll are a work of art. Each ingredient is carefully chosen and expertly prepared. #SushiLover #FoodArt #FoodPhotography" (Include a close-up shot of the sushi roll showcasing the details)

- **Food Styling:** "Styled this pasta dish with fresh herbs and a drizzle of olive oil. It's a feast for the eyes as well as the taste buds! #PastaPerfection #FoodStyling #FoodPhotography" (Include a photo of the pasta dish with thoughtful styling)

- **Minimal Editing:** "Captured the natural beauty of this fresh fruit salad. No filters needed! #HealthyEating #FruitSalad #FoodPhotography" (Include a photo of the fruit salad with minimal editing)

Engaging in Foodie Conversations: Connecting with the Culinary Community

Twitter is not just a platform for sharing your own culinary adventures. It's also a great place to connect with other food enthusiasts, engage in foodie conversations, and learn from each other's experiences.

Tips for Engaging in Foodie Conversations:

- **Follow other foodies:** Search for hashtags related to your culinary interests and follow other users who are sharing similar content.

- **Participate in Twitter chats:** Many online communities host Twitter chats focused on food, cooking, and dining. Participating in these chats can be a great way to connect with other foodies, share your knowledge, and learn from others.

- **Ask questions and share your opinions:** Don't be afraid to ask questions about recipes, cooking techniques, or restaurant recommendations. Share your own opinions and experiences to contribute to the conversation.

- **Retweet and amplify interesting content:** When you see a tweet that you find interesting or informative, retweet it to share it with your followers.

- **Be respectful and supportive:** The foodie community on Twitter is generally very welcoming and supportive. Be respectful of others' opinions, even if you disagree with them.

Examples of Engaging in Foodie Conversations:

- **Following Foodies:** "Just discovered some amazing #foodies on Twitter! So excited to connect with others who share my passion for food and cooking. #FoodieCommunity #FoodLovers"

- **Participating in Twitter Chats:** "Excited to join the #FoodChat tonight at 8pm EST! Let's discuss our favorite recipes, cooking tips, and restaurant recommendations. #FoodieConversations #CulinaryCommunity"

- **Asking Questions:** "I'm looking for recommendations for the best Italian restaurants in [City Name]. Any suggestions? #ItalianFood #RestaurantRecommendations #FoodieHelp"

- **Sharing Opinions:** "I believe that pineapple DOES belong on pizza. Fight me! 🍍 #PizzaDebate #PineappleOnPizza #ControversialFoodOpinions"

- **Retweeting Content:** "Just read a fascinating article about the history of [Dish Name]. Sharing it here for fellow food nerds! #FoodHistory #CulinaryCulture #FoodieFacts" (Include a link to the article)

Using Twitter for Foodie Inspiration: Discovering New Recipes, Restaurants, and Trends

Twitter can be a fantastic source of inspiration for your next culinary adventure. Whether you're looking for new recipes to try, restaurants to visit, or food trends to explore, the Twitter community can provide a wealth of ideas and recommendations.

Tips for Using Twitter for Foodie Inspiration:

- **Follow food bloggers and chefs:** Food bloggers and chefs often share their latest recipes, cooking tips, and restaurant recommendations on Twitter. Following them can provide a constant stream of culinary inspiration.

- **Explore food-related hashtags:** Search for hashtags related to your culinary interests, such as #recipes, #restaurants, #foodtrends, #[CuisineType], or #[DishName]. This can help you discover new content and connect with other foodies who share your passions.

- **Save tweets for later:** If you see a recipe or restaurant recommendation that you want to try later, use Twitter's bookmarking feature to save the tweet for future reference.

- **Create Twitter lists to organize your foodie inspiration:** Create Twitter lists of accounts that share recipes, restaurant recommendations, or food trends that you're interested in. This can help you keep your foodie inspiration organized and easily accessible.

- **Participate in food-related challenges and events:** Many online communities host food-related challenges and events, such as recipe contests, cooking challenges, or virtual food festivals. Participating in these events can be a fun and inspiring way to explore new culinary horizons.

Examples of Tweets Using Twitter for Foodie Inspiration:

- **Following Food Bloggers:** "Just discovered a new food blog with amazing recipes and stunning food photography. Give them a follow for some serious foodie inspiration! #FoodBloggers #RecipeInspiration #CulinaryCreativity"

- **Exploring Hashtags:** "Scrolling through the #[CuisineType] hashtag for some dinner inspiration tonight. So many delicious options to choose from! #FoodieAdventures #CulinaryExploration"

- **Saving Tweets:** "Just bookmarked this recipe for [Dish Name]. It looks so delicious and I can't wait to try it this weekend! #RecipeGoals #WeekendCooking #FoodieFinds"

- **Creating Twitter Lists:** "I've created a Twitter list of my favorite food bloggers and chefs. It's my go-to resource for recipe inspiration and cooking tips. #FoodieResources #CulinaryExperts #TwitterLists"

- **Participating in Challenges:** "Excited to participate in the #RecipeChallenge this month! I'm going to try to create a new dish every week. Wish me luck! #CookingChallenge #FoodieFun #CreativeCooking"

Using Twitter for Food-Related Support and Advice: Troubleshooting Culinary Dilemmas

We all encounter culinary dilemmas from time to time, whether it's a recipe that went wrong, a cooking technique we're struggling with, or a question about food safety or storage. Twitter can be a valuable resource for getting support and advice from experienced cooks and food experts.

Tips for Using Twitter for Food-Related Support and Advice:

- **Be specific with your questions:** Clearly state the problem you're encountering or the question you have. The more specific you are, the more likely you are to get helpful responses.

- **Use relevant hashtags:** Hashtags can help increase the visibility of your tweets and connect you with people who have the expertise to answer your questions. Use hashtags like #cookinghelp, #recipesos, #foodsafety, #kitchentips, #[CuisineType], or #[DishName].

- **Tag relevant experts or organizations:** If you know of any food experts, chefs, or organizations that might be able to help, consider tagging them in your tweet.

- **Be open to suggestions and feedback:** Be receptive to the suggestions and feedback you receive from others. Even if you don't agree with everything, you might learn something new or gain a different perspective.

- **Express your gratitude for the help you receive:** When someone takes the time to answer your question or offer advice, be sure to express your gratitude.

Examples of Tweets Seeking Food-Related Support and Advice:

- **Recipe Troubleshooting:** "Help! My cake didn't rise properly. What could have gone wrong? #BakingSOS #CakeDisaster #CookingHelp"

- **Cooking Technique Question:** "I'm trying to learn how to make a roux, but I'm having trouble getting the consistency right. Any tips? #CookingTechniques #Roux #CulinarySkills"

- **Food Safety Question:** "How long can I safely store cooked chicken in the refrigerator? #FoodSafety #FoodStorage #KitchenTips"

- **Tagging Experts:** "I'm having trouble getting my sourdough starter to activate. Any advice, @SourdoughExpert? #SourdoughBread #BakingHelp #FoodieSOS"

- **Expressing Gratitude:** "Thank you to everyone who offered advice on my cake dilemma! I really appreciate your help. I'm going to try again tomorrow. #CookingCommunity #FoodieSupport #Grateful"

Using Twitter to Discover Food Events and Festivals: Expanding Your Culinary Horizons

Twitter can be a great resource for discovering food events and festivals in your area or around the world. From food truck rallies and farmers' markets to culinary festivals and wine tasting events, there's a world of foodie experiences waiting to be explored.

Tips for Using Twitter to Discover Food Events and Festivals:

- **Follow food event organizers and venues:** Many food event organizers and venues have Twitter accounts where they announce upcoming events and share details about ticket sales, schedules, and participating vendors.

- **Explore food-related hashtags:** Search for hashtags related to food events and festivals, such as #foodevents, #foodfestivals, #[CityName]foodevents, #[CuisineType]festival, or #[EventName]. This can help you discover events that you might not have otherwise known about.

- **Use Twitter's advanced search features:** Twitter's advanced search features allow you to filter your search results by location, date, and other criteria. This can be helpful for finding food events that are happening near you or on a specific date.

- **Engage with other attendees:** If you're attending a food event or festival, use Twitter to connect with other attendees, share your experiences, and discover new food and drinks to try.

- **Share your photos and videos from the event:** Capture the sights, sounds, and flavors of the event by sharing photos and videos on Twitter. This can help to promote the event and inspire others to attend in the future.

Examples of Tweets Discovering Food Events and Festivals:

- **Following Event Organizers:** "Just followed the Twitter account for the [Food Festival]. Can't wait to see what delicious treats they have in store this year! #FoodieEvents #[CityName]Food #FestivalSeason"

- **Exploring Hashtags:** "Scrolling through the #[CityName]FoodieEvents hashtag to see what's happening this weekend. Looks like there's a food truck rally and a farmers' market! #FoodTruckFun #LocalProduce #WeekendPlans"

- **Using Advanced Search:** "Using Twitter's advanced search to find food festivals that are happening within a 50-mile radius of me in the next month. #FoodieAdventures #CulinaryExploration #RoadTripReady"

- **Engaging with Attendees:** "Anyone else going to the [Food Festival] this weekend? Let's connect and share our favorite food finds! #FoodieMeetup #FestivalFun #[EventName]"

- **Sharing Event Experiences:** "Having an amazing time at the [Food Festival]! Just tried the most delicious [Dish Name] from [Vendor Name]. Highly recommend! #FoodieHeaven #FestivalFood #[EventName]" (Include a photo of the dish)

Building Your Foodie Brand on Twitter: Becoming a Culinary Influencer

If you're passionate about food and enjoy sharing your culinary adventures on Twitter, you might consider building your foodie brand and becoming a culinary influencer. A strong foodie brand can open up opportunities for collaborations with restaurants, brands, and other food-related businesses.

Tips for Building Your Foodie Brand on Twitter:

- **Choose a niche:** What are you most passionate about when it comes to food? Do you specialize in a particular cuisine? Are you a baking enthusiast? Do you focus on healthy eating or vegan cooking? Choosing a niche can help you to stand out from the crowd and attract a targeted audience.

- **Develop a consistent brand voice:** How do you want to be perceived by your audience? Are you witty and sarcastic? Are you informative and educational? Are you passionate and enthusiastic? Developing a consistent brand voice will help you to create a recognizable and memorable identity.

- **Create high-quality content:** Share visually appealing photos, engaging videos, informative articles, and well-written tweets that provide value to your audience.

- **Engage with your followers:** Respond to comments and questions, participate in conversations, and build relationships with your followers.

- **Collaborate with other foodies:** Partner with other food bloggers, chefs, or restaurants to cross-promote each other's content and reach a wider audience.

- **Use relevant hashtags:** Use hashtags strategically to increase the visibility of your tweets and connect with a wider audience.

- **Promote your other platforms:** If you have a food blog, a YouTube channel, or an Instagram account, be sure to promote them on your Twitter profile and in your tweets.

- **Be patient and persistent:** Building a strong foodie brand takes time and effort. Don't get discouraged if you don't see results overnight. Keep creating great content, engaging with your audience, and promoting your brand, and you'll eventually start to see success.

Examples of Tweets Building Your Foodie Brand:

- **Niche Focus:** "I'm a #vegan #baker who loves creating delicious and healthy treats. Follow me for plant-based baking inspiration! #VeganBaking #PlantBasedDesserts #HealthyEating"

- **Brand Voice:** "I'm a #foodie with a sarcastic sense of humor. Follow me for witty commentary on all things food-related. #FoodHumor #CulinarySarcasm #FoodieLife"

- **High-Quality Content:** "Just published a new blog post with my favorite #glutenfree #pasta recipes. Check it out for some delicious and easy-to-make dishes! #GlutenFreeCooking #HealthyPasta #RecipeInspiration" (Include a link to the blog post)

- **Follower Engagement:** "I'm curious to know what your favorite #comfortfood is. Share your answers in the comments! #FoodieConversation #FoodLovers #CulinaryDebate"

- **Collaboration:** "Excited to be partnering with [Restaurant Name] to host a #cookingclass on [CuisineType] cuisine. Sign up now to learn some new culinary skills! #FoodieEvent #CulinaryCollaboration #[CuisineType]Cooking" (Include a link to the event registration page)

A Few Final Tips for Foodie Tweets

- **Be mindful of food allergies and dietary restrictions:** When sharing recipes or restaurant recommendations, be mindful of food allergies and dietary restrictions. Clearly label your content with relevant information, such as #glutenfree, #vegan, #vegetarian, or #dairyfree.

- **Be respectful of cultural food traditions:** When discussing or sharing recipes from different cultures, be respectful of the cultural significance of the food and avoid making generalizations or stereotypes.

- **Promote healthy eating habits:** While indulging in delicious food is part of the foodie experience, it's important to promote healthy eating habits as well. Share recipes and tips for creating balanced and nutritious meals.

- **Support local food businesses:** Use your platform to support local restaurants, farmers' markets, and food producers. Sharing your experiences and recommendations can help to promote these businesses and strengthen your local food community.

- **Have fun!** Food is meant to be enjoyed. Let your passion and enthusiasm for food shine through in your tweets and inspire others to explore the world of culinary delights.

By following these tips and examples, you can use Twitter to transform your culinary adventures into engaging and inspiring content that will tantalize your followers' taste buds and establish you as a culinary influencer in the Twitterverse. So go forth, explore the world of food, and share your delicious discoveries with the world!

CHAPTER TEN: Travel Tales: Tweeting Your Journeys

The world is a book, and those who don't travel read only one page. So said Saint Augustine, and he wasn't wrong. Travel opens our eyes to new cultures, breathtaking landscapes, and experiences that broaden our horizons and leave us with lasting memories.

And in the age of social media, what better way to share those memories – and inspire a little wanderlust in others – than through Twitter (or X)?

This chapter is your guide to crafting engaging and memorable travel-related tweets. From pre-trip excitement to hilarious travel mishaps, we'll explore a variety of tweet types, examples, and tips to help you document your journeys, connect with fellow travelers, and perhaps even become the next big travel influencer.

Pre-Trip Buzz: Tweeting the Anticipation

The excitement leading up to a trip is almost as good as the trip itself. Packing lists, travel apps, daydreaming about exotic destinations – it's all part of the fun. Share your pre-trip buzz on Twitter and let your followers in on the adventure.

Tweet Examples:

- "Packing my bags and getting ready for an adventure to [Destination]! Any must-see recommendations? #TravelPlanning #Wanderlust #[Destination]Bound"

- "Finally booked my dream trip to [Destination]! Counting down the days until I can explore [Highlight of Destination]. #BucketListTrip #TravelDreams #AdventureAwaits"

- "Anyone else get ridiculously excited about creating travel playlists? My [Destination] playlist is going to be epic. #TravelMusic #SoundtrackToMyAdventure #[Destination]Vibes"

- "Trying to pack light for my trip, but my suitcase seems to have other plans. #OverpackerProblems #TravelStruggles #SendHelp"

- "Just realized I don't speak a word of [Language of Destination]. Time to brush up on some key phrases! #LanguageLearning #TravelPrep #WishMeLuck"

Pro-Tip: Use relevant hashtags to connect with other travelers who are planning trips to the same destination or who share similar travel interests. Hashtags like #TravelPlanning, #Wanderlust, #[Destination]Travel, #[TravelStyle] (e.g., #SoloTravel, #Backpacking), and #TravelTips can help expand the reach of your tweets.

In-Transit Tweets: Sharing the Journey

The journey is just as important as the destination, as they say. Whether you're soaring through the skies, cruising along scenic highways, or navigating bustling train stations, your in-transit experiences can be tweet-worthy moments.

Tweet Examples:

- "Window seat secured! Soaking up the views as we fly over [Landmark/Scenery]. #TravelViews #WindowSeatPerks #FlyingHigh"

- "Road tripping through [Region/Country] and loving the scenic landscapes. Every turn reveals a new postcard-worthy vista. #RoadTripAdventures #ScenicDrives #[Region]RoadTrip"

- "Navigating the train system in [City] is an adventure in itself. But hey, at least I'm getting my steps in! #TrainTravel #CityAdventures #[City]Life"

- "Airport delays are the worst, but at least there's free Wi-Fi. Time to catch up on some reading/Netflix. #TravelDelays #AirportLife #MakingTheMostOfIt"

- "Met some interesting people on the train today. Travel is such a great way to connect with others from all walks of life. #TravelEncounters #HumanConnection #[Destination]Train"

Pro-Tip: If you're comfortable sharing your location, use Twitter's location tagging feature to add context to your tweets. You can also use live-tweeting to document your journey in real time, sharing updates and photos as you go.

First Impressions: Tweeting Your Arrival

You've arrived at your destination, and the excitement is palpable. Share your first impressions of the city, the culture, the people, and the overall vibe. Let your followers know what's captivating your senses.

Tweet Examples:

- "Just arrived in [City]! The energy here is electric, the streets are bustling with life, and I can't wait to explore every corner. #[City]Adventures #FirstImpressions #TravelVibes"

- "Stepping off the plane in [Country] and immediately hit with a wave of [Sensory Detail: e.g., warm air, exotic spices]. I'm officially in love with this place. #[Country]Travel #SensoryOverload #DreamDestination"

- "Checked into my hotel room with a view of [Landmark/Scenery]. Pinch me, I must be dreaming! #[City]Views #HotelLife #TravelLuxury"

- "First meal in [City] was a culinary delight! [Dish Name] from [Restaurant Name] was absolutely incredible. My taste buds are dancing. #[City]Food #CulinaryAdventures #FoodieTravel"

- "The people in [City] are so friendly and welcoming. Already had several interesting conversations with locals. #CulturalExchange #TravelEncounters #[City]People"

Pro-Tip: Include photos or videos to capture the essence of your first impressions. A shot of the city skyline, a vibrant street scene, or a short video clip capturing the sounds and sights of your arrival can add depth to your tweets.

Sightseeing and Activities: Tweeting Your Adventures

From iconic landmarks to hidden gems, every destination offers a unique tapestry of experiences. Share your sightseeing adventures, cultural encounters, and the activities that are filling your days with excitement and wonder.

Tweet Examples:

- "Just visited [Landmark] and it was even more impressive in person than in pictures. The history and architecture are simply awe-inspiring. #[Landmark] #[City]Sightseeing #TravelGoals"

- "Exploring the backstreets of [City] and discovering hidden cafes, charming boutiques, and local art studios. Loving the off-the-beaten-path adventures. #[City]HiddenGems #UrbanExploration #TravelDiscoveries"

- "Took a cooking class in [City] and learned how to make traditional [Dish Name]. It was a delicious and immersive cultural experience. #[City]CookingClass #CulturalImmersion #FoodieTravel"

- "Hiked to the top of [Mountain/Viewpoint] today and the panoramic views were breathtaking. Definitely worth the effort! #HikingAdventures #[Destination]Views #NatureLover"

- "Spent the day at [Museum/Art Gallery] and was blown away by the collection of [Art/Artifacts]. A must-visit for any art/history enthusiast. #[Museum/Art Gallery] #[City]Culture #TravelInspiration"

Pro-Tip: Use Twitter's threading feature to create a series of tweets that tell a more comprehensive story about your adventures. You can include multiple photos, videos, and anecdotes to capture the highlights of your day.

Food and Drink: Tweeting Your Culinary Discoveries

Food is an integral part of any travel experience, and Twitter is the perfect platform to document your culinary discoveries. From street food stalls to Michelin-starred restaurants, share your foodie adventures and tantalize your followers' taste buds.

Tweet Examples:

- "Just had the best [Dish Name] of my life at [Restaurant Name] in [City]! The flavors were incredible, the presentation was beautiful, and the service was impeccable. #[City]Food #FoodieFinds #CulinaryDelights"

- "Exploring the street food scene in [City] and loving the variety of flavors and aromas. [Dish Name] from [Street Vendor Name] was a standout. #StreetFood #[City]Eats #FoodieAdventures"

- "Sipping on a delicious [Drink Name] at a rooftop bar with stunning views of [City]. Cheers to travel and new experiences! #[City]Drinks #RooftopBar #TravelLuxury"

- "Learning about the local cuisine in [Region/Country] and trying all the traditional dishes. [Dish Name] is a new favorite! #CulturalFood #[Region/Country]Cuisine #FoodieTravel"

- "Taking a food tour in [City] and discovering hidden culinary gems. The local guides are so knowledgeable and passionate about their city's food scene. #FoodTour #[City]Eats #CulinaryExploration"

Pro-Tip: Include mouthwatering photos of your food and drinks to make your tweets more visually appealing. You can also use Twitter's location tagging feature to share the specific restaurants or cafes you're visiting.

Cultural Encounters: Tweeting Your Interactions

Travel is about more than just sightseeing and trying new foods. It's also about connecting with people from different cultures and gaining new perspectives. Share your cultural encounters on Twitter and highlight the moments that broadened your understanding of the world.

Tweet Examples:

- "Had a fascinating conversation with a local in [City] today about [Cultural Topic]. Learning about different perspectives is one of the most rewarding aspects of travel. #CulturalExchange #TravelEncounters #OpenMindOpenHeart"

- "Attending a traditional [Cultural Event] in [City] and it's an incredible experience. The music, the costumes, and the energy are captivating. #[City]Culture #CulturalImmersion #TravelInspiration"

- "Learning a few basic phrases in [Language of Destination] and it's amazing how much a simple 'hello' or 'thank you' can enhance your interactions with locals. #LanguageLearning #TravelTips #CulturalRespect"

- "The hospitality in [Country] is truly remarkable. The people are so welcoming and generous, making me feel right at home. #[Country]Travel #WarmWelcome #CulturalCharm"

- "Volunteering at a local [Organization] in [City] and it's been a humbling and rewarding experience. Giving back to the communities you visit is a meaningful way to travel. #VolunteerTravel #MakingADifference #[City]Community"

Pro-Tip: Be respectful of the cultures you're encountering and avoid making generalizations or stereotypes. Focus on sharing your personal experiences and insights in a way that is both authentic and culturally sensitive.

Travel Mishaps: Tweeting the Unexpected

Let's face it, travel isn't always smooth sailing. Delayed flights, lost luggage, language barriers, and unexpected detours are all part of the adventure. Embrace the unexpected and share your travel mishaps on Twitter with a touch of humor and self-deprecation.

Tweet Examples:

- "Just missed my connecting flight by 5 minutes. Looks like I'll be spending the night in the airport. At least there's a Starbucks. #TravelDelays #AirportLife #MakingTheMostOfIt"

- "My luggage decided to take a solo vacation to [Random Destination]. Hoping it reunites with me soon! #LostLuggage #TravelStruggles #PackingLightNextTime"

- "Tried to order [Dish Name] in [Language of Destination] and ended up with [Hilarious Misunderstanding]. Guess I'll be sticking to pointing at the menu from now on. #LanguageBarrier #TravelFails #FoodieAdventures"

- "Got lost in the labyrinthine streets of [City] today. Turns out, my sense of direction is worse than I thought. #LostInTranslation #CityAdventures #EmbraceTheChaos"

- "My hotel room is the size of a shoebox and the air conditioning is broken. But hey, at least I'm in [Destination]! #TravelRealityCheck #MakingTheMostOfIt #[Destination]Bound"

Pro-Tip: Use humor to lighten the mood and make your travel mishaps more relatable. Your followers will appreciate your ability to laugh at yourself and embrace the unexpected twists and turns of travel.

Travel Reflections: Tweeting Your Insights

As your trip draws to a close, take some time to reflect on your experiences and share your insights on Twitter. What did you learn about yourself, the world, or the places you visited?

Tweet Examples:

- "Leaving [Destination] with a heart full of memories and a renewed appreciation for [Cultural Insight/Personal Reflection]. Travel has a way of changing your perspective. #TravelReflections #LifeLessons #[Destination]Memories"

- "This trip has taught me to [Personal Growth/Skill Learned]. Stepping outside of your comfort zone is the best way to grow. #TravelInspiration #PersonalDevelopment #[Destination]Experience"

- "The world is a beautiful and diverse place, full of wonder and possibility. Travel is a privilege that I'll never take for granted. #GratefulForTravel #Wanderlust #ExploreTheWorld"

- "Returning home from my trip feeling refreshed, inspired, and ready to embrace new adventures. Until next time, [Destination]! #TravelPostcard #[Destination]Bound #AlreadyPlanningMyNextTrip"

- "Travel isn't just about the destinations you visit, it's about the journey, the people you meet, and the memories you make. #TravelQuotes #LifeIsAJourney #[Destination]Adventures"

Pro-Tip: Use Twitter's photo collage feature to create a visual summary of your trip highlights. You can also create a Moment to curate a collection of your travel-related tweets.

Travel Tips and Recommendations: Sharing Your Knowledge

If you've become a seasoned traveler, share your hard-earned wisdom with your followers by tweeting travel tips and recommendations. From packing hacks to budget-friendly travel strategies, your insights can be a valuable resource for fellow adventurers.

Tweet Examples:

- **Packing Hack:** "Roll your clothes instead of folding them to save space in your suitcase and prevent wrinkles. #PackingTips #TravelHacks #TravelLight"

- **Budget-Friendly Travel:** "Travel doesn't have to be expensive. Consider staying in hostels, cooking your own meals, and taking advantage of free activities. #BudgetTravel #TravelTips #AffordableAdventures"

- **Travel Insurance:** "Never travel without travel insurance! It's a small investment that can save you a lot of money and hassle in case of emergencies. #TravelInsurance #TravelSafety #PeaceOfMind"

- **Language Learning:** "Learning a few basic phrases in the local language can enhance your travel experience and show respect for the culture. #LanguageLearning #TravelTips #CulturalImmersion"

- **Destination Recommendation:** "If you're looking for a unique and off-the-beaten-path destination, I highly recommend [Destination]. The [Highlight of Destination] is incredible! #TravelInspiration #HiddenGems #[Destination]Travel"

Pro-Tip: Use Twitter's threading feature to create a series of tweets that provide a more comprehensive guide to a specific travel topic, such as packing tips, budget-friendly travel strategies, or destination recommendations.

Building Your Travel Brand: Becoming a Travel Influencer

If you're passionate about travel and enjoy sharing your adventures on Twitter, you might consider building your travel brand and becoming a travel influencer. A strong travel brand can open up opportunities for collaborations with travel companies, brands, and tourism boards.

Tips for Building Your Travel Brand on Twitter:

- **Choose a niche:** What type of travel are you most passionate about? Do you specialize in solo travel, budget travel, luxury travel, adventure travel, or family travel? Choosing a niche can help you to target a specific audience and establish yourself as an expert in that area.

- **Develop a consistent brand voice:** How do you want to be perceived by your audience? Are you adventurous and daring? Are you informative and helpful? Are you humorous and relatable? Developing a consistent brand voice will help you to create a recognizable and memorable identity.

- **Create high-quality content:** Share visually appealing photos, engaging videos, informative articles, and well-written tweets that provide value to your audience.

- **Engage with your followers:** Respond to comments and questions, participate in conversations, and build relationships with your followers.

- **Collaborate with other travel influencers:** Partner with other travel bloggers, photographers, or videographers to cross-promote each other's content and reach a wider audience.

- **Use relevant hashtags:** Use hashtags strategically to increase the visibility of your tweets and connect with a wider audience.

- **Promote your other platforms:** If you have a travel blog, a YouTube channel, or an Instagram account, be sure to promote them on your Twitter profile and in your tweets.

- **Be patient and persistent:** Building a strong travel brand takes time and effort. Don't get discouraged if you don't see results overnight. Keep creating great content, engaging with your audience, and promoting your brand, and you'll eventually start to see success.

Examples of Tweets Building Your Travel Brand:

- **Niche Focus:** "I'm a #solo #female #traveler who loves exploring the world on a budget. Follow me for tips, inspiration, and adventures! #SoloTravel #BudgetTravel #AdventureTime"

- **Brand Voice:** "I'm a travel blogger with a quirky sense of humor. Follow me for hilarious travel mishaps, relatable travel stories, and offbeat destination recommendations. #TravelHumor #AdventureComedy #Wanderlust"

- **High-Quality Content:** "Just published a new blog post with my top tips for packing for a long-term trip. Check it out for some packing hacks that will save you space and stress! #PackingTips #TravelHacks #LongTermTravel" (Include a link to the blog post)

- **Follower Engagement:** "I'm curious to know what your dream travel destination is. Share your answers in the comments! #TravelDreams #BucketList #Wanderlust"

- **Collaboration:** "Excited to be partnering with [Travel Company] on a trip to [Destination]. Follow along on my Twitter and Instagram for updates and behind-the-scenes insights! #TravelCollaboration #[Destination]Adventure #TravelInfluencer"

Travel Photography: Capturing the Essence of Your Journey

Travel photography is an art form that allows you to capture the essence of your journey and share your experiences with others in a visually compelling way. Twitter, with its focus on visual content, is a great platform for showcasing your travel photography skills.

Tips for Taking and Sharing Stunning Travel Photos on Twitter:

- **Invest in a good camera:** While smartphone cameras have come a long way, investing in a dedicated camera with interchangeable lenses can significantly improve the quality of your travel photos.

- **Learn the basics of photography:** Take some time to learn the fundamentals of photography, such as composition, lighting, and exposure. There are many online resources and tutorials available.

- **Capture a variety of shots:** Don't just focus on taking wide-angle shots of landscapes. Capture details, portraits, action shots, and candid moments to create a diverse and engaging collection of photos.

- **Tell a story with your photos:** Think about the story you want to convey with your photos and choose shots that will help you to tell that story.

- **Edit your photos thoughtfully:** Use photo editing software to enhance your photos, but avoid over-editing. You want your photos to look natural and authentic.

- **Share your photos with captions that provide context:** Write captions that describe the location, the story behind the photo, or the emotions you were feeling when you took the shot.

- **Use relevant hashtags:** Use hashtags related to the location, the type of photography, or the theme of your photos to increase the visibility of your tweets.

Examples of Tweets Showcasing Travel Photography:

- **Landscape Photography:** "Captured this breathtaking view of the [Landmark/Scenery] in [Destination]. The beauty of nature never ceases to amaze me. #LandscapePhotography #[Destination]Travel #TravelInspiration" (Include a stunning landscape photo)

- **Portrait Photography:** "Met this friendly local in [City] who shared their stories and culture with me. A reminder that travel is about connecting with people as much as it is about seeing places. #PortraitPhotography #CulturalEncounters #[City]Travel" (Include a portrait of the local person)

- **Action Shot:** "Hiked to the summit of [Mountain] today and the sense of accomplishment was incredible. The views were breathtaking and the challenge was rewarding. #HikingAdventures #ActionPhotography #[Destination]Travel" (Include an action shot of yourself hiking)

- **Candid Moment:** "Captured this candid moment of children playing in the streets of [City]. The joy and innocence of childhood is universal. #CandidPhotography #StreetPhotography #[City]Life" (Include a candid photo of children playing)

- **Storytelling:** "My journey through [Destination] has been a transformative experience. These photos tell the story of my adventures, encounters, and reflections. #TravelPhotography #Storytelling #[Destination]Memories" (Include a collage of photos from your trip)

Etiquette for Travel Tweeting: Being a Respectful Traveler

While Twitter can be a great way to share your travel experiences, it's important to be mindful of etiquette and be a respectful traveler, both online and offline.

Tips for Respectful Travel Tweeting:

- **Be mindful of privacy:** Don't share personal information about others without their consent. Avoid posting photos or videos of people who haven't given you permission to do so.

- **Be respectful of cultures:** Avoid making generalizations or stereotypes about the cultures you're encountering. Be sensitive to local customs and traditions.

- **Be mindful of your surroundings:** Don't let your social media use distract you from enjoying the present moment. Put your phone away and engage with your surroundings.

- **Avoid geo-tagging sensitive locations:** Don't geo-tag locations that are sacred, private, or potentially dangerous. This can help to protect these places and the people who live there.

- **Be a responsible traveler:** Practice Leave No Trace principles and minimize your impact on the environment. Support local businesses and communities.

Examples of Respectful Travel Tweeting:

- **Privacy:** "Met some wonderful people in [Destination] who shared their stories and culture with me. Grateful for the connections I made. (Photos shared with consent)"

- **Cultural Sensitivity:** "Learning about the traditional customs and beliefs in [Destination] has been a fascinating experience. Appreciating the diversity and richness of human culture. "

- **Mindfulness:** "Putting my phone away for a while to fully immerse myself in the beauty of [Destination]. Sometimes, the best experiences are the ones you don't capture on camera. "

- **Geo-Tagging:** "Enjoying the stunning views from [Viewpoint]. The natural beauty of this place is breathtaking. (Geo-tagging a general location instead of a specific sensitive spot)"

- **Responsible Travel:** "Supporting local businesses and communities in [Destination]. Travel is a great way to make a positive impact on the places you visit. "

A Few Final Tips for Tweeting Your Travel Tales

- **Be authentic and enthusiastic:** Share your genuine love for travel and your unique experiences with your followers.

- **Use a variety of content formats:** Mix up your tweets with photos, videos, anecdotes, tips, reflections, and humor to keep your audience engaged.

- **Engage with other travelers:** Connect with other travel enthusiasts on Twitter, share your experiences, ask for advice, and participate in travel-related conversations.

- **Use Twitter's features to enhance your storytelling:** Take advantage of features like threading, Moments, polls, and live-tweeting to create more engaging and interactive travel content.

- **Have fun!** Travel is an adventure, and your tweets should reflect that. Let your personality shine through and inspire others to explore the world.

CHAPTER ELEVEN: Bookworm Tweets: Sharing Your Literary Love

Books. They transport us to other worlds, introduce us to unforgettable characters, expand our minds, and touch our hearts. And in the age of social media, they provide a constant source of conversation, debate, and, let's be honest, some pretty epic Twitter (or X) rants about plot twists and character betrayals.

Whether you're a voracious reader who devours books like candy or a casual bibliophile who enjoys a good read now and then, this chapter will help you navigate the world of book-related tweets. We'll explore different ways to express your literary love, share your reading experiences, connect with fellow bookworms, and maybe even inspire others to pick up a book (or e-reader) and discover the magic of storytelling.

Sharing Your Current Read: Tweeting Your Literary Journey

One of the simplest and most effective ways to engage with the bookish community on Twitter is by sharing what you're currently reading. It's a great way to spark conversations, get recommendations, and track your reading progress.

Tweet Examples:

- "Currently engrossed in [Book Title] by [Author Name]. The writing is captivating, the characters are complex, and I can't wait to see where the story takes me. #CurrentlyReading #Bookworm #[Genre]"

- "Just started reading [Book Title] and I'm already hooked! The premise is intriguing, the pacing is perfect, and I can't put it down. #NewRead #BookRecommendation #[AuthorName]"

- "Struggling to get through [Book Title]. The plot is dragging, the characters are unrelatable, and I'm tempted to DNF (Did Not Finish). #ReadingSlump #BookStruggles #MaybeNextTime"

- "Reading [Book Title] for my book club and it's sparking some interesting discussions. Can't wait for our meeting next week! #BookClub #LiteraryDiscussions #[AuthorName]"

- "Listening to the audiobook of [Book Title] and loving the narrator's performance. It's bringing the story to life in a whole new way. #Audiobook #[NarratorName] #[Genre]"

Pro-Tip: Include a photo of the book cover, your e-reader displaying the book, or a cozy reading nook setup to make your tweet more visually appealing. You can also use relevant hashtags to connect with other readers who are interested in the same genre, author, or book.

Book Reviews: Sharing Your Thoughts and Recommendations

Book reviews are a staple of the bookish community on Twitter. Whether you loved a book, hated it, or fell somewhere in between, sharing your thoughts and recommendations can be a valuable resource for other readers.

Tips for Crafting Engaging Book Reviews:

- **Provide a brief synopsis of the book:** Give a brief overview of the plot, the setting, and the main characters without giving away any major spoilers.

- **Highlight the strengths of the book:** What did you enjoy most about the book? Was it the writing style, the characters, the plot, the themes, or something else?

- **Acknowledge any weaknesses:** If there were aspects of the book that you didn't enjoy, be honest and constructive in your criticism. Avoid being overly negative or personal.

- **Offer your overall recommendation:** Would you recommend this book to others? If so, who would you recommend it to? Be specific about your target audience.

- **Use relevant hashtags:** Hashtags can help increase the visibility of your review and connect you with other readers who are interested in the same genre, author, or book. Use hashtags like #bookreview, #[Genre]Review, #[AuthorName], and #BookRecommendation.

- **Be spoiler-free (unless you explicitly state otherwise):** Avoid revealing any major plot twists or surprises that could ruin the reading experience for others. If you do need to discuss spoilers, use a spoiler warning and hide the text behind a spoiler tag.

Examples of Engaging Book Reviews:

- **Positive Review:** "Just finished [Book Title] by [Author Name] and it was absolutely breathtaking! The writing was lyrical, the characters were unforgettable, and the story stayed with me long after I finished reading. Highly recommend for fans of [Genre]. #BookReview #[Genre]Review #[AuthorName]"

- **Mixed Review:** "I had mixed feelings about [Book Title]. The writing was strong and the premise was intriguing, but the pacing was uneven and I didn't connect with the main character. It's a solid read, but not one I'd rave about. #BookReview #HonestReview #[Genre]"

- **Negative Review:** "Unfortunately, I didn't enjoy [Book Title]. The writing was clunky, the characters were one-dimensional, and the plot was predictable. I wouldn't recommend it. #BookReview #DNF #[Genre]"

- **Specific Strength Highlight:** "The character development in [Book Title] is exceptional. [Author Name] has a gift for creating complex and relatable characters that jump off the page. #BookReview #CharacterDriven #[AuthorName]"

- **Target Audience Recommendation:** "I would highly recommend [Book Title] to anyone who enjoys historical fiction with a strong female lead. It's a captivating story of love, loss, and resilience. #BookRecommendation #HistoricalFiction #[AuthorName]"

Reacting to Plot Twists and Character Developments: Tweeting Your Emotional Rollercoaster

Books have a way of evoking a wide range of emotions, from joy and excitement to sadness and anger. And Twitter is the perfect platform to share your emotional rollercoaster as you react to plot twists, character developments, and other surprising moments in your reading journey.

Tips for Tweeting Your Emotional Reactions:

- **Use emojis to express your feelings:** Emojis can be a great way to convey your emotional state without having to write a lengthy explanation. A simple "☹" or "☺" can speak volumes.

- **Use GIFs to capture your reaction:** A well-chosen GIF can perfectly capture your reaction to a shocking plot twist or a heartbreaking character death.

- **Use humor to lighten the mood:** If you're feeling overwhelmed by the emotional intensity of a book, use humor to diffuse the tension and connect with other readers who are experiencing the same thing.

- **Use spoiler warnings:** If you're tweeting about a specific plot point or character development, use a spoiler warning to avoid ruining the surprise for others who haven't read that far in the book.

- **Don't be afraid to be vulnerable:** Sharing your emotional reactions to books can be a way to connect with other readers on a deeper level. Don't be afraid to express your true feelings, whether they're positive or negative.

Examples of Tweets Reacting to Books:

- **Shocking Plot Twist:** "OMG! I can't believe that just happened! 😨 #PlotTwist #[BookTitle] #MindBlown"

- **Heartbreaking Character Death:** "I'm not crying, you're crying! 😭😭 #[CharacterName] #[BookTitle] #RIP"

- **Humorous Reaction:** "This book is giving me anxiety! I need a glass of wine and a therapy session. 🍷 #BookStress #[BookTitle] #SendHelp"

- **Spoiler Warning:** "Spoiler Alert for [Book Title]! I can't believe [Plot Point]! What did you guys think? #BookDiscussion #SpoilerAlert #[AuthorName]"

- **Vulnerable Reaction:** "[Book Title] really hit me hard. It made me think about [Theme/Personal Connection] in a new way. #BookReflections #EmotionalRead #[AuthorName]"

Bookish Humor: Tweeting Your Literary Laughs

The bookish world is full of quirky characters, absurd situations, and relatable struggles that are ripe for humor. Share your literary laughs on Twitter and connect with other readers who appreciate a good book-related joke.

Tips for Using Bookish Humor:

- **Use puns and wordplay:** Puns and wordplay are classic forms of humor that can be particularly effective when applied to book titles, characters, or literary themes.

- **Share relatable bookish memes:** The internet is a treasure trove of bookish memes that perfectly capture the joys and struggles of being a reader. Share your favorites with your followers.

- **Create your own bookish memes:** If you're feeling creative, try your hand at creating your own bookish memes using meme generators or photo editing software.

- **Use self-deprecating humor:** Don't be afraid to poke fun at your own bookish quirks, such as your overflowing TBR (To Be Read) pile, your tendency to judge people by their bookshelves, or your inability to resist buying new books even though you have a stack of unread ones at home.

Examples of Tweets Using Bookish Humor:

- **Book Pun:** "I'm so glad I decided to read [Book Title]. It's been a real page-turner! #Punny #BookLover #[Genre]"

- **Bookish Meme:** [Share a meme about the struggles of choosing what to read next, the disappointment of a bad ending, or the joy of finding a new favorite author.] #BookMeme #Relatable #BookwormProblems"

- **Self-Deprecating Humor:** "My TBR pile is so high, it's practically touching the ceiling. I'm not sure I'll ever be able to read all these books, but I can't resist buying more! #BookwormProblems #TBRPile #Bibliophile"

Connecting with Fellow Bookworms: Building Your Literary Community

Twitter is a great platform for connecting with other book lovers, sharing recommendations, discussing your favorite reads, and building a supportive literary community.

Tips for Connecting with Fellow Bookworms:

- **Follow bookish accounts:** Search for hashtags related to your reading interests and follow other users who share your love for books. Look for book bloggers, reviewers, authors, publishers, libraries, and book clubs.

- **Participate in Twitter chats:** Many online communities host Twitter chats focused on books, reading, and writing. Participating in these chats can be a great way to connect with other bookworms, share your thoughts, and get new recommendations.

- **Join bookish Twitter communities:** There are many Twitter communities dedicated to specific genres, authors, or book series. Joining these communities can provide a more focused space for discussing your favorite reads and connecting with like-minded readers.

- **Start your own book club:** If you're looking for a more structured way to connect with other readers, consider starting your own online book club on Twitter. You can choose a book to read together, set a discussion schedule, and use a specific hashtag to keep the conversation organized.

Examples of Tweets Connecting with Fellow Bookworms:

- **Following Bookish Accounts:** "Just discovered some amazing book bloggers and reviewers on Twitter! So excited to connect with other book lovers and get new recommendations. #BookCommunity #BookTwitter #Bibliophile"

- **Participating in Twitter Chats:** "Excited to join the #BookChat tonight at 8pm EST! Let's discuss our favorite recent reads and get some new recommendations. #BookDiscussions #BookLovers #TwitterChat"

- **Joining Bookish Communities:** "Just joined the #[Genre]Twitter community! Looking forward to connecting with other fans of [Genre] and discussing our favorite books. #[Genre]Lovers #BookNerds #Community"

- **Starting a Book Club:** "Starting an online book club on Twitter for fans of [Genre]. Our first read will be [Book Title] by [Author Name]. Join the conversation using the hashtag #[BookClubName]! #BookClub #[Genre]Readers #LiteraryDiscussions"

Fangirling (or Fanboying) Over Your Favorite Authors: Tweeting Your Literary Crushes

We all have our favorite authors, those whose words have touched our hearts, expanded our minds, or simply kept us entertained for hours on end. And Twitter provides the perfect platform to express your admiration, share your enthusiasm, and connect with other fans.

Tips for Fangirling (or Fanboying) Over Authors on Twitter:

- **Follow your favorite authors:** Many authors have an active presence on Twitter, sharing updates on their writing projects, engaging with fans, and participating in literary conversations. Following your favorite authors can give you a glimpse into their creative process and personality.

- **Tweet about their books:** Share your thoughts on their books, your favorite quotes, or your favorite characters. Tag the author in your tweets to let them know how much you enjoy their work.

- **Attend virtual events:** Many authors participate in virtual events, such as book signings, Q&A sessions, or writing workshops. Attending these events can give you a chance to interact with the author directly and ask them questions.

- **Be respectful:** While it's okay to express your enthusiasm, remember to be respectful of the author's boundaries. Avoid sending overly personal or intrusive messages.

- **Support their work:** Buy their books, leave reviews, and recommend their work to others. Word-of-mouth is a powerful form of marketing for authors, and your support can make a big difference.

Examples of Tweets Fangirling (or Fanboying) Over Authors:

- **Following Authors:** "Just followed [Author Name] on Twitter! So excited to get updates on their writing and insights into their creative process. #[AuthorName] #LiteraryCrush #AuthorLove"

- **Tweeting About Books:** "Just finished rereading [Book Title] by [Author Name] and it's even better the second time around! [Favorite Quote] #[AuthorName] #[BookTitle] #LiteraryMasterpiece"

- **Attending Virtual Events:** "Excited to attend the virtual book signing with [Author Name] tonight! Can't wait to ask them about their new book. #[AuthorName] #BookSigning #VirtualEvent"

- **Respectful Interaction:** "[Author Name], your books have had a profound impact on me. Thank you for sharing your gift of storytelling with the world. #[AuthorName] #LiteraryInspiration #GratefulReader"

- **Supporting Authors:** "Just pre-ordered [Author Name]'s new book! Can't wait to read it! #[AuthorName] #NewRelease #SupportAuthors"

Participating in Bookish Challenges and Events: Expanding Your Literary Horizons

The online bookish community is full of challenges and events that can help you to expand your reading horizons, discover new authors, and connect with other readers.

Examples of Bookish Challenges and Events:

- **Reading Challenges:** Many websites and online communities host reading challenges that encourage you to read a certain number of books in a year, explore different genres, or read books by authors from diverse backgrounds.

- **Book Bingo:** Book bingo is a fun and engaging way to challenge yourself to read books that fit specific categories, such as "a book with a one-word title," "a book set in a different country," or "a book recommended by a friend."

- **Readathons:** Readathons are events where participants try to read as many books as they can within a certain time frame, often 24 or 48 hours. Readathons can be a great way to motivate yourself to read, connect with other readers, and support charitable causes.

- **Virtual Book Festivals:** Many book festivals have gone virtual in recent years, offering online events, author interviews, and panel discussions that can be accessed from anywhere in the world.

Tips for Participating in Bookish Challenges and Events:

- **Choose challenges that align with your interests:** Don't feel pressured to participate in every challenge you see. Focus on challenges that genuinely interest you and that will help you to achieve your reading goals.

- **Use relevant hashtags:** Use hashtags related to the challenge or event to connect with other participants and share your progress.

- **Share your reading experiences:** Tweet about the books you're reading, your favorite quotes, and your thoughts on the challenge or event.

- **Engage with other participants:** Connect with other readers who are participating in the same challenge or event. Share your experiences, offer encouragement, and celebrate each other's successes.

Examples of Tweets Participating in Bookish Challenges:

- **Reading Challenge:** "I'm participating in the #[ReadingChallengeName] this year. My goal is to read 50 books! Wish me luck! #BookChallenge #ReadingGoals #Bibliophile"

- **Book Bingo:** "Just got a bingo on my #BookBingo card! I read a book set in a different country, a book with a blue cover, and a book recommended by a friend. #BookChallenge #ReadingFun #Bookworm"

- **Readathon:** "Excited to participate in the #[ReadathonName] this weekend! I'm going to try to read as many books as I can in 24 hours. Wish me luck! #Readathon #BookMarathon #ReadingChallenge"

- **Virtual Book Festival:** "Attending the virtual #[BookFestivalName] this week. Looking forward to the author interviews and panel discussions! #BookFestival #VirtualEvents #LiteraryLove"

Supporting Independent Bookstores and Libraries: Tweeting Your Bookish Loyalty

Independent bookstores and libraries are essential parts of the literary landscape. They provide access to books, foster a love of reading, and support local communities. Use your Twitter platform to show your support for these vital institutions.

Tips for Supporting Independent Bookstores and Libraries on Twitter:

- **Follow their accounts:** Many independent bookstores and libraries have active Twitter accounts where they share updates on new arrivals, events, and community initiatives. Following their accounts can help you to stay informed and show your support.

- **Share your favorite bookstores and libraries:** Tweet about your favorite local bookstores and libraries, highlighting their unique qualities and the reasons why you love them.

- **Promote their events:** If your local bookstore or library is hosting an event, such as a book signing, a reading, or a workshop, help spread the word by tweeting about it.

- **Buy books from independent bookstores:** When you're looking to buy a new book, consider purchasing it from an independent bookstore instead of a large online retailer. Independent bookstores often offer a curated selection of books, personalized recommendations, and a supportive environment for book lovers.

- **Donate to libraries:** Libraries rely on donations to provide free access to books and resources for their communities. Consider making a donation to your local library or a library in need.

Examples of Tweets Supporting Independent Bookstores and Libraries:

- **Following Bookish Accounts:** "Just followed [Bookstore/Library Name] on Twitter! Loving their updates on new arrivals, events, and community initiatives. #SupportLocal #BookstoreLove #LibraryLife"

- **Sharing Favorites:** "[Bookstore Name] is my favorite local bookstore! They have a fantastic selection of books, a knowledgeable staff, and a cozy atmosphere. #BookwormHaven #IndependentBookstore #[CityName]"

- **Promoting Events:** "[Library Name] is hosting a book signing with [Author Name] on [Date]. Don't miss this chance to meet the author and get your book signed! #BookSigning #[AuthorName] #[LibraryName]"

- **Buying Books:** "Just bought a new book from [Bookstore Name]. Supporting independent bookstores is important for fostering a love of reading and supporting local communities. #ShopLocal #BookstoreLove #Bibliophile"

- **Donating to Libraries:** "Just made a donation to [Library Name]. Libraries are vital resources for our communities, providing free access to books, information, and technology. #SupportLibraries #LibraryLove #GiveBack"

Sharing Your Reading Nook: Tweeting Your Cozy Bookish Space

For many bookworms, having a dedicated reading nook is essential for creating a relaxing and immersive reading experience. Share your cozy bookish space on Twitter and inspire others to create their own reading sanctuaries.

Tips for Sharing Your Reading Nook:

- **Take a photo or video of your space:** Showcase your reading nook with a visually appealing photo or video. Highlight the elements that make your space cozy and inviting, such as comfortable seating, good lighting, blankets, pillows, and bookish decor.

- **Describe the ambiance:** Use descriptive language to convey the ambiance of your reading nook. Is it a quiet and peaceful space? Is it a bright and airy room? Is it a cozy and intimate corner?

- **Share your favorite reading accessories:** What are your must-have reading accessories? Do you have a favorite blanket, a special mug for your tea or coffee, or a reading lamp that creates the perfect ambiance?

- **Use relevant hashtags:** Hashtags can help increase the visibility of your tweet and connect you with other bookworms who are interested in reading nooks and cozy spaces. Use hashtags like #readingnook, #cozyspace, #bookishdecor, #readinglife, and #bibliophile.

- **Engage with other bookworms who share their spaces:** Connect with other bookworms who are sharing their reading nooks on Twitter. Comment on their photos, share your own tips, and exchange ideas for creating the perfect reading environment.

Examples of Tweets Sharing Your Reading Nook:

- **Photo with Description:** "My cozy reading nook is my happy place. Comfortable chair, good lighting, and a stack of books – what more could I ask for? #ReadingNook #CozySpace #BookwormLife" (Include a photo of your reading nook)

- **Ambiance Focus:** "Curled up in my reading nook with a cup of tea and a good book. The rain is pattering outside, creating the perfect ambiance for a cozy afternoon of reading. #RainyDayReads #ReadingLife #PeacefulVibes"

- **Favorite Accessories:** "My essential reading accessories: a soft blanket, a warm mug of coffee, and a reading lamp that creates the perfect glow. #ReadingEssentials #CozyVibes #BookwormMustHaves"

- **Engagement with Others:** "Loving all the #ReadingNook photos on Twitter! So many inspiring spaces! What are your must-have elements for a cozy reading nook? #BookishDecor #ReadingLife #Community"

Using Twitter for Book Recommendations: Finding Your Next Great Read

Twitter can be a fantastic resource for finding your next great read. With so many book lovers sharing their recommendations, reviews, and reading experiences, you're sure to discover books that you'll love.

Tips for Using Twitter for Book Recommendations:

- **Follow bookish accounts:** Follow book bloggers, reviewers, authors, publishers, libraries, and book clubs to get a steady stream of book recommendations.

- **Use relevant hashtags:** Search for hashtags related to your reading interests, such as #bookrecommendations, #[Genre]Recommendations, #[AuthorName], or #[Theme].

- **Participate in Twitter chats:** Many online communities host Twitter chats focused on book recommendations. These chats can be a great way to discover new books and connect with other readers who share your tastes.

- **Ask for recommendations from your followers:** Don't be afraid to ask your followers for book recommendations. Be specific about your reading preferences, such as your favorite genres, authors, or themes.

- **Create a "Want to Read" list:** Use Twitter's bookmarking feature or create a dedicated list to keep track of the book recommendations that you want to check out.

Examples of Tweets Seeking Book Recommendations:

- **Following Bookish Accounts:** "Looking for new books to add to my TBR pile. Any recommendations from my fellow bookworms? #BookRecommendations #ReadingList #Bibliophile"

- **Using Hashtags:** "Scrolling through the #[Genre]Recommendations hashtag for some new reading material. Any hidden gems I should check out? #[Genre]Lover #BookNerds #ReadingInspiration"

- **Participating in Twitter Chats:** "Excited to join the #BookRecommendationChat tonight at 8pm EST! Let's share our favorite books and discover some new reads. #BookLovers #TwitterChat #ReadingCommunity"

- **Asking for Recommendations:** "I'm looking for a book with a strong female protagonist and a captivating plot. Any suggestions? #[Genre] #BookRecommendations #StrongFemaleLeads"

- **Creating a "Want to Read" List:** "Just added [Book Title] to my "Want to Read" list after seeing so many glowing reviews on Twitter. Can't wait to check it out! #Bookworm #TBRPile #ReadingGoals"

Using Twitter to Enhance Your Reading Experience: From Book Clubs to Author Q&As

Twitter can enhance your reading experience in a variety of ways, from connecting you with other readers to providing insights from authors and experts.

Tips for Using Twitter to Enhance Your Reading Experience:

- **Join online book clubs:** Twitter is a great platform for online book clubs. You can connect with other readers who are reading the same book, share your thoughts, and participate in discussions.

- **Participate in author Q&As:** Many authors host Q&A sessions on Twitter, where you can ask them questions about their books, their writing process, or their inspirations.

- **Follow literary magazines and journals:** Following literary magazines and journals can provide you with insights into the world of literature, including book reviews, author interviews, and essays on literary topics.

- **Use Twitter to research books and authors:** If you're interested in learning more about a particular book or author, use Twitter to search for reviews, interviews, and articles. You can also use Twitter to find out if the author has an active presence on the platform.

- **Share your reading progress and thoughts:** Use Twitter to share your reading progress, your favorite quotes, and your thoughts on the books you're reading. This can help you to stay motivated and engaged with your reading.

Examples of Tweets Enhancing Your Reading Experience:

- **Joining Book Clubs:** "Just joined an online book club on Twitter for [Book Title]. Looking forward to discussing the book with other readers! #BookClub #[BookTitle] #LiteraryDiscussions"

- **Participating in Author Q&As:** "Excited to participate in the #Ask[AuthorName] Q&A session today! I have so many questions about their new book. #AuthorQ&A #[AuthorName] #BookNerd"

- **Following Literary Magazines:** "Just followed [Literary Magazine] on Twitter. Loving their book reviews, author interviews, and essays on literary topics. #LiteraryWorld #BookReviews #AuthorInsights"

- **Researching Books and Authors:** "Using Twitter to research [Book Title] by [Author Name]. So far, the reviews are overwhelmingly positive! Can't wait to read it. #BookResearch #[BookTitle] #[AuthorName]"

- **Sharing Reading Progress:** "Halfway through [Book Title] and I'm completely hooked! The plot is thickening and the characters are so well-developed. #[BookTitle] #PageTurner #ReadingUpdate"

A Few Final Tips for Bookworm Tweets

- **Be authentic and passionate:** Let your love for books shine through in your tweets. Share your genuine thoughts and feelings, and don't be afraid to be yourself.

- **Use a variety of content formats:** Mix up your tweets with book reviews, recommendations, reading updates, humorous observations, and engaging discussions to keep your audience interested.

- **Use visuals:** Include photos of book covers, reading nooks, or bookish merchandise to make your tweets more visually appealing.

- **Use relevant hashtags:** Hashtags are essential for connecting with other bookworms and increasing the visibility of your tweets. Use a mix of general bookish hashtags (e.g., #booklover, #bibliophile) and specific hashtags related to your reading interests (e.g., #[Genre], #[AuthorName], #[BookTitle]).

- **Engage with others:** Respond to comments, participate in discussions, and connect with other book lovers to build a supportive community.

- **Spread the love of reading:** Encourage others to discover the joy of reading by sharing your favorite books, recommendations, and inspiring quotes.

Twitter can be a fantastic platform for book lovers to connect, share their passion, and discover new literary adventures. By following these tips and examples, you can use Twitter to enhance your reading experience, build a community of fellow bookworms, and spread the love of reading to the world. Happy tweeting (and reading)!

CHAPTER TWELVE: Music Mania: Tweeting Your Favorite Tunes

Music. It's the soundtrack to our lives, the rhythm that moves our souls, and the melodies that echo in our hearts. And in the age of streaming services and social media, it's easier than ever to share our musical passions with the world.

Twitter (or X), despite its 280-character limit, can be a surprisingly effective platform for expressing your love of music, connecting with fellow music lovers, and even discovering new artists and genres.

This chapter will explore the many ways you can use Twitter to amplify your musical experiences, from sharing your favorite songs and albums to live-tweeting concerts and engaging in music-related debates. Get ready to turn up the volume on your Twitter presence and become a music maven in the digital world.

Sharing Your Current Jam: Tweeting the Soundtrack of Your Day

What better way to start your musical journey on Twitter than by sharing what you're currently listening to? Whether it's a classic tune that's been on repeat all week, a new release that's blowing your mind, or a hidden gem that you just discovered, your current jam can spark conversations, introduce your followers to new artists, and even reveal a bit about your personality and mood.

Tweet Examples:

- "Currently vibing to [Song Title] by [Artist Name]. This song always puts me in a good mood. What's your go-to feel-good anthem? #NowPlaying #MusicLover #[Genre]"

- "Obsessed with the new [Album Title] by [Artist Name]. Every track is a banger! What new releases are you digging lately? #NewMusicFriday #AlbumOfTheYear #[ArtistName]"

- "Just discovered this amazing band called [Band Name]. Their sound is so unique and refreshing. Give them a listen if you're looking for something different. #HiddenGems #IndieMusic #MusicDiscovery"

- "Feeling nostalgic today and listening to my favorite [Artist Name] album from high school. Music has a way of transporting you back in time. #ThrowbackThursday #MusicMemories #[ArtistName]"

- "The soundtrack to my workout today is [Playlist/Album Title]. Pumping me up and getting me through those last few reps. #WorkoutMusic #FitnessMotivation #[Genre]"

Pro-Tip: Enhance your tweets by including links to the song or album on streaming services like Spotify, Apple Music, or YouTube Music. This makes it easy for your followers to listen to your recommendations. You can also use Twitter's audio card feature to embed a short audio clip of the song directly in your tweet.

Album Reviews: Sharing Your Musical Opinions

Album reviews are a great way to share your musical tastes with your followers, spark discussions, and recommend albums that you think others might enjoy. Whether you're a seasoned music critic or simply a passionate listener, your opinions can help others discover new music and appreciate different perspectives.

Tips for Crafting Engaging Album Reviews:

- **Provide context:** Start your review by providing some context about the album, such as the artist's background, the genre, and the overall concept or theme of the album.

- **Highlight the strengths of the album:** What are the standout tracks? What aspects of the music impressed you the most? Focus on the elements that make the album unique and noteworthy.

- **Acknowledge any weaknesses:** If there are aspects of the album that you didn't enjoy, be honest and constructive in your criticism. Avoid being overly negative or attacking the artist personally.

- **Offer your overall assessment:** Is this an album that you would recommend to others? If so, who would you recommend it to? Be specific about your target audience.

- **Use relevant hashtags:** Hashtags can help increase the visibility of your review and connect you with other music lovers who are interested in the same genre, artist, or album. Use hashtags like #albumreview, #musicreview, #[Genre]Review, #[ArtistName], and #[AlbumTitle].

- **Be mindful of spoilers:** Avoid revealing too much about the album's content or plot (if it's a concept album). You want to pique your followers' interest without ruining the listening experience for them.

Examples of Engaging Album Reviews:

- **Positive Review:** "Just finished listening to [Album Title] by [Artist Name] and it's a masterpiece! The songwriting is brilliant, the production is top-notch, and every track is a journey. Highly recommend for fans of [Genre]. #AlbumReview #[Genre]Review #[ArtistName]"

- **Mixed Review:** "I had mixed feelings about [Album Title]. Some tracks are fantastic, while others fall flat. The production is solid, but the songwriting is inconsistent. Overall, it's a decent album, but not one I'd put on repeat. #AlbumReview #HonestReview #[Genre]"

- **Negative Review:** "Unfortunately, I was disappointed by [Album Title]. The songs are uninspired, the production is lackluster, and the whole thing feels like a missed opportunity. I wouldn't recommend it. #AlbumReview #SkipIt #[Genre]"

- **Specific Strength Highlight:** "The vocals on [Album Title] are absolutely stunning. [Artist Name] has a voice that can melt your heart and move your soul. #AlbumReview #VocalPowerhouse #[ArtistName]"

- **Target Audience Recommendation:** "I would highly recommend [Album Title] to anyone who loves experimental electronic music with a touch of jazz influence. It's a mind-bending and genre-defying experience. #AlbumRecommendation #ElectronicMusic #[ArtistName]"

Concert Reviews: Reliving the Live Music Experience

Live music is an electrifying experience that can create lasting memories and forge a deep connection between artist and audience. Twitter is a great platform for sharing your concert experiences, reliving the highlights, and expressing your appreciation for the artists who moved you.

Tips for Crafting Engaging Concert Reviews:

- **Set the scene:** Start your review by describing the venue, the atmosphere, the crowd's energy, and any other details that set the stage for the performance.

- **Highlight the performance highlights:** What were the most memorable moments of the concert? Did the artist perform any unexpected covers? Were there any special guests or surprise appearances? Focus on the elements that made the performance unique and unforgettable.

- **Share your emotional response:** How did the concert make you feel? Did the music move you, inspire you, or energize you? Share your personal connection to the performance.

- **Include photos and videos (if allowed):** Many concerts allow attendees to take photos and videos. Capture some of the highlights of the performance to share with your followers.

- **Use relevant hashtags:** Hashtags can help increase the visibility of your review and connect you with other fans who attended the concert or who are interested in the artist. Use hashtags like #concert, #liveshow, #[ArtistName], #[VenueName], and #[CityName].

- **Be respectful of the artist and other attendees:** Avoid posting negative or derogatory comments about the artist or other concertgoers. Focus on sharing your positive experiences and spreading good vibes.

Examples of Engaging Concert Reviews:

- **Setting the Scene:** "The energy at the [Artist Name] concert tonight was electric! The crowd was packed, the lights were dazzling, and everyone was singing along to every word. #ConcertVibes #[ArtistName] #[VenueName]"

- **Performance Highlights:** "[Artist Name] absolutely killed it tonight! The setlist was perfect, the band was tight, and they even played a surprise cover of [Song Title]! #ConcertReview #[ArtistName] #LiveMusic"

- **Emotional Response:** "The [Artist Name] concert was more than just a show – it was an experience. The music touched my soul and left me feeling inspired and uplifted. #MusicIsLife #[ArtistName] #ConcertMagic"

- **Photos and Videos:** "Here's a clip of [Artist Name] performing my favorite song, [Song Title]. The crowd went wild! #ConcertMoments #[ArtistName] #[VenueName]" (Include a short video clip of the performance)

- **Respectful Fan Appreciation:** "Huge shoutout to [Artist Name] for an incredible performance tonight. You put on an amazing show and made everyone feel connected through the power of music. #FanLove #[ArtistName] #Grateful"

Music Recommendations: Sharing Your Favorite Songs, Artists, and Playlists

Sharing your favorite songs, artists, and playlists on Twitter is a great way to introduce your followers to new music, spark discussions, and discover shared musical tastes. Whether it's a classic album that everyone should hear, an emerging artist that you think deserves more recognition, or a curated playlist that perfectly captures a certain mood or theme, your recommendations can expand your followers' musical horizons and create a sense of community through shared listening experiences.

Tips for Sharing Music Recommendations:

- **Be specific and provide context:** Instead of simply saying "You should listen to [Artist Name]," provide some context about the artist's genre, style, and why you enjoy their music. If you're recommending a specific song or album, highlight what makes it special or noteworthy.

- **Share links to streaming services:** Make it easy for your followers to listen to your recommendations by including links to the songs, albums, or playlists on streaming services like Spotify, Apple Music, or YouTube Music.

- **Use descriptive language:** Use evocative language to describe the music and create a sense of anticipation for your followers. Words like "atmospheric," "uplifting," "soulful," "energetic," or "haunting" can help paint a picture of the musical experience.

- **Use relevant hashtags:** Hashtags can help increase the visibility of your recommendations and connect you with other music lovers who are interested in similar genres, artists, or playlists. Use hashtags like #musicrecommendation, #[Genre], #[ArtistName], #[PlaylistName], and #MusicLover.

- **Engage with followers who listen to your recommendations:** Ask your followers what they think of the music you recommended. Start discussions about the artists, the songs, or the themes that resonate with them.

Examples of Music Recommendations:

- **Classic Album Recommendation:** "If you haven't listened to [Album Title] by [Artist Name], you're missing out on a classic! This album is a masterpiece of [Genre] and it's influenced countless artists since its release. #MusicRecommendation #[Genre] #EssentialListening" (Include a link to the album on a streaming service)

- **Emerging Artist Recommendation:** "Check out this amazing new artist, [Artist Name]. Their sound is a blend of [Genre] and [Genre] with a unique twist. I'm hooked on their latest single, [Song Title]. #NewMusic #[Genre] #MusicDiscovery" (Include a link to the song on a streaming service)

- **Curated Playlist Recommendation:** "I just created a new playlist called [Playlist Name] that's perfect for [Mood/Activity]. It features a mix of [Genre] and [Genre] tracks that will set the vibe for your [Activity]. Enjoy! #Playlist #MusicFor[Mood/Activity] #[Genre]" (Include a link to the playlist on a streaming service)

- **Descriptive Language:** "Get ready to be transported to another world with [Album Title] by [Artist Name]. This album is an atmospheric journey through sound and emotion, with haunting melodies, ethereal vocals, and intricate instrumentation. #MusicRecommendation #[Genre] #DreamyVibes"

- **Follower Engagement:** "Has anyone listened to [Song/Album/Playlist Title] that I recommended? What did you think? #MusicDiscussion #[Genre] #SharingIsCaring"

Live-Tweeting Concerts and Music Festivals: Sharing the Experience in Real Time

Live-tweeting concerts and music festivals allows you to share the excitement and energy of live music with your followers in real time, creating a virtual concert experience for those who couldn't attend in person. It's also a great way to connect with other fans who are at the event or who are following along from home.

Tips for Live-Tweeting Concerts and Music Festivals:

- **Set the scene:** Start your live-tweeting session by describing the venue, the atmosphere, the crowd's energy, and any pre-show rituals or observations.

- **Use a dedicated hashtag:** Use a dedicated hashtag for the event, such as #[ArtistName]Concert or #[FestivalName], to make it easy for other fans to find your tweets and join the conversation.

- **Share photos and videos (if allowed):** Capture the highlights of the performance with photos and videos, if allowed. Be sure to respect the artist's and venue's policies regarding photography and videography.

- **Comment on the setlist:** Share your thoughts on the songs the artist is performing. Are they playing your favorites? Are they surprising you with any deep cuts or covers?

- **Interact with other fans:** Respond to tweets from other fans who are at the event or who are following along from home. Ask questions, share your excitement, and create a sense of community.

- **Avoid spoilers:** If the artist is performing any new or unreleased material, be mindful of spoilers and avoid revealing too much detail about the songs.

- **Be present and enjoy the experience:** While live-tweeting can enhance the concert experience, don't let it distract you from enjoying the moment. Put your phone down periodically and immerse yourself in the music.

Examples of Live-Tweeting Concerts and Music Festivals:

- **Setting the Scene:** "Just arrived at the [Venue Name] for the [Artist Name] concert! The crowd is buzzing with excitement and the stage looks amazing. Can't wait for the show to start! #[ArtistName]Concert #[CityName]"

- **Using a Dedicated Hashtag:** "Live-tweeting the #[FestivalName] all weekend long! Follow along for updates, photos, and musical discoveries. #MusicFestival #[Genre]"

- **Sharing Photos and Videos:** "Here's a sneak peek of the stage setup for the [Artist Name] concert. The lights are insane! #[ArtistName] #ConcertProduction #[VenueName]" (Include a photo of the stage)

- **Commenting on the Setlist:** "[Artist Name] just opened with [Song Title]! This is my favorite song! The crowd is going wild! #SetlistGoals #[ArtistName] #[SongTitle]"

- **Interacting with Other Fans:** "Anyone else at the #[FestivalName] this weekend? What artists are you most excited to see? #MusicLovers #FestivalCommunity"

- **Avoiding Spoilers:** "[Artist Name] just debuted a new song! It sounds amazing! I won't spoil it for those who aren't here, but let's just say it's a banger! #NewMusic #[ArtistName] #[FestivalName]"

- **Being Present:** "Putting my phone down for a while to fully immerse myself in the music. [Artist Name] is putting on an incredible show! #ConcertVibes #MusicMagic #InTheMoment"

Music Debates: Engaging in Friendly (or Not-So-Friendly) Banter

Music is a subjective experience, and passionate fans often have strong opinions about their favorite artists, genres, and songs. Twitter can be a breeding ground for music-related debates, from playful banter to heated arguments about musical tastes and preferences.

Tips for Engaging in Music Debates:

- **Be respectful:** Even when you disagree with someone, remember to be respectful of their opinions. Avoid personal attacks, name-calling, or inflammatory language.

- **Focus on the music:** Keep the debate focused on the music itself, rather than attacking the person who holds a different opinion. Discuss the elements of the music, such as the songwriting, the production, the vocals, or the instrumentation.

- **Provide evidence:** If you're making a claim about an artist's influence, a genre's historical significance, or a song's cultural impact, provide evidence to support your argument. Link to articles, interviews, or other sources that back up your points.

- **Know when to disengage:** Not every debate is worth having. If a conversation becomes unproductive, disrespectful, or personal, it's okay to disengage and move on.

- **Don't take it too seriously:** Remember that music is subjective, and what one person loves, another person might hate. Embrace the diversity of musical tastes and enjoy the banter, even if you don't agree with everything you hear.

Examples of Music Debates:

- **Genre Debate:** "I think [Genre A] is much more innovative and influential than [Genre B]. [Genre A] has a richer history, more diverse subgenres, and has pushed the boundaries of music further. #MusicDebate #[GenreA]vs[GenreB]"

- **Artist Comparison:** "I think [Artist A] is a much more talented songwriter than [Artist B]. [Artist A]'s lyrics are more poetic, their melodies are more memorable, and their songs have a deeper emotional impact. #[ArtistA]vs[ArtistB] #Songwriting"

- **Song Ranking:** "I'm ranking the songs on [Album Title] from best to worst. My top 3 are [Song Title A], [Song Title B], and [Song Title C]. What's your ranking? #AlbumRanking #[AlbumTitle] #MusicDiscussion"

- **Disagreement with Respect:** "I disagree with your assessment of [Artist Name]. While I respect your opinion, I think their music is groundbreaking and has had a significant impact on [Genre]. #MusicDebate #RespectfulDisagreement #[Genre]"

- **Disengagement:** "I'm not interested in engaging in a debate that's based on personal attacks and insults. Let's keep the conversation focused on the music. #MusicDiscussion #RespectfulDebate #EndofDiscussion"

Sharing Music-Related News and Articles: Staying Informed and Engaging in Discussions

Twitter is a great source for staying up-to-date on the latest music-related news, releases, and discussions. By following music journalists, publications, and industry insiders, you can stay informed about the happenings in the music world and engage in conversations about the topics that matter to you.

Examples of Music-Related Accounts to Follow:

- **Music Journalists:** Follow music journalists who write for publications you admire or who specialize in genres or artists that you enjoy.

- **Music Publications:** Follow the Twitter accounts of music magazines, websites, and blogs that cover the music you're interested in.

- **Music Industry Insiders:** Follow record labels, producers, managers, and other industry professionals to get behind-the-scenes insights into the music business.

- **Music Charts and Awards Shows:** Follow the Twitter accounts of music charts, such as Billboard (@billboard) or the Official Charts (@officialcharts), and awards shows, such as the Grammy Awards (@RecordingAcad), to stay informed about the latest trends and accolades.

- **Music Streaming Services:** Follow the Twitter accounts of streaming services like Spotify (@Spotify), Apple Music (@AppleMusic), and YouTube Music (@YouTubeMusic) to get updates on new releases, curated playlists, and exclusive content.

Pro-Tip: Engage with the accounts you follow by asking questions, sharing your thoughts on articles, and participating in discussions. Twitter provides a unique opportunity to interact directly with music journalists, industry professionals, and other music lovers.

Music and Memes: Adding a Touch of Humor to Your Musical Tweets

Memes have become a ubiquitous part of internet culture, and the music world is no exception. A well-chosen meme can perfectly capture the essence of a song, an artist's personality, or a relatable music-related experience, adding a touch of humor and relatability to your tweets.

Tips for Using Music-Related Memes:

- **Choose relevant memes:** Select memes that are relevant to the topic of your tweet, whether it's a specific song, an artist, a genre, or a music-related experience.

- **Use high-quality memes:** Avoid using low-resolution or poorly formatted memes, as they can detract from the overall quality of your tweet.

- **Give credit where credit is due:** If you're using a meme that someone else created, be sure to give them credit if possible.

- **Don't overuse them:** While memes can be fun, don't overuse them. Too many memes can make your tweets appear unoriginal and spammy.

- **Be mindful of copyright:** Some memes may use copyrighted images or music. Be aware of the potential for copyright infringement and avoid using memes that could get you into trouble.

Examples of Tweets Using Music-Related Memes:

- **Drakeposting Meme:** "Me trying to decide which [Artist Name] album to listen to first: [Drakeposting meme with

Drake looking disgusted at one option and approving of the other]" #[ArtistName] #AlbumChoices #MusicLover"

- **Distracted Boyfriend Meme:** "Me trying to focus on work: [Distracted Boyfriend meme with the boyfriend representing work and the girlfriend representing music]" #CantStopListening #MusicDistraction #[SongTitle]"

- **Woman Yelling at a Cat Meme:** "Me trying to explain to my friends why [Artist Name] is a genius: [Woman Yelling at a Cat meme with the woman representing you and the cat representing your friends]" #MusicDebate #UnderratedArtist #[ArtistName]"

- **Success Kid Meme:** "Me finally finding that song that's been stuck in my head all day: [Success Kid meme]" #Earworm #MusicMysterySolved #[SongTitle]"

- **Change My Mind Meme:** "[Song Title] is the best song of all time. Change my mind. [Change My Mind meme]" #MusicDebate #BestSongEver #[SongTitle]"

Music and Nostalgia: Tweeting Your Musical Memories

Music has a powerful ability to evoke memories and transport us back to specific times and places in our lives. Sharing your musical memories on Twitter can be a nostalgic and heartwarming experience, allowing you to connect with your followers on a personal level and spark conversations about the songs that shaped their lives.

Tips for Tweeting Your Musical Memories:

- **Share specific memories:** Instead of simply saying "This song reminds me of my childhood," share a specific memory associated with the song. Describe the time, the place, the people involved, and the emotions you felt.

- **Use vivid language:** Use descriptive language to paint a picture of the memory and transport your followers back in time with you.

- **Include photos or videos:** If you have any photos or videos that relate to the memory, include them in your tweet to make it more visually engaging.

- **Use relevant hashtags:** Hashtags can help increase the visibility of your tweets and connect you with other people who share similar musical memories. Use hashtags like #MusicMemories, #ThrowbackThursday, #Nostalgia, #[ArtistName], and #[SongTitle].

- **Engage with followers who share similar memories:** Respond to comments from followers who share similar memories or who have been touched by the same songs. Music can be a powerful bond, and sharing these experiences can create a sense of connection.

Examples of Tweets Sharing Musical Memories:

- **Childhood Memory:** "This song always reminds me of summers spent at my grandparents' house. We'd listen to it on their old record player while playing in the backyard. #MusicMemories #SummerVibes #[SongTitle]"

- **First Concert:** "My first concert was [Artist Name] when I was 16. I remember being blown away by the energy of the crowd and the power of the music. It was a night I'll never forget. #ConcertMemories #[ArtistName] #LifeChanging"

- **High School Dance:** "This song was our prom theme song, and it always takes me back to that magical night. #ThrowbackThursday #PromNight #[SongTitle]" (Include a photo from your prom night)

- **Road Trip Soundtrack:** "This album was the soundtrack to our epic cross-country road trip. Every time I hear it, I'm transported back to those endless highways and unforgettable adventures. #RoadTripMemories #[AlbumTitle] #Wanderlust"

- **Shared Memory with a Friend:** "This song reminds me of our crazy college days, [Friend's Twitter Handle]. Remember all those late-night singalongs? Good times! #MusicMemories #FriendshipAnthem #[SongTitle]"

Supporting Musicians: Tweeting Your Appreciation and Spreading the Word

In the digital age, it's easier than ever to support the musicians you love. Use your Twitter platform to express your appreciation, spread the word about their music, and contribute to their success.

Tips for Supporting Musicians on Twitter:

- **Share their music:** Tweet links to their songs, albums, and music videos. Encourage your followers to give them a listen.

- **Promote their shows and events:** If they're playing a show in your area, tweet about it and encourage your followers to attend.

- **Buy their merchandise:** If you love their music, support them by purchasing their merchandise, such as t-shirts, albums, or concert tickets.

- **Leave positive reviews:** Leave positive reviews on their music on streaming services and online retailers. Positive reviews can help boost their visibility and attract new listeners.

- **Tag them in your tweets:** Tag them in your tweets about their music to show your appreciation and let them know that you're a fan.

- **Engage with their content:** Like, retweet, and comment on their tweets to show your support and help their content reach a wider audience.

- **Contribute to their crowdfunding campaigns:** Many independent musicians use crowdfunding platforms like Kickstarter or Patreon to fund their projects. Consider contributing to their campaigns to help them achieve their goals.

Examples of Tweets Supporting Musicians:

- **Sharing Music:** "Loving the new single from [Artist Name], [Song Title]. Give it a listen if you're a fan of [Genre]. #[ArtistName] #NewMusic #[Genre]" (Include a link to the song on a streaming service)

- **Promoting Shows:** "[Artist Name] is playing at [Venue Name] on [Date]. Don't miss this chance to see them live! #ConcertAlert #[ArtistName] #[VenueName]"

- **Buying Merchandise:** "Just ordered a new [Artist Name] t-shirt! Supporting the artists I love by buying their merch. #[ArtistName] #MerchLove #FanSupport"

- **Leaving Reviews:** "Left a glowing review for [Album Title] by [Artist Name] on Spotify. This album is a masterpiece! #[ArtistName] #[AlbumTitle] #PositiveReview"

- **Tagging Artists:** "[Artist Name], your new album is incredible! Every track is a banger! Thank you for sharing your music with the world. #[ArtistName] #[AlbumTitle] #FanAppreciation"

- **Engaging with Content:** "Retweeting this amazing performance by [Artist Name]. Their vocals are incredible! #[ArtistName] #LiveMusic #Talent"

- **Contributing to Crowdfunding:** "Just contributed to [Artist Name]'s Kickstarter campaign for their new album. Excited to support their creative journey! #Crowdfunding #MusicSupport #[ArtistName]"

Discovering New Music: Using Twitter to Expand Your Musical Horizons

Twitter can be a fantastic tool for discovering new music. With so many music lovers, artists, and industry professionals sharing their recommendations and insights, you're sure to find something that piques your interest and expands your musical tastes.

Tips for Discovering New Music on Twitter:

- **Follow music discovery accounts:** There are many Twitter accounts dedicated to sharing new music from a variety of genres and artists. Following these accounts can expose you to a wider range of sounds and styles.

- **Explore music-related hashtags:** Search for hashtags related to your musical interests, such as #newmusic, #[Genre], #musicdiscovery, or #underratedartists. You can also explore hashtags based on moods or activities, such as #musicforstudying, #musicforworkingout, or #musicforrelaxing.

- **Participate in Twitter chats:** Many online communities host Twitter chats focused on music discovery and recommendations. Participating in these chats can introduce you to new artists and genres that you might not have otherwise found.

- **Ask for recommendations from your followers:** Don't be afraid to ask your followers for music recommendations. Be specific about your musical tastes and preferences, such as your favorite genres, artists, or moods.

- **Create a "Want to Listen" list:** Use Twitter's bookmarking feature or create a dedicated list to keep track of the music recommendations that you want to check out.

Examples of Tweets Discovering New Music:

- **Following Music Discovery Accounts:** "Just followed @NewMusicDaily for my daily dose of musical discoveries. Excited to explore new genres and artists! #MusicDiscovery #NewMusicFriday #OpenToAnything"

- **Exploring Hashtags:** "Scrolling through the #[Genre] hashtag to find some new bands and artists to listen to. Any recommendations? #MusicExploration #[Genre]Lover #HiddenGems"

- **Participating in Twitter Chats:** "Excited to join the #MusicDiscoveryChat tonight at 8pm EST! Let's share our favorite new music finds and expand our musical horizons. #NewMusic #TwitterChat #MusicCommunity"

- **Asking for Recommendations:** "I'm looking for new music that's upbeat, energetic, and perfect for working out. Any suggestions? #WorkoutMusic #MusicMotivation #[Genre]Recommendations"

- **Creating a "Want to Listen" List:** "Just added [Artist Name] to my "Want to Listen" list after seeing them mentioned in several tweets. Their music sounds intriguing! #MusicDiscovery #NewArtistAlert #[Genre]"

Music and Mental Health: Tweeting the Therapeutic Power of Music

Music has a profound impact on our mental and emotional well-being. It can soothe our anxieties, lift our spirits, and provide comfort and solace during difficult times. Sharing the therapeutic power of music on Twitter can create a sense of community, offer support to others who are struggling, and raise awareness about the importance of music for mental health.

Tips for Tweeting About Music and Mental Health:

- **Share your personal experiences:** If you've found music to be helpful in managing your mental health, share your experiences with your followers. Be honest and vulnerable about how music has helped you to cope with stress, anxiety, depression, or other mental health challenges.

- **Recommend songs and playlists:** Share songs and playlists that you find to be calming, uplifting, or inspiring. Create playlists for specific moods or activities, such as relaxation, meditation, or motivation.

- **Use relevant hashtags:** Use hashtags like #MusicAndMentalHealth, #MusicTherapy, #MentalHealthAwareness, #SelfCare, #AnxietyRelief, #DepressionSupport, and #Mindfulness to connect with others who are interested in the topic.

- **Follow mental health organizations:** Follow mental health organizations on Twitter to get updates on resources, support groups, and events.

- **Be mindful of triggering content:** Avoid sharing content that could be triggering for others who are struggling with mental health issues. Be sensitive to the experiences of others and create a safe and supportive space.

Examples of Tweets About Music and Mental Health:

- **Personal Experience:** "Music has been a lifeline for me during times of anxiety and stress. Certain songs have a way of calming my mind and grounding me in the present moment. #MusicAndMentalHealth #AnxietyRelief #SelfCare"

- **Song Recommendation:** "If you're feeling anxious or overwhelmed, I recommend listening to [Song Title] by [Artist Name]. It has a calming melody and soothing lyrics that always help me to relax. #MusicTherapy #AnxietySupport #[SongTitle]"

- **Playlist Recommendation:** "I just created a new playlist called "Mindful Moments" that's perfect for meditation, relaxation, or simply unwinding after a long day. It features instrumental music, nature sounds, and calming melodies. Enjoy! #Mindfulness #Meditation #MusicForRelaxation"

- **Mental Health Organization:** "Follow @MentalHealthAm for resources, support, and advocacy related to mental health. #MentalHealthAwareness #Support #EndTheStigma"

- **Trigger Warning:** "Trigger Warning: This tweet discusses themes of depression and suicide. If you're struggling, please reach out for help. The National Suicide Prevention Lifeline is available 24/7 at 988. #MentalHealthMatters #SuicidePrevention #YouAreNotAlone"

Engaging with Musicians on Twitter: Building Connections and Showing Support

Twitter provides a unique opportunity to connect directly with musicians, from emerging artists to established stars. Engaging with musicians on Twitter can be a rewarding experience, allowing you to express your appreciation, ask questions, and contribute to their creative journey.

Tips for Engaging with Musicians on Twitter:

- **Follow them:** Start by following the Twitter accounts of the musicians you admire.

- **Tag them in your tweets:** When you tweet about their music, tag them in your tweets to let them know that you're a fan.

- **Comment on their posts:** Leave thoughtful comments on their posts, sharing your thoughts on their music, their performances, or their creative process.

- **Ask questions:** If you have questions about their music, their inspirations, or their upcoming projects, don't be afraid to ask.

- **Share their content:** Retweet their posts, share their music videos, and help spread the word about their work.

- **Attend their virtual events:** Many musicians host virtual events, such as listening parties, Q&A sessions, or live performances. Participating in these events can give you a chance to interact with the artist directly and show your support.

- **Be respectful:** While it's great to be enthusiastic, remember to be respectful of their boundaries. Avoid sending overly personal or intrusive messages.

Examples of Tweets Engaging with Musicians:

- **Tagging an Artist:** "[Artist Name], your new album is blowing my mind! The songwriting is incredible, the production is top-notch, and your vocals are out of this world! #[ArtistName] #[AlbumTitle] #FanForLife"

- **Commenting on a Post:** "Love the behind-the-scenes glimpse of your recording process, [Artist Name]. It's fascinating to see how your music comes together. #[ArtistName] #StudioLife #CreativeProcess"

- **Asking a Question:** "[Artist Name], what was your inspiration for writing [Song Title]? The lyrics are so powerful and relatable. #[ArtistName] #[SongTitle] #Songwriting"

- **Sharing Content:** "Retweeting this amazing live performance by [Artist Name]. Their energy on stage is infectious! #[ArtistName] #LiveMusic #MustSeeShow" (Include a link to the video of the performance)

- **Attending a Virtual Event:** "Excited to join the virtual listening party for [Artist Name]'s new album tonight! Can't wait to hear the new music and chat with other fans. #[ArtistName] #AlbumRelease #VirtualEvent"

Using Twitter to Discover Live Music Events: Finding Shows in Your Area

Twitter can be a valuable resource for discovering live music events in your area. Many venues, promoters, and artists use Twitter to announce upcoming shows, share ticket information, and promote their events.

Tips for Using Twitter to Discover Live Music Events:

- **Follow venues and promoters:** Follow the Twitter accounts of music venues, concert halls, and promoters in your area. They often tweet about upcoming shows, ticket sales, and special events.

- **Follow artists you love:** Follow the Twitter accounts of your favorite artists to get updates on their tour dates and announcements of shows in your area.

- **Explore music-related hashtags:** Search for hashtags related to live music events, such as #concerts, #liveshows, #[Genre]Shows, #[CityName]Music, or #[VenueName].

- **Use Twitter's advanced search features:** Twitter's advanced search features allow you to filter your search results by location, date, and other criteria. This can be helpful for finding specific types of events, such as concerts by a particular artist or shows in a particular genre.

- **Create Twitter lists:** Create Twitter lists to organize the accounts you follow based on your musical interests, such as "Local Venues," "Favorite Artists," or "[Genre] Shows." This can make it easier to keep track of upcoming events and announcements.

Examples of Tweets Discovering Live Music Events:

- **Following Venues:** "Just followed @[VenueName] on Twitter to stay up-to-date on upcoming shows and events. Love their eclectic lineup of artists! #[VenueName] #[CityName]Music #

CHAPTER THIRTEEN: Movie Magic: Tweeting About Films

Movies. They transport us to other worlds, make us laugh, cry, and think, and stay with us long after the credits roll. And in the age of social media, they spark endless conversations, debates, and memes. Twitter (or X), with its fast-paced nature and vibrant community, is a fantastic platform to share your love for movies, connect with fellow cinephiles, and maybe even inspire others to discover their next cinematic obsession.

This chapter will explore the myriad ways you can use Twitter to engage with the world of film, from sharing your instant reactions to new releases to recommending hidden gems and delving into the depths of film analysis. Get ready to unleash your inner film critic and light up the Twitterverse with your cinematic insights.

Sharing Your Movie Night: Tweeting Your Viewing Experiences

Whether you're settling in for a cozy night at home with a classic film or venturing out to catch the latest blockbuster, Twitter provides the perfect platform to share your movie night with your followers. It's a simple yet effective way to connect with other film enthusiasts, get recommendations, and spark conversations about the movies that are captivating audiences.

Tweet Examples:

- **Classic Movie Night:** "Curling up on the couch with a bowl of popcorn and a classic film tonight: [Movie Title]. This movie never gets old. What's your favorite classic movie to revisit? #MovieNight #ClassicCinema #[Genre]"

- **New Release Excitement:** "Heading to the theater to see the new [Movie Title] tonight! I've heard great things about it. Anyone else planning to see it? #NewRelease #MoviePremiere #[Genre]"

- **Streaming Surprise:** "Just discovered [Movie Title] on [Streaming Platform] and I'm blown away! It's a hidden gem that I somehow missed. Highly recommend checking it out. #StreamingFind #HiddenGem #[Genre]"

- **Themed Movie Marathon:** "Having a [Theme] movie marathon this weekend! Starting with [Movie Title], followed by [Movie Title], and ending with [Movie Title]. Join me in the comments for a virtual watch party! #MovieMarathon #[Theme]Movies #WeekendVibes"

- **Movie Night Fail:** "Well, my movie night didn't go as planned. The Wi-Fi is down, the popcorn burned, and I accidentally spilled my drink on the remote. Maybe I should just try again tomorrow. #MovieNightFail #TechnicalDifficulties #FirstWorldProblems"

Pro-Tip: Enhance your tweets by including photos or videos related to your movie night. A shot of your cozy setup, a selfie at the theater, or a short clip of a memorable scene can make your tweets more engaging and visually appealing. You can also use relevant hashtags to connect with other movie lovers who are watching the same film or who share similar cinematic tastes.

Instant Reactions: Tweeting Your First Impressions

Movies have a way of eliciting immediate reactions, whether it's a gasp of surprise, a burst of laughter, or a tear-jerking moment. Twitter, with its fast-paced nature, is the perfect platform to share those instant reactions and connect with other viewers who are experiencing the film's emotional rollercoaster alongside you.

Tips for Tweeting Your Instant Reactions:

- **Keep it brief and impactful:** Twitter's character limit encourages brevity. Capture the essence of your reaction in a concise and impactful way.

- **Use emojis to express your emotions:** Emojis can be a powerful tool for conveying your feelings without having to write a lengthy explanation. A simple "😱" or "😭" can speak volumes.

- **Use GIFs to amplify your reaction:** A well-chosen GIF can perfectly capture your response to a shocking plot twist, a hilarious one-liner, or a heartwarming scene.

- **Use spoiler warnings:** If you're tweeting about a specific plot point or scene, use a spoiler warning to avoid ruining the experience for others who haven't seen the film.

- **Don't overthink it:** Instant reactions are all about capturing your raw emotions in the moment. Don't spend too much time crafting the perfect tweet – just share what you're feeling!

Examples of Instant Reactions:

- **Shock and Awe:** "That plot twist was insane! I did not see that coming! □ #[MovieTitle] #MindBlown #Shook"

- **Laughter Out Loud:** "I just laughed so hard I cried! [Character Name] is hilarious! 😂 #[MovieTitle] #ComedyGold #BestLineEver"

- **Heartwarming Moment:** "That scene was so heartwarming! I'm a puddle of tears right now. 😢 #[MovieTitle] #FeelGoodMovie #TouchingMoment"

- **Spoiler Warning:** "Spoiler Alert for [Movie Title]! That ending was heartbreaking! 💔 What did you guys think? #MovieDiscussion #SpoilerAlert #[MovieTitle]"

- **Raw Emotion:** "I'm speechless. [Movie Title] just hit me on such a deep level. I need a moment to process everything I just saw. #EmotionalMovie #PowerfulStorytelling #[MovieTitle]"

Movie Reviews: Sharing Your Cinematic Insights

Movie reviews are a staple of film discourse, allowing you to share your opinions, analyze the film's strengths and weaknesses, and recommend (or not recommend) it to others. Whether you're a seasoned film critic or simply a passionate viewer, your insights can contribute to the conversation and help others make informed decisions about their movie choices.

Tips for Crafting Engaging Movie Reviews:

- **Provide a brief synopsis without spoilers:** Give a general overview of the movie's premise, setting, and characters without revealing any major plot points or surprises.

- **Analyze the key elements of the film:** Discuss the aspects of the film that stood out to you, such as the acting, the directing, the screenplay, the cinematography, the score, or the special effects.

- **Support your opinions with evidence:** Instead of simply stating your opinions, provide specific examples from the film to support your claims. Refer to particular scenes, dialogue, or visual elements that illustrate your points.

- **Offer your overall assessment:** Would you recommend this movie to others? If so, who would you recommend it to? Be specific about your target audience.

- **Use relevant hashtags:** Hashtags can help increase the visibility of your review and connect you with other film enthusiasts who are interested in the same genre, director, actors, or themes. Use hashtags like #moviereview,

#filmreview, #[Genre]Review, #[DirectorName], #[ActorName], and #[MovieTitle].

- **Be objective and respectful:** While it's okay to express your personal preferences, try to be as objective as possible in your assessment of the film. Avoid making personal attacks on the filmmakers or actors, and respect the opinions of others, even if you disagree with them.

Examples of Engaging Movie Reviews:

- **Positive Review:** "Just saw [Movie Title] and it was absolutely phenomenal! The acting was superb, the directing was masterful, and the story was both thought-provoking and emotionally resonant. Highly recommend for fans of [Genre]. #MovieReview #[Genre]Review #[DirectorName]"

- **Mixed Review:** "I had mixed feelings about [Movie Title]. The visuals were stunning, but the plot was convoluted and the pacing was uneven. It's a visually impressive film, but it lacks substance. #MovieReview #HonestReview #[Genre]"

- **Negative Review:** "Unfortunately, I was disappointed by [Movie Title]. The acting was wooden, the dialogue was cheesy, and the special effects were laughably bad. I wouldn't recommend it. #MovieReview #SkipIt #[Genre]"

- **Specific Element Highlight:** "The cinematography in [Movie Title] is breathtaking. Every shot is like a work of art, and the use of light and shadow is masterful. #MovieReview #CinematographyGoals #[DirectorName]"

- **Target Audience Recommendation:** "I would highly recommend [Movie Title] to anyone who enjoys thought-provoking sci-fi films with a philosophical bent. It's a film that will stay with you long after you've seen it. #MovieRecommendation #SciFi #[DirectorName]"

Dissecting Details: Tweeting About Specific Movie Elements

Sometimes, you just want to gush about a particular aspect of a film that blew you away. Whether it's a stunning performance, a clever plot twist, a thought-provoking theme, or a breathtaking visual effect, Twitter provides the perfect platform to dissect those details and share your appreciation with fellow cinephiles.

Tips for Tweeting About Specific Movie Elements:

- **Be specific and focused:** Choose a particular element of the film that you want to discuss and focus your tweet on that aspect. Avoid rambling or trying to cover too much ground in a single tweet.

- **Provide context:** Give enough context so that your followers understand what you're referring to, even if they haven't seen the film. Briefly describe the scene, the character, or the theme that you're discussing.

- **Use descriptive language:** Use vivid language to convey your appreciation for the specific element. Paint a picture in your followers' minds and evoke the same sense of awe or wonder that you experienced.

- **Use relevant hashtags:** Hashtags can help increase the visibility of your tweets and connect you with other film enthusiasts who are interested in similar topics. Use hashtags related to the specific element you're discussing, such as #acting, #screenwriting, #cinematography, #score, #specialeffects, or #[Theme].

- **Avoid spoilers (unless you explicitly state otherwise):** Be mindful of spoilers and avoid revealing any major plot twists or surprises that could ruin the experience for others who haven't seen the film. If you do need to discuss spoilers, use a spoiler warning and hide the text behind a spoiler tag.

Examples of Tweets Dissecting Movie Details:

- **Acting Performance:** "[Actor Name] delivers a tour-de-force performance in [Movie Title]. Their portrayal of [Character Name] is both nuanced and heartbreaking. #ActingGoals #[ActorName] #[MovieTitle]"

- **Plot Twist:** "That plot twist in [Movie Title] was mind-bending! I'm still trying to wrap my head around it. □ #PlotTwistMasterpiece #[MovieTitle] #ScreenwritingGoals"

- **Theme:** "[Movie Title] explores the complex themes of [Theme A] and [Theme B] in a thought-provoking and emotionally resonant way. #[ThemeA] #[ThemeB] #[MovieTitle]"

- **Visual Effects:** "The special effects in [Movie Title] are absolutely breathtaking! The [Specific Visual Effect] scene is a visual masterpiece. #VisualEffectsGoals #[MovieTitle] #MovieMagic"

- **Spoiler Warning:** "Spoiler Alert for [Movie Title]! That scene where [Spoiler] was heartbreaking! I'm still recovering. 💔 #[MovieTitle] #SpoilerAlert #EmotionalScene"

Movie Recommendations: Sharing Your Cinematic Gems

Sharing movie recommendations on Twitter is a fantastic way to spread your love for film, introduce your followers to new cinematic experiences, and maybe even spark a new obsession. Whether it's a classic film that everyone should see, a hidden gem that deserves more recognition, or a film that perfectly captures a certain mood or theme, your recommendations can expand your followers' cinematic horizons and create a sense of community through shared viewing experiences.

Tips for Sharing Movie Recommendations:

- **Be specific and provide context:** Instead of simply saying "You should watch [Movie Title]," provide some context about the film's genre, director, actors, and why you enjoy it. Highlight what makes the film unique or noteworthy.

- **Offer recommendations for different moods and interests:** Consider recommending films for different moods, such as feel-good movies, thought-provoking films, action-packed adventures, or heartwarming romances.

- **Create themed lists:** Create themed lists of movie recommendations, such as "Best Sci-Fi Movies," "Movies That Will Make You Cry," or "Movies to Watch on a Rainy Day."

- **Use relevant hashtags:** Hashtags can help increase the visibility of your recommendations and connect you with other film enthusiasts who are interested in similar genres, directors, actors, or themes. Use hashtags like #movierecommendation, #filmrecommendation, #[Genre], #[DirectorName], #[ActorName], and #MovieLover.

- **Engage with followers who watch your recommendations:** Ask your followers what they think of the movies you recommended. Start discussions about the films, the characters, the themes, or the performances.

Examples of Movie Recommendations:

- **Classic Film Recommendation:** "If you've never seen [Movie Title], you're missing out on a cinematic masterpiece. This film is a timeless classic that will stay with you long after you've seen it. #MovieRecommendation #ClassicCinema #[Genre]"

- **Hidden Gem Recommendation:** "Check out [Movie Title], a hidden gem that deserves more recognition. It's a

185

beautifully crafted film with a powerful story and memorable performances. #MovieRecommendation #HiddenGem #[Genre]"

- **Themed List:** "Here's my list of the best sci-fi movies of all time: [Movie Title], [Movie Title], [Movie Title], [Movie Title], [Movie Title]. What are your favorites? #SciFiMovies #MovieRecommendations #GenreLove"

- **Mood-Based Recommendation:** "If you're looking for a feel-good movie to brighten your day, I highly recommend [Movie Title]. It's a heartwarming story with charming characters and a positive message. #FeelGoodMovies #MovieRecommendation #[Genre]"

- **Follower Engagement:** "Has anyone seen [Movie Title] that I recommended? What did you think? #MovieDiscussion #[Genre] #SharingIsCaring"

Movie Trivia and Behind-the-Scenes Insights: Tweeting Fun Facts and Trivia

The world of film is full of fascinating trivia, behind-the-scenes stories, and little-known facts that can enhance your appreciation for the movies you love. Sharing these insights on Twitter can spark conversations, impress your followers with your cinematic knowledge, and add a touch of fun and intrigue to your tweets.

Tips for Tweeting Movie Trivia and Behind-the-Scenes Insights:

- **Choose interesting and relevant facts:** Select trivia that is both interesting and relevant to the movies you're discussing. Avoid sharing obscure or irrelevant facts that are unlikely to engage your followers.

- **Provide context:** Give enough context so that your followers understand the significance of the trivia or behind-the-scenes story.

- **Use visuals:** Include photos, videos, or GIFs related to the trivia to make your tweets more visually appealing.

- **Use relevant hashtags:** Hashtags can help increase the visibility of your tweets and connect you with other film enthusiasts who are interested in similar topics. Use hashtags like #movietrivia, #behindthescenes, #filmfacts, #[MovieTitle], and #[ActorName].

- **Verify your facts:** Before sharing trivia or behind-the-scenes stories, make sure that your information is accurate. Double-check your sources and avoid spreading misinformation.

Examples of Tweets Sharing Movie Trivia and Behind-the-Scenes Insights:

- **Casting Trivia:** "Did you know that [Actor Name] was originally considered for the role of [Character Name] in [Movie Title]? Can you imagine how different the film would have been? #MovieTrivia #CastingChoices #[MovieTitle]"

- **Filming Location:** "The iconic [Scene] in [Movie Title] was filmed on location in [Location]. I'd love to visit that place someday! #BehindTheScenes #MovieLocations #[MovieTitle]" (Include a photo of the filming location)

- **Special Effects:** "The groundbreaking special effects in [Movie Title] were created using [Technique]. It's amazing how far filmmaking technology has come! #SpecialEffects #MovieMagic #[MovieTitle]"

- **Hidden Meaning:** "There's a hidden meaning in [Scene] in [Movie Title]. The [Symbol] represents [Meaning]. I love how films can be layered with symbolism and deeper meanings. #FilmAnalysis #Symbolism #[MovieTitle]"

- **Director's Cameo:** "Keep an eye out for director [Director Name]'s cameo appearance in [Movie Title]. They can be spotted briefly in [Scene]. #DirectorsCameo #HiddenDetails #[MovieTitle]"

Movie Debates: Engaging in Cinematic Discussions

Movies often spark passionate debates about their themes, characters, interpretations, and overall quality. Twitter, with its fast-paced and interactive nature, is a great platform for engaging in cinematic discussions, sharing your opinions, and challenging (or defending) your favorite films.

Tips for Engaging in Movie Debates on Twitter:

- **Be respectful:** Even when you disagree with someone, remember to be respectful of their opinions. Avoid personal attacks, name-calling, or inflammatory language.

- **Focus on the film:** Keep the debate focused on the film itself, rather than attacking the person who holds a different opinion. Discuss the elements of the film, such as the plot, the characters, the themes, the acting, the directing, or the overall message.

- **Support your opinions with evidence:** Instead of simply stating your opinions, provide specific examples from the film to support your claims. Refer to particular scenes, dialogue, or visual elements that illustrate your points.

- **Acknowledge different interpretations:** Recognize that films can be interpreted in different ways, and there's no single "right" answer. Be open to hearing other perspectives, even if they differ from your own.

- **Know when to disengage:** Not every debate is worth having. If a conversation becomes unproductive, disrespectful, or personal, it's okay to disengage and move on.

- **Don't take it too seriously:** Remember that movies are meant to be enjoyed, and debates about them should be fun and engaging. Embrace the diversity of opinions and enjoy the banter, even if you don't agree with everything you hear.

Examples of Movie Debates:

- **Best Movie of All Time:** "I believe that [Movie Title] is the best movie ever made. The story is timeless, the characters are unforgettable, and the filmmaking is masterful. Change my mind! #MovieDebate #BestMovieEver #[MovieTitle]"

- **Character Interpretation:** "I think [Character Name]'s motivations in [Movie Title] are more complex than they appear on the surface. They're not simply a [Label], but a deeply flawed and conflicted individual. #CharacterAnalysis #[MovieTitle] #[CharacterName]"

- **Theme Debate:** "I think the main theme of [Movie Title] is [Theme]. The film explores this theme through the characters' actions, the dialogue, and the symbolism throughout the story. #ThemeAnalysis #[MovieTitle] #[Theme]"

- **Disagreement with Respect:** "I respectfully disagree with your interpretation of [Movie Title]. While I see your point, I think the film is more about [Theme] than [Theme]. #MovieDebate #DifferentPerspectives #[MovieTitle]"

- **Disengagement:** "This conversation is becoming unproductive and disrespectful. I'm not interested in engaging in a debate that's based on personal attacks. #MovieDiscussion #RespectfulDebate #EndofDiscussion"

Sharing Movie Quotes and Dialogue: Tweeting Memorable Lines

Movies are full of memorable quotes and lines of dialogue that resonate with audiences, capture the essence of a character, or perfectly encapsulate a theme. Sharing your favorite movie quotes on Twitter is a great way to express your love for film, spark conversations, and remind others of the power of cinematic storytelling.

Tips for Tweeting Movie Quotes:

- **Choose impactful quotes:** Select quotes that are memorable, thought-provoking, humorous, or otherwise impactful. Avoid sharing generic or uninspired lines of dialogue.

- **Provide context:** Give enough context so that your followers understand the significance of the quote, even if they haven't seen the film. Briefly describe the scene, the character who said it, or the theme it relates to.

- **Use visuals:** Include a photo, video, or GIF related to the quote to make your tweets more visually appealing.

- **Use relevant hashtags:** Hashtags can help increase the visibility of your tweets and connect you with other film enthusiasts who are interested in similar topics. Use hashtags like #moviequotes, #filmquotes, #[MovieTitle], #[CharacterName], and #[Theme].

Examples of Tweets Sharing Movie Quotes:

- **Inspirational Quote:** ""Life moves pretty fast. If you don't stop and look around once in a while, you could miss it." - Ferris Bueller, Ferris Bueller's Day Off #MovieQuotes #Inspirational #FerrisBuellersDayOff"

- **Humorous Quote:** ""My mama always said life was like a box of chocolates. You never know what you're gonna get." - Forrest Gump, Forrest Gump #MovieQuotes #ComedyGold #ForrestGump"

- **Character-Defining Quote:** ""I'll be back." - The Terminator, The Terminator #MovieQuotes #IconicLines #TheTerminator"

- **Theme-Related Quote:** ""The greatest trick the devil ever pulled was convincing the world he didn't exist." - Verbal Kint, The Usual Suspects #MovieQuotes #MindBending #TheUsualSuspects"

- **Visual Enhancement:** ""Here's looking at you, kid." - Rick Blaine, Casablanca #MovieQuotes #RomanticClassics #Casablanca" (Include a GIF of the iconic scene)

Fancasting: Tweeting Your Dream Movie Casts

Fancasting is a fun and imaginative exercise where you envision your ideal cast for a movie adaptation, a remake, or a sequel. Twitter is a great platform for sharing your fancasting ideas, sparking discussions, and engaging with other film enthusiasts who share your passion for cinematic dream teams.

Tips for Tweeting Your Fancasting Ideas:

- **Choose a specific project:** Select a specific movie or TV show that you want to fancast. It could be an upcoming adaptation, a remake of a classic film, or a sequel to a beloved franchise.

- **Be clear and concise:** State the role you're casting and the actor you're envisioning for the part. Avoid rambling or providing lengthy explanations.

- **Provide visuals:** Include photos of the actors you're suggesting to make your tweets more visually appealing. You can create collages or use side-by-side comparisons to showcase your casting choices.

- **Use relevant hashtags:** Hashtags can help increase the visibility of your tweets and connect you with other film enthusiasts who are interested in fancasting. Use hashtags like #fancasting, #dreamcast, #moviecasting, #[MovieTitle], and #[CharacterName].

- **Be respectful of actors and filmmakers:** Avoid making negative or derogatory comments about actors or filmmakers. Fancasting is meant to be a fun and imaginative exercise, so keep it lighthearted and positive.

Examples of Tweets Sharing Fancasting Ideas:

- **Movie Adaptation:** "My dream cast for the movie adaptation of [Book Title]: [Actor Name] as [Character Name], [Actor Name] as [Character Name], and [Actor Name] as [Character Name]. #Fancasting #[BookTitle] #DreamCast" (Include a photo collage of the actors)

- **Remake:** "If they ever remake [Movie Title], I think [Actor Name] would be perfect for the role of [Character Name]. They have the charisma, the acting chops, and the perfect look for the part. #Fancasting #Remake #[MovieTitle]" (Include a side-by-side photo comparison of the original actor and the suggested actor)

- **Sequel:** "I'm hoping that [Actor Name] will reprise their role as [Character Name] in the sequel to [Movie Title]. They brought so much depth and complexity to the character, and I can't wait to see what they do next. #Fancasting #Sequel #[MovieTitle]"

- **Engagement with Followers:** "Who would you fancast in your dream adaptation of [Book Title]? Share your ideas in the comments! #Fancasting #[BookTitle] #DreamCast"

Movie-Inspired Creative Writing: Tweeting Your Cinematic Stories

Movies often inspire us to create our own stories, whether it's fanfiction, short stories, poems, or screenplays. Twitter can be a great platform for sharing your movie-inspired creative writing, connecting with other fans, and exploring the worlds and characters that have captured your imagination.

Tips for Tweeting Movie-Inspired Creative Writing:

- **Choose a format:** Decide on a format for your creative writing, such as a short story, a poem, a screenplay excerpt, or a series of tweets that tell a larger story.

- **Set the scene:** Establish the setting, the characters, and the conflict in your writing. Draw inspiration from the movie, but feel free to add your own unique twists and interpretations.

- **Use descriptive language:** Use vivid language to bring your story to life and engage your readers' senses.

- **Include dialogue:** Dialogue can add depth and personality to your characters and move the story forward.

- **Use relevant hashtags:** Hashtags can help increase the visibility of your tweets and connect you with other fans who are interested in similar creative writing. Use hashtags like #fanfiction, #shortstories, #poetry, #screenwriting, #[MovieTitle], and #[CharacterName].

- **Respect copyright:** Avoid directly copying or plagiarizing from the original movie. Your creative writing should be inspired by the film, but it should be your own original work.

Examples of Tweets Sharing Movie-Inspired Creative Writing:

- **Short Story:** "[Character Name] stood at the edge of the cliff, gazing out at the vast expanse of the [Setting]. The events of [Movie Title] had changed them forever, and they were uncertain of what the future held. (Continues in a thread with multiple tweets telling the story) #Fanfiction #[MovieTitle] #[CharacterName]"

- **Poem:** "The stars twinkled like diamonds in the night sky, / A reflection of the hope that flickered within [Character Name]'s heart. / Though the journey had been fraught with peril, / They had emerged stronger, braver, and ready to face the unknown. #[MovieTitle] #Poetry #Hope"

- **Screenplay Excerpt:**

INT. SPACESHIP - COCKPIT - NIGHT

[CHARACTER A] sits at the controls, staring out at the vast expanse of space. [CHARACTER B] approaches them.

CHARACTER B

We're approaching the [Destination]. Are you ready?

CHARACTER A

(a long pause)

As ready as I'll ever be.

```
CHARACTER B

                              (placing a hand on
their shoulder)

                              We'll get through
this together.
```

[CHARACTER A] nods, a determined look in
their eyes.

- **Engagement with Followers:** "I'm writing a fanfiction
  story inspired by [Movie Title]. What would you like to see
  happen to [Character Name] in the sequel? #Fanfiction
  #[MovieTitle] #[CharacterName]"

Using Twitter to Connect with Fellow Film Buffs: Building a Cinematic Community

Twitter is a fantastic platform for connecting with other film
enthusiasts, sharing your love for movies, and engaging in
cinematic discussions. By building a community of like-minded
individuals, you can expand your cinematic horizons, discover
new films, and deepen your appreciation for the art of filmmaking.

Tips for Connecting with Fellow Film Buffs on Twitter:

- **Follow film-related accounts:** Follow film critics,
  reviewers, bloggers, podcasters, directors, actors, studios,
  and film festivals to stay up-to-date on the latest news,
  releases, and discussions in the film world.

- **Participate in Twitter chats:** Many online communities host Twitter chats focused on film, providing a platform for discussing specific movies, genres, directors, actors, or themes. Participating in these chats can introduce you to new perspectives, spark debates, and expand your cinematic knowledge.

- **Join film-related Twitter communities:** There are many Twitter communities dedicated to specific genres, directors, actors, or film franchises. Joining these communities can provide a more focused space for discussing your favorite films and connecting with like-minded individuals.

- **Start or join a virtual movie club:** If you're looking for a more structured way to connect with other film enthusiasts, consider starting or joining a virtual movie club on Twitter. You can choose a movie to watch together, set a discussion schedule, and use a specific hashtag to keep the conversation organized.

Examples of Tweets Connecting with Fellow Film Buffs:

- **Following Film-Related Accounts:** "Just followed @[FilmCritic] on Twitter. Love their insightful movie reviews and their passion for cinema! #FilmCritic #MovieReviews #CinematicInsights"

- **Participating in Twitter Chats:** "Excited to join the #FilmChat tonight at 8pm EST! Let's discuss our favorite movies of the year so far and debate the Oscars contenders. #MovieDiscussions #FilmLovers #TwitterChat"

- **Joining Film-Related Communities:** "Just joined the #[Genre]Twitter community! Looking forward to connecting with other fans of [Genre] and discussing our favorite films. #[Genre]Lovers #FilmNerds #Community"

- **Starting a Virtual Movie Club:** "Starting a virtual movie club on Twitter for fans of classic cinema. Our first watch will be [Movie Title]. Join the conversation using the hashtag #[MovieClubName]! #MovieClub #ClassicCinema #FilmDiscussions"

Using Twitter to Find Movie Screenings and Events: Exploring Cinematic Experiences

Twitter can be a valuable resource for discovering movie screenings and events in your area, from new releases at your local multiplex to special screenings of classic films at independent theaters or film festivals.

Tips for Using Twitter to Find Movie Screenings and Events:

- **Follow local theaters and film festivals:** Follow the Twitter accounts of movie theaters, art house cinemas, and film festivals in your area to get updates on their screening schedules, ticket information, and special events.

- **Follow film distributors and studios:** Follow the Twitter accounts of film distributors and studios to get updates on the release dates of new films and announcements of special screenings or events.

- **Explore film-related hashtags:** Search for hashtags related to movie screenings and events, such as #moviescreenings, #filmevents, #[CityName]Movies, #[Genre]Screenings, or #[FilmFestivalName].

- **Use Twitter's advanced search features:** Twitter's advanced search features allow you to filter your search results by location, date, and other criteria. This can be helpful for finding specific types of events, such as screenings of a particular film or events happening on a particular date.

- **Create Twitter lists:** Create Twitter lists to organize the accounts you follow based on your cinematic interests, such as "Local Theaters," "Film Festivals," or "Movie Distributors." This can make it easier to keep track of upcoming screenings and announcements.

Examples of Tweets Discovering Movie Screenings and Events:

- **Following Local Theaters:** "Just followed @[TheaterName] on Twitter to stay up-to-date on their screening schedule. They always have a great selection of independent and foreign films. #[TheaterName] #[CityName]Movies #SupportLocalCinema"

- **Following Film Festivals:** "Excited to follow @[FilmFestivalName] on Twitter! Can't wait to see what films they'll be showcasing this year. #[FilmFestivalName] #FilmFestivalLover #CinemaBuzz"

- **Exploring Hashtags:** "Scrolling through the #[CityName]Movies hashtag to see what's playing this weekend. Looks like there's a special screening of [Movie Title] at the [Theater Name]! #ClassicCinema #MovieNight #[CityName]"

- **Using Advanced Search:** "Using Twitter's advanced search to find screenings of [Movie Title] near me. I'm determined to see this film on the big screen! #[MovieTitle] #MustSeeMovie #CinemaSearch"

- **Creating Twitter Lists:** "I've created a Twitter list of my favorite local theaters and film festivals. It's my go-to resource for finding movie screenings and events in my area. #MovieLover #CinemaGuide #[CityName]Events"

Using Twitter to Promote Your Own Filmmaking Projects: Connecting with an Audience

If you're a filmmaker, Twitter can be a valuable tool for promoting your projects, connecting with an audience, and building a following for your work. Whether you're a seasoned professional or an aspiring filmmaker, Twitter provides a platform to share your passion, showcase your talent, and engage with the film community.

Tips for Promoting Your Filmmaking Projects on Twitter:

- **Create a professional profile:** Use a professional profile picture and header image that represent your filmmaking brand. Write a compelling bio that highlights your experience, your skills, and your current projects.

- **Share your work:** Tweet links to your films, trailers, behind-the-scenes footage, and other content related to your projects. Use visually appealing images and videos to capture your followers' attention.

- **Engage with the film community:** Follow other filmmakers, film critics, reviewers, bloggers, and film enthusiasts. Participate in Twitter chats, comment on others' posts, and share your thoughts on the film industry.

- **Use relevant hashtags:** Use hashtags strategically to increase the visibility of your tweets and connect with a wider audience. Use hashtags related to your genre, your filmmaking style, your projects, and the film industry in general.

- **Promote your screenings and events:** If you're screening your films at festivals, theaters, or other events, use Twitter to promote these screenings and encourage people to attend.

- **Build a following:** The more followers you have, the wider your reach will be. Engage with your followers, respond to comments and questions, and build relationships with other members of the film community.

- **Be patient and persistent:** Building a following and promoting your filmmaking projects takes time and effort. Don't get discouraged if you don't see results overnight. Keep creating great content, engaging with your audience, and promoting your work, and you'll eventually start to see success.

Examples of Tweets Promoting Your Filmmaking Projects:

- **Sharing Your Work:** "Check out my latest short film, [Film Title], now available to watch on [Platform]. It's a [Genre] film that explores the themes of [Theme A] and [Theme B]. #[FilmTitle] #[Genre] #ShortFilm #Filmmaker" (Include a link to the film)

- **Engaging with the Film Community:** "Excited to join the #FilmmakerChat tonight at 8pm EST! Let's discuss the challenges and rewards of independent filmmaking. #IndieFilm #FilmmakingCommunity #TwitterChat"

- **Promoting a Screening:** "My film, [Film Title], will be screening at the [Film Festival] on [Date]! Come see it on the big screen! #FilmFestival #[FilmTitle] #[FilmFestivalName]"

- **Building a Following:** "Thanks to everyone who has followed me and supported my filmmaking journey. I appreciate your encouragement! #Filmmaker #FilmCommunity #Grateful"

- **Be Patient and Persistent:** "Keep creating, keep hustling, keep believing in yourself. Success in filmmaking takes time and dedication. #FilmmakerLife #NeverGiveUp #DreamBig"

A Few Final Tips for Tweeting About Movies

- **Be authentic and passionate:** Share your genuine love for movies and your unique perspective with your followers.

- **Use a variety of content formats:** Mix up your tweets with reviews, recommendations, reactions, trivia, fancasting, creative writing, and discussions to keep your audience engaged.

- **Use visuals:** Include photos, videos, GIFs, and other visual elements to make your tweets more eye-catching and memorable.

- **Use relevant hashtags:** Hashtags are essential for connecting with other film enthusiasts and increasing the visibility of your tweets.

- **Engage with others:** Respond to comments, participate in discussions, and build relationships with other members of the film community.

- **Respect copyright:** Avoid sharing copyrighted material without permission.

- **Have fun!** Movies are meant to be enjoyed, and your tweets should reflect that. Let your personality shine through and inspire others to discover the magic of cinema.

CHAPTER FOURTEEN: Tech Talk: Tweeting About Gadgets and Gizmos

We live in a world saturated with technology. From the smartphones in our pockets to the smart homes we inhabit, gadgets and gizmos have become integral parts of our daily lives. And what better platform to discuss, dissect, and sometimes even drool over these technological marvels than Twitter (or X)?

This chapter is your guide to navigating the exciting, ever-evolving world of tech-related tweets. Whether you're an early adopter who camps out for the latest releases, a tech enthusiast who loves to tinker and explore, or simply someone who appreciates the convenience and innovation that technology brings, this chapter will equip you with the tools and inspiration to share your tech passions, connect with fellow techies, and maybe even spark a few viral tech trends along the way.

New Gadget Day: Tweeting Your Tech Excitement

There's a certain thrill that comes with unboxing a shiny new gadget. The sleek design, the cutting-edge features, the promise of enhanced productivity or entertainment – it's enough to make any tech enthusiast giddy with excitement. Sharing that unboxing experience and your first impressions on Twitter can be a fun way to connect with other tech lovers, spark conversations, and perhaps even inspire a little tech envy along the way.

Tweet Examples:

- **Unboxing Excitement:** "New gadget day! Just got my hands on the new [Gadget Name] and I can't wait to put it through its paces. #Unboxing #TechEnthusiast #[GadgetName]" (Include a photo or video of the unboxing)

- **First Impressions:** "First impressions of the [Gadget Name]: sleek design, intuitive interface, and impressive performance. So far, I'm impressed! #[GadgetName]Review #TechReview #FirstLook"

- **Feature Highlight:** "Loving the [Specific Feature] on the new [Gadget Name]. It's a game-changer for [Task/Activity]. #[GadgetName] #TechFeatures #Innovation"

- **Comparison with Previous Model:** "The [Gadget Name] is a significant upgrade from the previous model. The [Specific Improvement] is a welcome addition. #TechUpgrade #[GadgetName] #WorthTheUpgrade"

- **Humorous Take:** "My wallet is crying, but my heart is singing. The new [Gadget Name] is just too good to resist. #TechAddiction #WorthEveryPenny #[GadgetName]"

Pro-Tip: Make your tweets more engaging by including visuals, such as photos or videos of the unboxing, the gadget itself, or you using the gadget. You can also use relevant hashtags to connect with other tech enthusiasts who are interested in the same gadget or technology.

Tech Reviews: Sharing Your Expert Opinions

As a tech enthusiast, you probably have a knack for evaluating gadgets and software, dissecting their features, and determining their strengths and weaknesses. Sharing your tech reviews on Twitter can be a valuable resource for others who are considering purchasing a new device, trying out a new app, or exploring a new technology.

Tips for Crafting Engaging Tech Reviews:

- **Be clear and concise:** Get straight to the point and state your overall assessment of the gadget or software in a clear and concise manner. Avoid rambling or using overly technical jargon.

- **Focus on the key features and benefits:** Highlight the most important features and benefits of the gadget or software, and explain how they can improve users' lives or solve specific problems.

- **Provide real-world examples:** Illustrate your points with real-world examples of how you've used the gadget or software. Share your personal experiences, both positive and negative, to provide a more relatable and authentic perspective.

- **Offer comparisons with competitors:** If there are similar gadgets or software available, compare the product you're reviewing with its competitors, highlighting its strengths and weaknesses relative to the competition.

- **Include visuals:** Use photos, videos, or screenshots to showcase the gadget or software's design, features, and functionality.

- **Use relevant hashtags:** Hashtags can help increase the visibility of your review and connect you with other tech enthusiasts who are interested in the same topics. Use hashtags like #techreview, #gadgets, #software, #[GadgetName], #[AppName], and #[Technology].

- **Be objective and fair:** While it's okay to express your personal opinions, try to be as objective and fair as possible in your review. Avoid making unsubstantiated claims or exaggerating the product's capabilities.

Examples of Engaging Tech Reviews:

- **Smartphone Review:** "The [Smartphone Name] is a solid all-around phone with a stunning display, a powerful processor, and an impressive camera system. Highly

204

recommend it for users who prioritize performance and photography. #SmartphoneReview #[SmartphoneName] #Android #iOS"

- **Laptop Review:** "The [Laptop Name] is a lightweight and portable laptop with excellent battery life and a comfortable keyboard. It's perfect for students and professionals who need a reliable device for work or travel. #LaptopReview #[LaptopName] #Productivity #Portability"

- **App Review:** "The [App Name] is a game-changer for [Task/Activity]. It's intuitive, easy to use, and packed with useful features. Highly recommend it for anyone who wants to [Benefit]. #AppReview #[AppName] #Productivity #[Benefit]"

- **Software Review:** "The [Software Name] is a powerful and versatile tool for [Task/Activity]. It offers a wide range of features and customization options, but it can be a bit overwhelming for beginners. #SoftwareReview #[SoftwareName] #[Task/Activity] #AdvancedUsers"

- **Comparison Review:** "Comparing the [Gadget A] to the [Gadget B]: both offer similar features, but the [Gadget A] has a better battery life and a more intuitive interface. #GadgetComparison #[GadgetA] #[GadgetB] #TechChoices"

Tech Tips and Tricks: Sharing Your Digital Expertise

As you explore the world of technology, you inevitably pick up valuable tips, tricks, and hacks that can enhance your digital experience. Sharing these insights on Twitter can be a great way to help others navigate the complexities of technology, solve common problems, and discover hidden features or shortcuts that can improve their productivity, entertainment, or overall digital literacy.

Tips for Sharing Tech Tips and Tricks:

- **Be clear and concise:** Get straight to the point and explain the tip or trick in a way that is easy to understand, even for those who are not tech-savvy. Use simple language and avoid technical jargon.

- **Focus on practical and actionable advice:** Share tips and tricks that are practical and actionable, something that your followers can easily implement themselves.

- **Use step-by-step instructions:** If your tip or trick involves multiple steps, break it down into a clear and concise set of instructions that are easy to follow.

- **Include visuals:** Use photos, screenshots, or videos to illustrate your tips and tricks, making them easier to understand and more engaging.

- **Use relevant hashtags:** Hashtags can help increase the visibility of your tweets and connect you with other tech enthusiasts who are interested in similar topics. Use hashtags like #techtips, #digitalhacks, #lifehacks, #[GadgetName]Tips, #[AppName]Tricks, and #[Technology]Hacks.

- **Engage with your followers:** Encourage your followers to try your tips and tricks and share their experiences. Respond to comments and questions, and offer help and support when needed.

Examples of Tech Tips and Tricks:

- **Smartphone Battery Life:** "Extend your smartphone's battery life by turning off location services when you're not using them, dimming your screen brightness, and closing apps that you're not actively using. #SmartphoneTips #BatteryLife #TechHacks"

- **Keyboard Shortcut:** "Save time and effort by using the keyboard shortcut [Shortcut] to [Action]. It's a simple trick that can make a big difference in your productivity. #KeyboardShortcuts #ProductivityHacks #TechTips"

- **Hidden Feature:** "Did you know that you can [Hidden Feature] on the [Gadget Name]? It's a little-known feature that can [Benefit]. #[GadgetName]Tips #HiddenFeatures #TechSecrets"

- **Troubleshooting Tip:** "If your [Gadget Name] is [Problem], try [Solution]. It's a common issue with an easy fix. #Troubleshooting #TechSupport #[GadgetName]"

- **App Integration:** "You can integrate [App A] with [App B] to [Benefit]. It's a great way to streamline your workflow and save time. #AppIntegration #[AppA] #[AppB] #ProductivityHacks"

Tech Humor: Tweeting the Lighter Side of Technology

The world of technology can be a source of both wonder and frustration. From software glitches to autocorrect fails, there's a certain humor that comes with navigating the digital landscape. Sharing tech-related humor on Twitter can be a great way to lighten the mood, connect with other techies who understand the struggle, and maybe even spark a viral tech meme along the way.

Tips for Using Tech Humor:

- **Embrace the relatable:** Focus on tech-related experiences that are relatable to a wide audience, such as software glitches, slow Wi-Fi, battery anxiety, or the constant barrage of notifications.

- **Use puns and wordplay:** Puns and wordplay are classic forms of humor that can be particularly effective when applied to technology and gadgets.

- **Share relatable tech memes:** The internet is a treasure trove of tech memes that perfectly capture the joys and frustrations of living in a digital world. Share your favorites with your followers and add your own witty captions.

- **Create your own tech memes:** If you're feeling creative, try your hand at creating your own tech memes using meme generators or photo editing software.

- **Don't be afraid to be self-deprecating:** Poking fun at your own tech mishaps or your obsessive gadget love can be incredibly endearing and humorous.

Examples of Tweets Using Tech Humor:

- **Software Glitch:** "My computer just crashed for the third time today. I'm starting to think it has a personal vendetta against me. #TechFail #SoftwareGlitch #SendHelp"

- **Tech Pun:** "I'm so addicted to my smartphone, I should probably check into a re-boot camp. #TechHumor #Punny #SmartphoneAddict"

- **Relatable Tech Meme:** [Share a meme about the frustration of slow Wi-Fi, the pain of a cracked phone screen, or the endless cycle of software updates.] #TechMeme #Relatable #TechLife"

- **Self-Deprecating Humor:** "I just spent two hours researching the best new earbuds, even though I already have three pairs that work perfectly fine. #TechObsessed #EarbudHoarder #HelpMe"

Tech News and Discussions: Tweeting the Latest Developments

The world of technology is constantly evolving, with new gadgets, software updates, and groundbreaking innovations emerging on a seemingly daily basis. Twitter is a great platform for staying informed about these developments, sharing your thoughts and insights, and engaging in discussions with other tech enthusiasts.

Tips for Tweeting About Tech News and Discussions:

- **Follow reliable sources:** Follow reputable tech journalists, publications, and industry experts to get accurate and timely information about the latest tech news.

- **Share links to articles and videos:** When you come across interesting tech news or articles, share them with your followers along with a brief summary or your own commentary.

- **Use relevant hashtags:** Hashtags can help increase the visibility of your tweets and connect you with others who are interested in the same topics. Use hashtags related to the specific technology, company, or event, as well as general tech hashtags like #technews, #technology, #innovation, and #futureoftech.

- **Engage in discussions:** Respond to tweets from others, share your opinions, and participate in discussions about the latest tech developments.

- **Be critical and discerning:** Not all tech news is created equal. Be critical of the information you come across and consider the source's credibility before sharing or retweeting.

Examples of Tweets About Tech News and Discussions:

- **Sharing an Article:** "Just read a fascinating article about the potential of [Emerging Technology] to revolutionize [Industry]. What are your thoughts on this development? #[EmergingTechnology] #[Industry] #TechNews" (Include a link to the article)

- **Commenting on a News Story:** "Excited about the announcement of the new [Gadget Name]. The [Specific Feature] sounds incredible! Can't wait to see it in action. #[GadgetName] #TechInnovation #NewRelease"

- **Engaging in a Discussion:** "Do you think [Technology A] will eventually replace [Technology B]? What are the pros and cons of each technology? #TechDebate #[TechnologyA] #[TechnologyB] #FutureofTech"

- **Sharing an Opinion:** "I believe that [Technology] has the potential to solve some of the world's most pressing problems, such as [Problem A] and [Problem B]. #TechForGood #[Technology] #Innovation"

- **Critical Thinking:** "While [Technology] sounds promising, I'm skeptical about the claims being made about its capabilities. More research is needed before we can jump to conclusions. #TechSkeptic #[Technology] #CriticalThinking"

Tech Support and Troubleshooting: Tweeting Your Help Requests

Even the most tech-savvy individuals encounter technical difficulties from time to time. Whether it's a software glitch, a hardware malfunction, or a simple user error, Twitter can be a surprisingly effective platform for getting tech support and troubleshooting advice.

Tips for Tweeting Tech Support Requests:

- **Be specific and clear:** Clearly state the problem you're experiencing, including the specific gadget, software, or error message involved.

- **Provide context:** Give as much context as possible, such as the steps you've already taken to troubleshoot the issue, the operating system you're using, or any relevant error messages.

- **Use relevant hashtags:** Hashtags can help increase the visibility of your tweet and connect you with people who might be able to help. Use hashtags like #techsupport, #troubleshooting, #[GadgetName]Help, #[AppName]Support, and #[Technology]Problems.

- **Tag relevant companies or experts:** If you're having trouble with a specific gadget or software, consider tagging the company's official Twitter account or any tech experts who specialize in that area.

- **Be patient and polite:** Remember that the people you're asking for help are likely volunteering their time and expertise. Be patient and polite, even if you're frustrated with the technical issue.

- **Express your gratitude:** When someone offers helpful advice or solves your problem, be sure to thank them for their assistance.

Examples of Tweets Seeking Tech Support:

- **Specific Problem:** "My [Gadget Name] is [Problem]. I've tried [Troubleshooting Steps], but nothing seems to work. Any suggestions? #[GadgetName]Help #TechSupport #Frustrated"

- **Error Message:** "I'm getting the error message [Error Message] when I try to [Action] on my [Gadget Name]. What does it mean and how can I fix it? #[GadgetName] #ErrorHelp #TechProblems"

- **Tagging a Company:** "Hey @[CompanyName], I'm having trouble with [Problem] on my [Gadget Name]. Can you help? #[GadgetName] #TechSupport #CustomerService"

- **Asking for Advice:** "Does anyone know how to [Action] on the [Gadget Name]? I'm struggling to find a solution in the user manual. #[GadgetName]Tips #TechHelp #Newbie"

- **Expressing Gratitude:** "Thank you so much to @[TwitterUser] for helping me fix my [Gadget Name] problem! You're a lifesaver! #TechSupportHero #Grateful #ProblemSolved"

Tech Communities: Tweeting Your Belonging

Twitter is home to a vibrant and diverse community of tech enthusiasts who share a passion for all things digital. Connecting with this community can provide a sense of belonging, offer opportunities for learning and collaboration, and keep you informed about the latest trends and innovations.

Tips for Engaging with Tech Communities on Twitter:

- **Follow tech influencers:** Follow tech influencers, bloggers, YouTubers, podcasters, and journalists who share your interests and whose insights you find valuable.

- **Participate in Twitter chats:** Many online communities host Twitter chats focused on specific tech topics, such as programming, cybersecurity, artificial intelligence, or digital marketing. Participating in these chats can be a great way to connect with other professionals, share your knowledge, and learn from others.

- **Join tech-related Twitter communities:** There are many Twitter communities dedicated to specific technologies, brands, or industries. Joining these communities can provide a more focused space for discussions, networking, and sharing resources.

- **Attend virtual events:** Many tech conferences, workshops, and meetups are now held virtually, providing opportunities to connect with other tech professionals from around the world. Follow the Twitter accounts of these events to stay informed about upcoming opportunities.

- **Share your knowledge and experiences:** Contribute to the community by sharing your own insights, experiences, and resources. Answer questions, offer advice, and participate in discussions to help others learn and grow.

Examples of Tweets Engaging with Tech Communities:

- **Following Tech Influencers:** "Just followed @[TechInfluencer] on Twitter. Loving their insights on the future of technology and the impact of AI on society. #TechInfluencer #FutureofTech #AI"

- **Participating in Twitter Chats:** "Excited to join the #[TechChatName] tonight at 8pm EST! Let's discuss the latest trends in [TechTopic]. #[TechTopic] #TechCommunity #TwitterChat"

- **Joining Tech Communities:** "Just joined the #[TechCommunityName] on Twitter. Looking forward to connecting with other [TechProfessionals] and discussing the challenges and opportunities in our field. #[TechProfessionals] #TechNetworking #Community"

- **Attending a Virtual Event:** "Attending the virtual #[TechEventName] this week. Looking forward to the keynote speeches, panel discussions, and networking opportunities. #[TechEventName] #VirtualConference #TechLearning"

- **Sharing Knowledge:** "Sharing my tips for [TechTask] using [Technology]. It's a simple process that can save you time and effort. #TechTips #[Technology] #ProductivityHacks"

Tech Advocacy: Tweeting Your Support for Innovation and Progress

Technology has the power to transform lives, solve problems, and create a better future for all. Using your Twitter platform to advocate for technological innovation and progress can help raise awareness, inspire others to embrace new ideas, and contribute to a more technologically advanced and equitable world.

Tips for Tweeting About Tech Advocacy:

- **Share stories of tech for good:** Highlight examples of how technology is being used to address social, environmental, or economic challenges, such as improving healthcare, combating climate change, or promoting education.

- **Advocate for STEM education:** Encourage support for STEM education (Science, Technology, Engineering, and Mathematics) to inspire the next generation of innovators and problem-solvers.

- **Promote digital literacy:** Share resources and tips for improving digital literacy and helping people of all ages and backgrounds navigate the digital world safely and effectively.

- **Support ethical and responsible tech development:** Advocate for ethical and responsible technology development, addressing issues such as privacy, security, bias, and accessibility.

- **Engage with policymakers and industry leaders:** Tag policymakers and industry leaders in your tweets to raise awareness and encourage them to support policies and initiatives that promote technological innovation and progress.

Examples of Tweets About Tech Advocacy:

- **Tech for Good:** "Amazing how [Technology] is being used to [Positive Impact] in [Community/Industry]. Technology has the power to make a real difference in the world. #TechForGood #[Technology] #SocialImpact"

- **STEM Education:** "We need to invest more in STEM education to inspire the next generation of innovators and problem-solvers. The future belongs to those who can create and use technology effectively. #STEMEducation #FutureofWork #Innovation"

- **Digital Literacy:** "Digital literacy is essential for navigating the modern world. Here are some resources for improving your digital skills and staying safe online: [Link to Resources] #DigitalLiteracy #OnlineSafety #TechSkills"

- **Ethical Tech Development:** "We need to ensure that technology is developed and used ethically and responsibly, addressing issues such as privacy, bias, and accessibility. #EthicalTech #ResponsibleAI #TechForEveryone"

- **Engaging with Policymakers:** "Hey @[Policymaker], I urge you to support policies that promote innovation, invest in STEM education, and ensure equitable access to technology for all. #TechPolicy #FutureofTech #[PolicyIssue]"

Building Your Tech Brand on Twitter: Becoming a Tech Influencer

If you're passionate about technology and enjoy sharing your insights and experiences on Twitter, you might consider building your tech brand and becoming a tech influencer. A strong tech brand can open up opportunities for collaborations with tech companies, brands, and media outlets, allowing you to share your expertise with a wider audience and potentially earn income from your passion.

Tips for Building Your Tech Brand on Twitter:

- **Choose a niche:** What aspect of technology are you most passionate about? Do you specialize in smartphones, laptops, software, gaming, artificial intelligence, cybersecurity, or another area of tech? Choosing a niche can help you to target a specific audience and establish yourself as an expert in that area.

- **Develop a consistent brand voice:** How do you want to be perceived by your audience? Are you technical and informative? Are you witty and humorous? Are you passionate and enthusiastic? Developing a consistent brand voice will help you to create a recognizable and memorable identity.

- **Create high-quality content:** Share insightful reviews, helpful tips and tricks, engaging discussions, and visually appealing content that provides value to your audience.

- **Engage with your followers:** Respond to comments and questions, participate in conversations, and build relationships with your followers.

- **Collaborate with other tech influencers:** Partner with other tech bloggers, YouTubers, podcasters, and journalists to cross-promote each other's content and reach a wider audience.

- **Use relevant hashtags:** Use hashtags strategically to increase the visibility of your tweets and connect with a wider audience.

- **Promote your other platforms:** If you have a tech blog, a YouTube channel, a podcast, or other online platforms, be sure to promote them on your Twitter profile and in your tweets.

- **Be patient and persistent:** Building a strong tech brand takes time and effort. Don't get discouraged if you don't see results overnight. Keep creating great content, engaging with your audience, and promoting your brand, and you'll eventually start to see success.

Examples of Tweets Building Your Tech Brand:

- **Niche Focus:** "I'm a tech enthusiast who specializes in [Tech Niche]. Follow me for the latest news, reviews, and insights on [Tech Niche]. #[TechNiche] #TechExpert #[TechIndustry]"

- **Brand Voice:** "I'm a tech blogger with a sarcastic sense of humor. Follow me for witty commentary on the world of technology and the occasional tech rant. #TechHumor #DigitalSarcasm #TechLife"

- **High-Quality Content:** "Just published a new blog post with my in-depth review of the [GadgetName]. Check it out for a detailed analysis of its features, performance, and value for money. #[GadgetName] #TechReview #[TechNiche]" (Include a link to the blog post)

- **Follower Engagement:** "What's your favorite tech gadget of all time? Share your answers in the comments! #TechDiscussion #GadgetLove #Nostalgia"

- **Collaboration:** "Excited to be partnering with @[TechCompany] on a review of their new [Gadget Name]. Stay tuned for my in-depth analysis and exclusive behind-the-scenes insights! #TechCollaboration #[GadgetName] #[TechNiche]"

A Few Final Tips for Tech Tweets

- **Be mindful of technical jargon:** While it's okay to use some technical terms, avoid overwhelming your followers with jargon that they might not understand. Explain complex concepts in a clear and concise way.

- **Be accurate and reliable:** Technology is a complex and rapidly evolving field. Double-check your facts and sources before sharing information to ensure that you're providing accurate and reliable content.

- **Respect intellectual property:** Avoid sharing copyrighted material without permission. Give credit to the original creators of content that you share or retweet.

- **Be aware of privacy and security concerns:** Be mindful of the privacy and security implications of the technology you're discussing. Avoid sharing personal information or sensitive data.

- **Promote a positive and inclusive tech community:** Technology should be accessible and beneficial to everyone. Promote a positive and inclusive tech community by supporting diversity, equity, and accessibility in the tech industry.

- **Have fun!** Technology can be both fascinating and fun. Let your passion for tech shine through in your tweets and inspire others to explore the exciting world of gadgets, gizmos, and digital innovations.

CHAPTER FIFTEEN: Gaming Glory: Tweeting Your Victories (and Defeats)

Gaming. It's a world of digital adventures, epic battles, and immersive stories that captivate millions of players worldwide. And with the rise of social media, it's become more than just a solitary pastime – it's a social phenomenon, a thriving community, and a source of endless entertainment and conversation.

Twitter (or X), with its fast-paced nature and passionate gaming community, is the perfect platform for sharing your gaming triumphs, venting your frustrations, connecting with fellow gamers, and celebrating the joy of all things gaming. Whether you're a casual mobile gamer, a hardcore esports competitor, or a dedicated console warrior, this chapter will guide you through the world of gaming-related tweets, helping you to level up your Twitter game and become a true digital champion.

Victory Lap: Tweeting Your Gaming Triumphs

There's nothing quite like the feeling of achieving a hard-fought victory in your favorite game. Whether it's finally defeating that challenging boss, completing a difficult quest, or achieving a new high score, your gaming triumphs deserve to be celebrated, and Twitter is the perfect platform to share your glory with the world.

Tips for Tweeting Your Gaming Victories:

- **Express your excitement:** Let your enthusiasm shine through in your tweets. Use exclamation points, emojis, and celebratory language to convey your joy and excitement.

- **Be specific about your achievement:** Instead of simply saying "I won!," describe the specific achievement you accomplished, such as the boss you defeated, the level you completed, or the score you achieved.

- **Share screenshots or videos:** Capture the moment of victory with a screenshot or video clip of your gameplay. This visual evidence adds credibility to your claim and allows your followers to share in your excitement.

- **Tag your teammates or opponents:** If you achieved the victory with teammates, be sure to tag them in your tweet to give them credit and celebrate together. If you were playing against a particularly challenging opponent, you can also tag them (respectfully, of course) to acknowledge their skill.

- **Use relevant hashtags:** Hashtags can help increase the visibility of your tweets and connect you with other gamers who are playing the same game or who appreciate your skills. Use hashtags related to the game, the achievement, your gaming platform, or your gamertag.

- **Engage with followers who congratulate you:** Respond to comments and questions from your followers, and engage in conversations about your victory.

Examples of Tweets Celebrating Gaming Victories:

- **Boss Battle Victory:** "Finally defeated [Boss Name] in [Game Name]! That was an epic battle! 🌀 #Victory #[GameName] #BossBattle #Gamer" (Include a screenshot of the victory screen)

- **Quest Completion:** "Just completed the [Quest Name] quest in [Game Name]! The rewards were worth the effort! 🗡 #QuestComplete #[GameName] #GamerLife #AchievementUnlocked"

- **High Score:** "New high score on [Game Name]! Beat my previous record by [Score Difference]! Who's got next? 🏆 #HighScore #[GameName] #GamerPride #ChallengeMe"

- **Team Victory:** "We did it! Team victory in [Game Name]! Great job, teammates! @[Teammate1] @[Teammate2] #Teamwork #[GameName] #VictoryRoyale #Esports"

- **Respectful Acknowledgment of Opponent:** "Tough match against @[OpponentGamertag] in [Game Name]. You gave me a run for my money! GG! #Respect #[GameName] #Gamer #CloseGame"

Rage Quit: Tweeting Your Gaming Frustrations (Politely)

Gaming, while often a source of joy and entertainment, can also be a source of intense frustration. From lag spikes and bugs to unfair opponents and seemingly impossible challenges, there are plenty of moments that can make you want to throw your controller (or phone) across the room. Venting your frustrations on Twitter can be a cathartic experience, but it's important to do so in a way that is constructive and respectful.

Tips for Tweeting Your Gaming Frustrations:

- **Avoid excessive negativity:** While it's okay to express your frustration, avoid excessive negativity, profanity, or personal attacks. Keep your tone constructive and focus on the specific issues that are causing you problems.

- **Be specific about the problem:** Instead of simply saying "This game is so frustrating!," describe the specific issues you're experiencing, such as lag, bugs, unfair gameplay mechanics, or toxic players.

- **Use humor to diffuse the tension:** Humor can be a great way to lighten the mood and make your tweets more relatable. Find the humor in your frustrations and share it with your followers.

- **Ask for advice or solutions:** If you're struggling with a particular problem, ask your followers for advice or solutions. The gaming community on Twitter is often helpful and supportive, and someone might have a solution that you haven't considered.

- **Tag the game developers (if appropriate):** If you're experiencing issues with a game, consider tagging the game developers in your tweet to bring the problem to their attention. However, avoid being overly demanding or aggressive in your tone.

- **Use relevant hashtags:** Hashtags can help increase the visibility of your tweets and connect you with other gamers who might be experiencing the same frustrations. Use hashtags related to the game, the issue, or the gaming platform.

Examples of Tweets Expressing Gaming Frustrations:

- **Lag Frustration:** "The lag in [Game Name] is making this game unplayable! I'm rubberbanding all over the place! 😫 #LagSpikes #[GameName] #FixYourServers"

- **Bug Report:** "Just encountered a game-breaking bug in [Game Name]. My character is stuck in a wall! 😕 #BugReport #[GameName] #HelpMe"

- **Unfair Gameplay Mechanic:** "The [Gameplay Mechanic] in [Game Name] is so unfair! It's impossible to win against players who abuse it. 😊 #[GameName] #GameBalance #FixYourGame"

- **Humorous Take on Frustration:** "I've died so many times in [Game Name] today that I'm starting to think I'm cursed. 💀 #GamingFails #[GameName] #ChallengeAccepted"

- **Request for Advice:** "Does anyone know how to fix the [Problem] in [Game Name]? I've tried everything I can think of, but nothing seems to work. #TechSupport #[GameName] #HelpMe"

Sharing Gaming News and Updates: Tweeting the Latest Buzz

The gaming world is constantly buzzing with news, announcements, and updates about new games, upcoming releases, esports tournaments, and industry trends. Twitter is a great platform for staying informed about the latest gaming buzz and sharing your thoughts and excitement with fellow gamers.

Tips for Tweeting About Gaming News and Updates:

- **Follow reliable sources:** Follow reputable gaming journalists, publications, and industry insiders to get accurate and timely information about the latest gaming news.

- **Share links to articles and videos:** When you come across interesting gaming news or articles, share them with your followers along with a brief summary or your own commentary.

- **Use relevant hashtags:** Hashtags can help increase the visibility of your tweets and connect you with others who are interested in the same topics. Use hashtags related to the specific game, company, event, or industry trend, as well as general gaming hashtags like #gamingnews, #videogames, #esports, and #gamingcommunity.

- **Engage in discussions:** Respond to tweets from others, share your opinions, and participate in discussions about the latest gaming news.

- **Be critical and discerning:** Not all gaming news is created equal. Be critical of the information you come across and consider the source's credibility before sharing or retweeting.

Examples of Tweets About Gaming News and Updates:

- **New Game Announcement:** "Excited about the announcement of the new [Game Name]! The trailer looks incredible! Can't wait to play it! #[GameName] #NewRelease #[Genre]" (Include a link to the trailer)

- **Esports Tournament Update:** "[Team Name] just won the [Tournament Name]! What an amazing performance! #Esports #[GameName] #[TeamName] #Victory"

- **Industry Trend Discussion:** "Do you think [Gaming Trend] is a positive or negative development for the gaming industry? Share your thoughts in the comments! #GamingDiscussion #[GamingTrend] #FutureofGaming"

- **Sharing an Opinion:** "I think the future of gaming is [Prediction]. What do you think? #GamingPredictions #FutureofGaming #TechTrends"

- **Critical Thinking:** "While I'm excited about the new [Gaming Technology], I'm concerned about the potential [Negative Impact] on the gaming industry. #GamingConcerns #[GamingTechnology] #CriticalThinking"

Streaming Your Gameplay: Tweeting Your Live Sessions

Live streaming your gameplay on platforms like Twitch or YouTube has become increasingly popular, allowing gamers to share their skills, their personalities, and their love of gaming with a wider audience. Twitter can be a great tool for promoting your live streams, engaging with your viewers, and building a community around your channel.

Tips for Tweeting About Your Gameplay Streams:

- **Announce your upcoming streams:** Let your followers know when you'll be streaming, what game you'll be playing, and any special events or giveaways that you might be hosting.

- **Share highlights from your streams:** Capture memorable moments from your streams, such as clutch plays, funny moments, or epic fails, and share them on Twitter with your followers.

- **Use relevant hashtags:** Use hashtags related to the game you're playing, your streaming platform, your gamertag, and your streaming schedule to help people discover your streams.

- **Engage with your viewers:** Respond to comments and questions from your viewers on Twitter, both during and after your streams. Create a sense of community by interacting with your audience and making them feel valued.

- **Promote your streaming channel:** Include a link to your streaming channel in your Twitter bio and in your tweets about your streams. This makes it easy for people to find and follow your channel.

Examples of Tweets Promoting Your Gameplay Streams:

- **Stream Announcement:** "Going live on Twitch in 30 minutes! Playing [Game Name] and answering your questions. Come hang out! #[GameName] #TwitchStreamer #LiveNow" (Include a link to your Twitch channel)

- **Highlight Clip:** "Check out this clutch play from my [Game Name] stream last night! I still can't believe I pulled that off! #[GameName] #TwitchHighlights #GamerSkills" (Include a video clip of the play)

- **Engaging with Viewers:** "Thanks to everyone who tuned in to my [Game Name] stream last night! It was a blast! What games would you like to see me play next? #[GameName] #TwitchCommunity #SuggestionsWelcome"

- **Promoting Your Channel:** "I stream [Game Name] and other games on Twitch every [Schedule]. Come hang out and join the community! #[GameName] #TwitchStreamer #[StreamingSchedule]" (Include a link to your Twitch channel)

Cosplay Showcase: Tweeting Your Gaming Style

Cosplay, the art of dressing up as your favorite video game characters, has become increasingly popular in recent years, allowing gamers to express their creativity, their passion for gaming, and their appreciation for character design. Twitter is a great platform for showcasing your cosplay creations, connecting with other cosplayers, and celebrating the artistry and craftsmanship of this unique form of self-expression.

Tips for Tweeting About Your Cosplay:

- **Share high-quality photos:** Showcase your cosplay with high-quality photos that capture the details of your costume, your makeup, and your posing. Use good lighting and a clean background to make your photos stand out.

- **Describe your cosplay process:** Share insights into your cosplay process, such as the materials you used, the techniques you employed, the challenges you faced, and the amount of time and effort you invested.

- **Tag the game and character:** Tag the game and character that you're cosplaying to make it easy for other fans to find your tweets and appreciate your work.

- **Use relevant hashtags:** Hashtags can help increase the visibility of your tweets and connect you with other cosplayers and gaming enthusiasts. Use hashtags like #cosplay, #[GameName]Cosplay, #[CharacterName]Cosplay, #Cosplayer, and #GamingFashion.

- **Engage with other cosplayers:** Follow other cosplayers on Twitter, comment on their work, and participate in discussions about cosplay techniques, materials, and conventions.

Examples of Tweets Showcasing Cosplay:

- **Cosplay Photo:** "Debuted my new [Character Name] cosplay at [Convention Name] this weekend! I had so much fun bringing this character to life. #[GameName]Cosplay #[CharacterName]Cosplay #Cosplay" (Include a high-quality photo of your cosplay)

- **Cosplay Process:** "The most challenging part of creating this [Character Name] cosplay was [Specific Detail]. I had to experiment with several different techniques before I found one that worked. #[GameName]Cosplay #CosplayProcess #BehindTheScenes"

- **Tagging the Game and Character:** "Feeling fierce in my [Character Name] cosplay! #[GameName] #[CharacterName] #Cosplay" (Include a photo of your cosplay)

- **Engaging with Other Cosplayers:** "Loving all the amazing cosplay I'm seeing on Twitter! You guys are so talented! #CosplayCommunity #Inspiration #GamingFashion"

- **Promoting Your Cosplay Page:** "If you're interested in seeing more of my cosplay, check out my Instagram page:

@[YourCosplayInstagram]. #Cosplayer #[GameName]Cosplay #[CharacterName]Cosplay"

Gaming Nostalgia: Tweeting Your Retro Gaming Memories

Retro gaming holds a special place in the hearts of many gamers, evoking fond memories of classic consoles, pixelated graphics, and groundbreaking gameplay experiences. Sharing your retro gaming memories on Twitter can be a nostalgic and heartwarming journey, connecting you with other gamers who grew up playing the same games and sparking conversations about the golden age of gaming.

Tips for Tweeting About Retro Gaming:

- **Share specific memories:** Instead of simply saying "I used to love playing [Game Name]," share a specific memory associated with the game, such as a challenging level you finally conquered, a memorable moment with friends, or the feeling of excitement you had when you first unboxed the console.

- **Use vivid language:** Use descriptive language to paint a picture of the memory and transport your followers back in time with you.

- **Include photos or videos:** If you have any photos or videos related to the memory, such as old screenshots, photos of your console collection, or videos of your gameplay, include them in your tweet to make it more visually engaging.

- **Use relevant hashtags:** Hashtags can help increase the visibility of your tweets and connect you with other gamers who share similar retro gaming memories. Use hashtags like #retrogaming, #classicgaming, #[ConsoleName], #[GameName], and #GamingNostalgia.

- **Engage with followers who share similar memories:** Respond to comments from followers who share similar memories or who have been touched by the same games. Retro gaming can be a powerful bond, and sharing these experiences can create a sense of community.

Examples of Tweets Sharing Retro Gaming Memories:

- **Childhood Memory:** "I'll never forget the first time I played [Game Name] on the [Console Name]. It was a groundbreaking experience that changed the way I looked at video games. #RetroGaming #[ConsoleName] #[GameName] #GamingMemories"

- **Challenging Level:** "Finally beat [Level Name] in [Game Name] after countless attempts! The feeling of satisfaction was immense. #RetroGamingChallenge #[GameName] #Victory #Persistence" (Include a screenshot of the victory screen)

- **Gaming with Friends:** "Spent countless hours playing [Game Name] with my friends on the [Console Name]. Those were the days! #RetroGaming #FriendshipGoals #[ConsoleName] #[GameName]"

- **Console Collection:** "Proud of my retro console collection! Still works perfectly! #RetroGamingCollection #[ConsoleName] #GamingNostalgia #VintageTech" (Include a photo of your console collection)

- **Shared Memory:** "[Twitter User], remember when we used to stay up all night playing [Game Name] on the [Console Name]? Good times! #RetroGaming #Friendship #[ConsoleName] #[GameName]"

Gaming Communities: Tweeting Your Tribe

The gaming world is all about community. Whether you're playing online with friends, participating in esports tournaments, or simply sharing your love of gaming on social media, connecting with other gamers can enhance your gaming experience, expand your network, and create lasting friendships. Twitter is a great platform for finding your gaming tribe, engaging in discussions, and building a community around your shared passion.

Tips for Connecting with Gaming Communities on Twitter:

- **Follow gaming influencers:** Follow gaming influencers, YouTubers, Twitch streamers, esports professionals, and game developers who share your interests and whose insights you find valuable.

- **Participate in Twitter chats:** Many online communities host Twitter chats focused on specific games, genres, platforms, or gaming topics. Participating in these chats can be a great way to connect with other gamers, share your thoughts, and get new recommendations.

- **Join gaming-related Twitter communities:** There are many Twitter communities dedicated to specific games, consoles, esports teams, or gaming interests. Joining these communities can provide a more focused space for discussions, networking, and sharing resources.

- **Attend virtual events:** Many gaming conventions, tournaments, and meetups are now held virtually, providing opportunities to connect with other gamers from around the world. Follow the Twitter accounts of these events to stay informed about upcoming opportunities.

- **Share your knowledge and experiences:** Contribute to the community by sharing your own insights, experiences, and resources. Answer questions, offer advice, and participate in discussions to help others learn and grow.

Examples of Tweets Engaging with Gaming Communities:

- **Following Gaming Influencers:** "Just followed @[GamingInfluencer] on Twitter. Loving their insights on the [Game Name] meta and their hilarious gameplay videos. #[GameName] #GamingInfluencer #TwitchStreamer"

- **Participating in Twitter Chats:** "Excited to join the #[GamingChatName] tonight at 8pm EST! Let's discuss our favorite [Game Genre] games and debate the best [Game Mechanic]. #[GameGenre] #GamingCommunity #TwitterChat"

- **Joining Gaming Communities:** "Just joined the #[GamingCommunityName] on Twitter. Looking forward to connecting with other [Game Name] fans and sharing tips and strategies. #[GameName] #GamingCommunity #Teamwork"

- **Attending a Virtual Event:** "Attending the virtual #[GamingEventName] this week. Looking forward to the esports tournaments, developer panels, and cosplay contests. #[GamingEventName] #VirtualConvention #GamingLife"

- **Sharing Knowledge:** "Sharing my tips for defeating [Boss Name] in [Game Name]. It took me a while to figure it out, but this strategy worked for me. Hope it helps! #[GameName] #BossBattle #GamingTips"

Building Your Gaming Brand: Becoming a Gaming Influencer

If you're passionate about gaming and enjoy sharing your experiences and insights on Twitter, you might consider building your gaming brand and becoming a gaming influencer. A strong gaming brand can open up opportunities for collaborations with game developers, esports teams, brands, and media outlets, allowing you to share your passion with a wider audience and potentially earn income from your love of gaming.

Tips for Building Your Gaming Brand on Twitter:

- **Choose a niche:** What aspect of gaming are you most passionate about? Do you specialize in a particular genre, platform, or game? Are you a skilled esports competitor, a knowledgeable game reviewer, or a charismatic streamer? Choosing a niche can help you to target a specific audience and establish yourself as an expert in that area.

- **Develop a consistent brand voice:** How do you want to be perceived by your audience? Are you competitive and driven? Are you informative and analytical? Are you funny and entertaining? Developing a consistent brand voice will help you to create a recognizable and memorable identity.

- **Create high-quality content:** Share insightful game reviews, helpful tips and strategies, engaging live streams, hilarious gaming memes, and visually appealing content that provides value to your audience.

- **Engage with your followers:** Respond to comments and questions, participate in conversations, and build relationships with your followers. Create a sense of community by interacting with your audience and making them feel valued.

- **Collaborate with other gaming influencers:** Partner with other gamers, streamers, YouTubers, and esports professionals to cross-promote each other's content and reach a wider audience.

- **Use relevant hashtags:** Use hashtags strategically to increase the visibility of your tweets and connect with a wider audience.

- **Promote your other platforms:** If you have a Twitch channel, a YouTube channel, a gaming blog, or other online platforms, be sure to promote them on your Twitter profile and in your tweets.

- **Be patient and persistent:** Building a strong gaming brand takes time and effort. Don't get discouraged if you don't see results overnight. Keep creating great content, engaging with your audience, and promoting your brand, and you'll eventually start to see success.

Examples of Tweets Building Your Gaming Brand:

- **Niche Focus:** "I'm a [Game Genre] gamer who specializes in [Specific Game/Skill]. Follow me for tips, strategies, and live streams of my gameplay. #[GameGenre] #[SpecificGame/Skill] #Gamer"

- **Brand Voice:** "I'm a gaming enthusiast with a sarcastic sense of humor. Follow me for hilarious gaming memes, relatable gaming struggles, and the occasional rage quit (but always respectful, of course). #GamingHumor #GamerLife #DigitalComedian"

- **High-Quality Content:** "Just published a new blog post with my in-depth review of [Game Name]. Check it out for a detailed analysis of the gameplay, the story, the graphics, and the overall gaming experience. #[GameName] #GameReview #[GameGenre]" (Include a link to the blog post)

- **Follower Engagement:** "What's the most frustrating gaming moment you've ever experienced? Share your stories in the comments! #GamingFrustrations #Relatable #GamerStruggles"

- **Collaboration:** "Excited to be partnering with @[EsportsTeam] on a live stream event this weekend! We'll be playing [Game Name] and giving away some awesome prizes. Tune in! #[EsportsTeam] #[GameName] #LiveStream #Giveaways"

A Few Final Tips for Gaming Tweets

- **Be mindful of spoilers:** Avoid spoiling the ending or key plot points of games for others who haven't played them yet. Use spoiler warnings when appropriate and consider hiding spoilers behind spoiler tags.

- **Promote a positive and inclusive gaming community:** Gaming should be a fun and welcoming experience for everyone. Promote a positive and inclusive gaming community by being respectful of others, avoiding toxic behavior, and supporting diversity and inclusion in gaming.

- **Balance your gaming and real life:** While gaming can be a fun and rewarding hobby, it's important to maintain a healthy balance between your gaming and your real life. Don't let gaming consume your life to the detriment of your relationships, your health, or your other responsibilities.

- **Have fun!** Gaming is all about entertainment and enjoyment. Let your passion for gaming shine through in your tweets, engage with the community, and have fun sharing your experiences and insights with the world.

Twitter can be a fantastic platform for gamers to connect, share their passion, and discover new adventures. By following these tips and examples, you can use Twitter to enhance your gaming experience, build a community of fellow gamers, and become a true digital champion. Game on!

CHAPTER SIXTEEN: Pet Peeves: Tweeting Your Frustrations (Politely)

We all have them – those little annoyances, those irksome habits, those things that make us want to scream into the void (or, you know, tweet about it). Pet peeves, those tiny thorns in the side of our otherwise blissful existence, are a universal human experience. And while it might be tempting to unleash a torrent of ALL CAPS rage on Twitter (or X) the next time someone commits a cardinal sin against your sensibilities, let's explore a more civilized approach to airing your grievances.

This chapter is all about navigating the delicate art of tweeting about your pet peeves without turning into *that* person – the one everyone secretly mutes. We'll explore various strategies for expressing your frustrations in a humorous, relatable, and (most importantly) polite manner. Get ready to unleash your inner rant-master while still maintaining your dignity (and your followers).

The Art of the Subtle Shade: Tweeting with a Wink

Sometimes, the most effective way to address a pet peeve is through a bit of subtle shade – a clever quip, a witty observation, or a sly remark that hints at your annoyance without explicitly stating it. It's like whispering your frustration in a crowded room, allowing those in the know to chuckle along while maintaining a veneer of politeness.

Tips for Tweeting Subtle Shade:

- **Master the art of the understated:** Instead of launching into a full-blown rant, opt for a more understated approach. A simple, "Is it just me, or does [Pet Peeve] drive anyone else crazy?" can be surprisingly effective.

- **Employ humor and wit:** Humor is your best friend when it comes to tweeting about pet peeves. A witty observation or a self-deprecating remark can make your annoyance more palatable and relatable.

- **Use emojis strategically:** Emojis can add a touch of playfulness and sarcasm to your tweets. A well-placed eye roll (□) or a weary sigh (☺) can speak volumes.

- **Avoid naming names:** Unless you're prepared for a public confrontation, it's best to avoid calling out specific individuals. Keep your complaints general and focus on the behavior rather than the person.

- **Don't be a hypocrite:** Before tweeting about a pet peeve, make sure you're not guilty of the same behavior yourself. Hypocrisy is never a good look, especially on social media.

Examples of Tweets with Subtle Shade:

- "I love how people leave their shopping carts in the middle of the parking lot. It really adds to the ambiance. □ #PetPeeve #ParkingLotEtiquette"

- "Nothing says 'I respect your time' like showing up 20 minutes late to a meeting. ☺ #TimeManagement #MeetingEtiquette"

- "Is it just me, or does the sound of someone chewing with their mouth open make you want to flee the country? ☏ #PetPeeve #TableManners"

- "I'm always amazed by people who can talk on their phones in a crowded movie theater. They must have superpowers. □♀□ #MovieTheaterEtiquette #ConsiderateMoviegoers"

- "My favorite hobby is listening to people have loud personal conversations on speakerphone in public places. It's so enriching. 🎧 #PublicTransitEtiquette #PersonalSpace"

The Relatable Rant: Turning Annoyances into Humor

Sometimes, subtle shade isn't enough. You need to let it all out – the frustration, the exasperation, the sheer absurdity of it all. But even when you're indulging in a full-blown rant, you can still maintain a sense of humor and relatability, turning your annoyance into a source of entertainment for your followers.

Tips for Crafting a Relatable Rant:

- **Find the humor in the situation:** Even the most frustrating pet peeves can be funny when viewed from a certain perspective. Exaggerate the absurdity of the situation, use self-deprecating humor, or find a way to make light of your annoyance.

- **Use relatable language and scenarios:** Choose language and scenarios that your followers can relate to. The more universal the experience, the more likely your rant will resonate with others.

- **Don't take yourself too seriously:** A touch of self-awareness and self-deprecation can make your rant more endearing and less preachy.

- **Use visuals to enhance the humor:** A well-chosen GIF or meme can perfectly capture the essence of your rant and add a visual element that will make your followers chuckle.

- **End on a positive note (if possible):** If you can find a way to end your rant on a positive or hopeful note, it will leave your followers feeling entertained rather than annoyed.

Examples of Relatable Rants:

- "I swear, people who leave their blinkers on for miles are sent to test my patience. Do they think it's a decorative feature? ☐ #BlinkerAbuse #DrivingPetPeeves"

- "Why is it so hard to find a matching pair of socks in the laundry? Is there a sock monster living in my dryer? □ #LaundryMysteries #SockMonster #PetPeeve"

- "I'm convinced that autocorrect is a sentient being that actively tries to sabotage my texts. Why else would it change 'duck' to 'ducking' every time? □ #AutocorrectFails #TechFail #PetPeeve"

- "I love how people stand right in the doorway of the subway car, blocking everyone from getting on or off. It's like a game of human Tetris. Ⓜ #SubwayEtiquette #PersonalSpace #PetPeeve"

- "My superpower is attracting the slowest walkers in the world. It's like I have a gravitational pull for people who meander. 🚶♀□ #WalkingPace #PetPeeve #LifeInTheSlowLane"

The Constructive Critique: Turning Pet Peeves into Teachable Moments

Sometimes, tweeting about your pet peeves can be an opportunity to educate others and promote better behavior. If you approach it with a constructive and informative tone, you can turn your annoyance into a teachable moment and perhaps even make the world a slightly less irksome place.

Tips for Offering Constructive Critiques:

- **Focus on the behavior, not the person:** Avoid making personal attacks or generalizations. Instead, focus on the specific behavior that you find annoying and explain why it's problematic.

- **Use a polite and respectful tone:** Even when you're addressing a frustrating issue, maintain a polite and respectful tone. Avoid using inflammatory language, sarcasm, or condescension.

- **Offer solutions or alternatives:** Don't just complain about the problem – offer solutions or alternatives. Suggest ways that people can improve their behavior or avoid causing annoyance to others.

- **Use visuals to illustrate your points:** Photos, infographics, or even humorous memes can be effective tools for illustrating your points and making your message more engaging.

- **Be open to feedback and discussion:** Be prepared to engage in constructive dialogue with your followers. Listen to their perspectives, answer their questions, and be open to the possibility that you might learn something new.

Examples of Constructive Critiques:

- **Public Transit Etiquette:** "A gentle reminder to please offer your seat to elderly passengers, pregnant women, or people with disabilities on public transit. A little kindness can go a long way. #PublicTransitEtiquette #BeConsiderate"

- **Email Etiquette:** "When sending emails, please use a clear and concise subject line that accurately reflects the content of your message. It helps recipients prioritize their inbox and find the information they need more easily. #EmailEtiquette #ProductivityTips"

- **Social Media Etiquette:** "Before sharing personal information or sensitive content on social media, please consider the potential impact on yourself and others. What you post online can have lasting consequences. #SocialMediaEtiquette #ThinkBeforeYouPost"

- **Environmental Awareness:** "Let's all do our part to reduce plastic waste by using reusable bags, bottles, and straws. Small changes can make a big difference for the environment. #ReducePlastic #Sustainability #EnvironmentalAwareness"

- **Respect for Personal Space:** "When standing in line or in crowded spaces, please be mindful of personal space. Give people enough room to move around comfortably and avoid invading their personal bubble. #PersonalSpace #RespectBoundaries"

The Humorous PSA: Using Humor for Social Change

Humor can be a powerful tool for promoting social change and raising awareness about important issues. By combining humor with your pet peeve complaints, you can create memorable and shareable tweets that entertain your followers while also encouraging them to reflect on their behavior.

Tips for Creating a Humorous PSA:

- **Choose a pet peeve that has a broader social impact:** Select a pet peeve that is not just a personal annoyance, but also has a broader social impact, such as littering, reckless driving, or online bullying.

- **Find the humor in the situation:** Find a humorous angle to approach the issue, using wit, sarcasm, or exaggeration to make your point.

- **Use visuals to enhance the humor:** A funny meme, a clever GIF, or a short video clip can make your message more memorable and shareable.

- **End with a call to action:** Don't just complain about the problem – encourage your followers to take action. Suggest ways that they can contribute to a solution or promote positive change.

Examples of Humorous PSAs:

- **Littering PSA:** "I'm convinced that some people think the ground is a giant trash can. Newsflash: it's not. Let's keep our planet clean, folks. #NoLittering #RespectOurPlanet #EarthDayEveryDay" (Include a funny meme of a person throwing trash on the ground with a caption like "This is not how you dispose of garbage.")

- **Reckless Driving PSA:** "To the drivers who weave in and out of traffic like they're in a Fast and Furious movie: please chill. We're all just trying to get to our destinations safely. #SafeDriving #RoadRage #ChillOut" (Include a GIF of a car swerving erratically)

- **Online Bullying PSA:** "Cyberbullying is not cool. Words can hurt, even if they're typed behind a screen. Let's spread kindness, not hate, online. #CyberbullyingAwareness #BeKindOnline #WordsMatter" (Include a meme of a person typing mean comments on a computer with a caption like "This is not how you treat others online.")

The Power of Positivity: Focusing on the Good

While it's tempting to dwell on the things that annoy us, sometimes the best way to combat pet peeves is by focusing on the positive. Instead of ranting about the things that drive you crazy, try tweeting about the things that make you happy, the people who inspire you, or the experiences that make life worthwhile. By shifting your focus to the positive, you can create a more uplifting and enjoyable Twitter experience for yourself and your followers.

Tips for Tweeting Positively:

- **Share your gratitude:** Take a moment to appreciate the good things in your life, no matter how small they may seem. Tweet about the things you're grateful for, the people who make you happy, or the experiences that bring you joy.

- **Celebrate the good in others:** Acknowledge the kindness, generosity, and accomplishments of others. Tweet about inspiring people, heartwarming stories, or acts of kindness that you witness.

- **Promote positivity and encouragement:** Share inspirational quotes, motivational messages, or words of encouragement to uplift your followers and spread good vibes.

- **Use visuals to enhance the positivity:** Include photos, videos, or GIFs that evoke positive emotions, such as beautiful scenery, smiling faces, or heartwarming moments.

Examples of Positive Tweets:

- **Expressing Gratitude:** "Today, I'm grateful for the sunshine, a good cup of coffee, and the love of my family and friends. What are you grateful for? #Gratitude #PositiveVibes #CountYourBlessings"

- **Celebrating Kindness:** "Just witnessed a random act of kindness that made my day. A stranger helped an elderly person carry their groceries. The world needs more of this! #KindnessMatters #PayItForward #GoodDeeds"

- **Inspirational Quote:** ""Be the change you wish to see in the world." - Mahatma Gandhi #Inspiration #Motivation #MakeADifference"

- **Motivational Message:** "You are capable of amazing things. Believe in yourself and never give up on your dreams. #YouGotThis #DreamBig #BelieveInYourself"

- **Visual Enhancement:** [Share a photo of a beautiful sunset, a blooming flower, or a happy moment with friends.] #NatureBeauty #JoyfulMoments #PositiveVibes"

A Few Final Tips for Tweeting About Pet Peeves

- **Know your audience:** Before tweeting about a pet peeve, consider your audience and their sensibilities. What might be funny or relatable to one group of people could be offensive or insensitive to another.

- **Use humor judiciously:** Humor can be a great way to make your tweets about pet peeves more engaging, but don't overdo it. Too much humor can make your complaints seem trivial or insincere.

- **Avoid being a chronic complainer:** No one likes a constant complainer. While it's okay to vent about your pet peeves occasionally, don't let your Twitter feed become a never-ending stream of negativity.

- **Focus on solutions, not just problems:** Don't just complain about the things that annoy you – offer solutions or alternatives. Suggest ways that people can improve their behavior or create a more positive environment.

- **Remember that everyone has different pet peeves:** What might be a major annoyance to you might be a minor inconvenience to someone else. Be respectful of others' perspectives and avoid getting into heated arguments about subjective experiences.

Tweeting about your pet peeves can be a fun, relatable, and even cathartic experience. By following these tips and examples, you can express your frustrations without alienating your followers, sparking unnecessary drama, or becoming *that* person on Twitter. Remember to use humor, wit, and a touch of kindness, and your tweets about pet peeves can be both entertaining and thought-provoking.

CHAPTER SEVENTEEN: Current Events: Sharing Your Thoughts on the News

The world is a whirlwind of events, and Twitter (or X) is often ground zero for breaking news, real-time reactions, and heated discussions. From political upheavals and natural disasters to viral trends and cultural moments, the platform provides a constant stream of information, opinions, and perspectives.

This chapter will navigate the complex landscape of tweeting about current events, offering strategies for staying informed, sharing your thoughts responsibly, engaging in constructive dialogue, and avoiding the pitfalls of misinformation and online negativity. Get ready to become a discerning news consumer and a thoughtful contributor to the ever-evolving conversation on current events.

Staying Informed: Curating Your News Feed

Before you can tweet intelligently about current events, you need to be informed. But in the age of information overload, it's easy to get lost in a sea of headlines, clickbait, and conflicting perspectives. Curating a balanced and reliable news feed is crucial for separating fact from fiction and developing a nuanced understanding of complex issues.

Tips for Curating Your News Feed:

- **Follow reputable news sources:** Seek out news organizations with a strong track record of accuracy, fairness, and objectivity. Look for publications that adhere to journalistic ethics and employ fact-checking procedures.

- **Diversify your sources:** Don't rely on a single news source for your information. Follow a variety of publications that represent different perspectives and ideologies. This helps to avoid echo chambers and ensures that you're exposed to a wider range of viewpoints.

- **Follow experts and analysts:** Seek out experts and analysts who specialize in the areas you're interested in, such as political commentators, economists, scientists, or historians. Their insights can provide valuable context and help you to understand complex issues more deeply.

- **Be wary of social media trends:** Social media platforms like Twitter can be breeding grounds for misinformation, rumors, and biased perspectives. Don't take everything you see on social media at face value. Verify information from multiple sources before accepting it as truth.

- **Use fact-checking resources:** Fact-checking websites like Snopes, PolitiFact, and FactCheck.org can help you to verify the accuracy of claims and debunk misinformation.

- **Be critical and discerning:** Question everything. Don't blindly accept information without considering the source, the context, and the potential for bias. Develop a healthy skepticism and a willingness to challenge your own assumptions.

Examples of Reputable News Sources:

- **Traditional News Organizations:** The New York Times (@nytimes), The Washington Post (@washingtonpost), The Associated Press (@AP), Reuters (@Reuters), BBC News (@BBCWorld), CNN (@CNN), ABC News (@ABC), CBS News (@CBSNews), NBC News (@NBCNews)

- **Investigative Journalism Outlets:** ProPublica (@propublica), The Intercept (@theintercept), Center for Investigative Reporting (@CIRonline)

- **International News Organizations:** Al Jazeera English (@AJEnglish), The Guardian (@guardian), The Economist (@TheEconomist)

- **Specialized News Outlets:** Science Magazine (@ScienceMagazine), Nature (@nature), The Atlantic (@TheAtlantic), The New Yorker (@NewYorker)

Sharing Breaking News: Tweeting Responsibly

Twitter is often the first place people turn to for breaking news, and it can be tempting to share the latest updates as soon as you see them. However, in the rush to be the first to tweet, it's crucial to prioritize accuracy and responsibility over speed.

Tips for Tweeting Breaking News:

- **Verify the information:** Before sharing breaking news, make sure that the information is accurate and comes from a reliable source. Double-check the facts and avoid spreading rumors or unconfirmed reports.

- **Provide context:** Don't just share a headline or a snippet of information. Provide context and background information to help your followers understand the significance of the news event.

- **Link to credible sources:** Include links to the original news sources so that your followers can read the full story and verify the information for themselves.

- **Avoid sensationalizing:** Stick to the facts and avoid using language that is overly dramatic, sensationalized, or designed to evoke fear or panic.

- **Be mindful of potential harm:** Consider the potential impact of the news you're sharing, especially if it involves sensitive topics like violence, tragedy, or natural disasters.

Avoid sharing graphic images or videos that could be upsetting or traumatic.

- **Update as needed:** Breaking news stories often evolve rapidly. Be prepared to update your tweets as new information becomes available, and acknowledge any corrections or retractions.

Examples of Responsible Breaking News Tweets:

- **Accurate and Verified:** "Breaking News: [News Event] confirmed by [Reliable News Source]. More details to follow. #[NewsEvent] #BreakingNews" (Include a link to the news source)

- **Context and Background:** "[News Event] is a significant development because [Explanation of Significance]. This follows [Previous Events] and could have implications for [Future Outcomes]. #[NewsEvent] #Analysis"

- **Linking to Credible Sources:** "For the latest updates on [News Event], follow these reliable news sources: [List of News Sources with Twitter Handles] #[NewsEvent] #StayInformed"

- **Avoiding Sensationalism:** "While [News Event] is a serious situation, it's important to remain calm and avoid spreading rumors or unconfirmed reports. Stick to the facts and rely on credible sources for information. #[NewsEvent] #StayCalm"

- **Mindful of Potential Harm:** "My thoughts are with those affected by [News Event]. Please avoid sharing graphic images or videos that could be upsetting or traumatic. #[NewsEvent] #Support #Compassion"

Expressing Your Opinions: Tweeting Thoughtfully

Current events often evoke strong opinions and emotions, and it's natural to want to share your thoughts on Twitter. However, it's essential to express your opinions in a way that is thoughtful, respectful, and constructive.

Tips for Tweeting Your Opinions on Current Events:

- **Be informed:** Before expressing your opinion, make sure you have a solid understanding of the issue. Research the facts, consider different perspectives, and be aware of the nuances of the situation.

- **Be clear and concise:** Twitter's character limit encourages brevity. Express your opinions in a clear and concise manner, focusing on the key points you want to convey.

- **Be respectful:** Even when disagreeing with others, maintain a respectful tone. Avoid personal attacks, name-calling, and inflammatory language.

- **Support your opinions with evidence:** Don't just state your opinions as facts. Support your claims with evidence from credible sources. Link to articles, studies, data, or other resources that back up your points.

- **Use "I" statements:** When expressing your opinions, use "I" statements to emphasize that you're sharing your personal perspective, not stating objective truths.

- **Be open to feedback:** Not everyone will agree with your opinions. Be prepared to engage in constructive dialogue with those who hold different perspectives, and be willing to consider alternative viewpoints.

Examples of Thoughtful Opinion Tweets:

- **Informed Perspective:** "I believe that [Policy/Action] is a necessary step to address [Issue] because [Reasoning

Supported by Evidence]. #[Issue] #[Policy/Action] #Opinion"

- **Respectful Disagreement:** "While I respect [Other Person/Group]'s opinion on [Issue], I disagree with their stance because [Reasoning Supported by Evidence]. #[Issue] #DifferentPerspectives #RespectfulDebate"

- **Personal Perspective:** "I'm deeply concerned about the impact of [Issue] on [Affected Group/Community] because [Personal Connection/Reasoning]. #[Issue] #Empathy #MyPerspective"

- **Call to Action:** "We need to take action to address [Issue]. I urge everyone to [Action Step] to make a difference. #[Issue] #CallToAction #GetInvolved"

- **Openness to Feedback:** "I'm open to hearing different perspectives on [Issue]. Please share your thoughts and insights in the comments. #[Issue] #OpenDialogue #LearningFromOthers"

Engaging in Discussions: Promoting Constructive Dialogue

Twitter can be a powerful platform for engaging in discussions about current events, exchanging ideas, and debating different perspectives. However, online discussions can easily devolve into unproductive arguments, personal attacks, and echo chambers. Promoting constructive dialogue requires a conscious effort to listen to others, respect different viewpoints, and focus on finding common ground.

Tips for Engaging in Constructive Dialogue on Twitter:

- **Listen actively:** Before responding to someone who disagrees with you, take the time to understand their perspective. Read their tweet carefully, consider their arguments, and try to see the issue from their point of view.

- **Ask clarifying questions:** If you're unsure about someone's position, ask them to clarify their views. This can help to avoid misunderstandings and promote a more productive conversation.

- **Find common ground:** Even when you disagree on fundamental issues, there may be areas of common ground that you can identify. Focusing on these shared values can help to build bridges and foster mutual understanding.

- **Challenge ideas, not people:** When responding to opposing views, focus on challenging the ideas presented, rather than attacking the person who holds them. Avoid personal insults, name-calling, and ad hominem attacks.

- **Be willing to change your mind:** Entering a conversation with the assumption that you're always right is not conducive to productive dialogue. Be open to the possibility that you might learn something new or change your mind based on the evidence and arguments presented.

- **Know when to disengage:** Not all conversations are worth having. If you find yourself in a discussion that is becoming unproductive or disrespectful, it's okay to disengage. You don't have to engage with everyone who disagrees with you.

Examples of Tweets Promoting Constructive Dialogue:

- **Active Listening:** "I appreciate your perspective on [Issue], [Twitter User]. I understand that you believe [Summary of Their Viewpoint]. I'm curious to hear more about your reasoning. #[Issue] #OpenDialogue #ListeningToOthers"

- **Clarifying Question:** "I'm not sure I understand your point about [Specific Point], [Twitter User]. Could you please clarify what you mean by that? #[Issue] #SeekingUnderstanding #OpenToLearning"

- **Finding Common Ground:** "While we may disagree on the best approach to solving [Issue], I think we can all agree that the goal is to [Shared Goal]. #[Issue] #CommonGround #WorkingTogether"

- **Challenging Ideas:** "I disagree with the idea that [Idea]. I believe that [Counterargument Supported by Evidence]. #[Issue] #ChallengingIdeas #RespectfulDebate"

- **Willingness to Change Your Mind:** "I'm open to hearing different perspectives on [Issue]. I'm always willing to learn and grow, and I'm not afraid to change my mind if presented with convincing evidence. #[Issue] #OpenMind #LifelongLearning"

Navigating Political Discussions: Tweeting Respectfully

Political discussions on Twitter can be particularly heated and divisive. Passions run high, opinions are often deeply entrenched, and the anonymity of the internet can embolden people to say things they might not say in person. Navigating political discussions on Twitter requires a delicate balance of expressing your views while maintaining civility and respect.

Tips for Tweeting Respectfully About Politics:

- **Focus on issues, not personalities:** Instead of attacking or praising specific politicians, focus on the issues and policies that matter to you. Discuss the potential impact of different policies, the arguments for and against specific proposals, and the values that inform your political beliefs.

- **Avoid generalizations and stereotypes:** Don't make sweeping generalizations about entire groups of people based on their political affiliations. Recognize that people hold diverse views within any political party or ideology.

- **Be mindful of your language:** Choose your words carefully and avoid using language that is inflammatory, divisive, or offensive. Remember that your tweets can have a real impact on others, even if you don't intend them to.

- **Don't spread misinformation:** Be diligent about verifying information before sharing it, especially during election cycles or when political tensions are high. Avoid spreading rumors, conspiracy theories, or unsubstantiated claims.

- **Seek out diverse perspectives:** Don't just follow people who share your political views. Seek out perspectives from people who hold different beliefs. This can help you to understand the complexities of political issues and challenge your own assumptions.

- **Remember that you're talking to real people:** It's easy to forget that there are real people behind the Twitter handles. Treat others with the same respect and empathy that you would extend to someone you were talking to face-to-face.

Examples of Respectful Political Tweets:

- **Focus on Issues:** "I'm concerned about the impact of [Policy] on [Affected Group/Community]. We need to find solutions that address [Issue] while also protecting the rights and well-being of all citizens. #[Policy] #[Issue] #PoliticalDiscussion"

- **Avoiding Generalizations:** "I disagree with [Political Party/Group]'s stance on [Issue], but I recognize that not everyone who identifies with that party/group shares the same views. #[Issue] #PoliticalDiversity #Nuance"

- **Mindful Language:** "I'm disappointed by the recent political discourse on [Issue]. We need to engage in more civil and respectful conversations if we want to find common ground. #[Issue] #CivilDiscourse #RespectfulDebate"

- **Fact-Checking:** "Before sharing political information on social media, please take a moment to verify it from multiple sources. Misinformation can spread quickly and have a negative impact on our democracy. #FactCheck #Misinformation #ElectionIntegrity"

- **Seeking Diverse Perspectives:** "I'm following people from across the political spectrum to get a more balanced understanding of the issues. It's important to listen to different viewpoints and challenge our own assumptions. #PoliticalDiversity #OpenMind #LearningFromOthers"

Addressing Social Justice Issues: Tweeting with Empathy and Action

Social justice issues, such as racial inequality, gender discrimination, LGBTQ+ rights, and environmental justice, are often at the forefront of current events. Twitter can be a powerful tool for raising awareness, amplifying marginalized voices, and advocating for social change. However, it's essential to approach these topics with sensitivity, empathy, and a commitment to action.

Tips for Tweeting About Social Justice Issues:

- **Amplify marginalized voices:** Center the voices of those who are most affected by the issue. Retweet their stories, share their perspectives, and amplify their calls to action.

- **Educate yourself:** Take the time to learn about the history, the complexities, and the nuances of the issue. Follow activists, organizations, and educators who are working to address the problem.

- **Be mindful of your language:** Use inclusive and respectful language, avoiding terms or phrases that could be offensive or insensitive.

- **Be an ally:** Use your platform to speak out against injustice, even if you're not directly affected by the issue. Stand in solidarity with marginalized communities and support their fight for equality.

- **Don't just talk, take action:** Tweeting about social justice issues is important, but it's not enough. Take concrete actions to support the cause, such as donating to organizations, volunteering your time, contacting your elected officials, or participating in protests or demonstrations.

Examples of Tweets Addressing Social Justice Issues:

- **Amplifying Marginalized Voices:** "Retweeting this powerful thread by [Activist/Organization] about the experiences of [Marginalized Group] facing [Issue]. We need to listen to their stories and amplify their voices. #[Issue] #SocialJustice #Amplify" (Include a link to the thread)

- **Educating Yourself:** "I'm learning more about [Social Justice Issue] by reading [Book/Article], following [Activist/Organization], and listening to [Podcast/Speech]. Education is the first step towards understanding and action. #[SocialJusticeIssue] #Education #Learning"

- **Being an Ally:** "As a [Your Identity], I stand in solidarity with [Marginalized Group] in their fight for [Goal]. We must work together to create a more just and equitable society for all. #[SocialJusticeIssue] #Ally #Solidarity"

- **Call to Action:** "We need to take action to address [Social Justice Issue]. Here are some ways you can get involved: [List of Action Steps with Links to Organizations/Resources] #[SocialJusticeIssue] #TakeAction #MakeADifference"

Dealing with Misinformation: Tweeting Corrections and Counterarguments

Misinformation is a pervasive problem on Twitter, and it can spread quickly and have a harmful impact on individuals and society. It's essential to be vigilant about identifying and addressing misinformation when you encounter it.

Tips for Tweeting Corrections and Counterarguments:

- **Verify the information:** Before responding to a tweet that you believe contains misinformation, verify the information from multiple credible sources. Don't spread misinformation yourself by accidentally retweeting or amplifying false claims.

- **Provide evidence from credible sources:** When correcting misinformation, provide links to reputable news sources, scientific studies, government data, or other credible sources that support your claims.

- **Be factual and avoid emotional appeals:** Stick to the facts and avoid making emotional appeals or using inflammatory language. Your goal is to correct the misinformation, not to engage in a heated argument.

- **Use a respectful tone:** Even when addressing misinformation, maintain a respectful tone. Avoid personal attacks or insults, as this can be counterproductive and make it less likely that the person will be receptive to your correction.

- **Know when to disengage:** Some people are entrenched in their beliefs and are unwilling to change their minds, even when presented with evidence to the contrary. If you find that your efforts to correct misinformation are being met with hostility or resistance, it's okay to disengage from the conversation.

Examples of Tweets Correcting Misinformation:

- **Factual Correction:** "This tweet contains misinformation. [Specific Claim] is false. According to [Credible Source], [Accurate Information]. #FactCheck #Misinformation #[Issue]" (Include a link to the credible source)

- **Counterargument:** "While it's true that [Partially True Statement], it's important to note that [Missing Context/Counterpoint]. #Nuance #[Issue] #MisleadingInformation"

- **Respectful Tone:** "I understand that you may have seen this information circulating online, but it's not accurate. Here's a link to a fact-check from [Credible Source]: [Link] #Misinformation #FactCheck #BeInformed"

- **Disengagement:** "I've provided evidence from multiple credible sources to show that [Specific Claim] is false, but you seem unwilling to consider alternative information. I'm ending this conversation. #Misinformation #FactResistance #EndofDiscussion"

Avoiding Negativity and Toxicity: Tweeting with Mindfulness

Twitter can be a breeding ground for negativity, hostility, and toxic behavior. It's easy to get caught up in the drama, the outrage, and the constant stream of bad news. However, it's important to be mindful of your own mental health and well-being, and to avoid contributing to the negativity.

Tips for Avoiding Negativity and Toxicity on Twitter:

- **Be selective about what you engage with:** You don't have to read or respond to every tweet that appears in your feed. Be selective about the conversations you choose to engage with and avoid topics or individuals that consistently trigger negativity or stress.

- **Use Twitter's mute and block features:** If you find that certain accounts or hashtags are consistently negative or toxic, use Twitter's mute and block features to remove them from your feed. You can also mute specific words or phrases that trigger negative emotions.

- **Take breaks from Twitter:** It's important to take breaks from social media to recharge and reconnect with the offline world. Set limits on your Twitter usage and schedule regular breaks to avoid getting overwhelmed by the negativity.

- **Focus on the positive:** Make a conscious effort to share and engage with positive content, such as inspiring stories, uplifting messages, or humorous observations. This can help to counterbalance the negativity and create a more enjoyable Twitter experience for yourself and your followers.

- **Remember that you can't control others:** You can't control what other people tweet, but you can control how you react to it. Choose to focus on the positive, engage in constructive conversations, and disengage from negativity whenever possible.

Examples of Tweets Promoting Mindfulness and Positivity:

- **Selective Engagement:** "I'm taking a break from Twitter today to focus on my mental health and well-being. It's important to set boundaries and avoid getting overwhelmed by the negativity. #SelfCare #DigitalDetox #MentalHealthMatters"

- **Using Mute and Block Features:** "I've muted the hashtag #[NegativeHashtag] because it's consistently filled with toxic and divisive content. I'm choosing to focus on more positive and constructive conversations. #Positivity #MindfulScrolling #CuratingMyFeed"

- **Focusing on the Positive:** "Sharing some good news today! [Positive News Story/Event]. It's important to celebrate the positive things happening in the world, even amidst the challenges. #GoodNews #Positivity #Hope"

- **Remembering Your Control:** "I can't control what other people tweet, but I can control how I react to it. I choose to focus on the positive, engage in constructive conversations, and disengage from negativity. #Mindfulness #PositiveChoices #CreatingMyOwnExperience"

Humor and Current Events: Tweeting with Wit and Satire

Humor can be a powerful tool for coping with the often overwhelming and disheartening nature of current events. A well-placed joke, a clever observation, or a dose of satire can help to lighten the mood, provide a fresh perspective, and even spark critical thinking about serious issues.

Tips for Using Humor in Current Events Tweets:

- **Be mindful of the context:** Not every current event is appropriate for humor. Be sensitive to the gravity of the situation and avoid making light of tragedy, suffering, or sensitive topics.

- **Punch up, not down:** Direct your humor towards those in positions of power or privilege, rather than towards marginalized groups or individuals who are already facing hardship.

- **Avoid stereotypes and offensive humor:** Be mindful of stereotypes and avoid using humor that could be offensive or insensitive to particular groups of people.

- **Use wit and satire to expose hypocrisy or absurdity:** Humor can be an effective tool for exposing hypocrisy, absurdity, or injustice. Use wit and satire to highlight the flaws in arguments, challenge the status quo, or spark critical thinking.

- **Don't be afraid to laugh at yourself:** Self-deprecating humor can be a great way to make your tweets more relatable and to show that you don't take yourself too seriously.

Examples of Tweets Using Humor in Current Events:

- **Witty Observation:** "[Politician/Public Figure] said [Quote]. It's like they're living in an alternate reality. #AlternativeFacts #[Issue] #PoliticalHumor"

- **Satire:** "In other news, the world is ending, but at least the stock market is doing well. #Priorities #LateStageCapitalism #Satire"

- **Self-Deprecating Humor:** "I'm so overwhelmed by the news that I'm starting to think I need a news detox. Maybe I should just unplug and live in a cave for a while. #NewsOverload #InformationFatigue #SendHelp"

- **Humorous Meme:** [Share a meme that satirizes a current event or a political figure, but be sure to avoid offensive or insensitive content.] #MemeCulture #CurrentEvents #Humor"

Using Twitter for Activism and Advocacy: Tweeting for Change

Twitter can be a powerful tool for activism and advocacy, allowing you to raise awareness, mobilize support for causes you care about, and put pressure on decision-makers. From organizing protests to amplifying marginalized voices, the platform has played a significant role in social and political movements around the world.

Tips for Using Twitter for Activism and Advocacy:

- **Identify your goals:** What are you trying to achieve with your activism or advocacy? Are you trying to raise awareness about an issue, change a policy, elect a particular candidate, or support a specific organization?

- **Target your audience:** Who are you trying to reach with your message? Are you trying to persuade undecided voters, mobilize supporters, or pressure elected officials?

- **Craft a compelling message:** Your message should be clear, concise, and persuasive. Use strong language, compelling visuals, and personal stories to connect with your audience.

- **Use relevant hashtags:** Hashtags can help increase the visibility of your tweets and connect you with others who are advocating for the same cause. Research relevant hashtags and use them strategically.

- **Engage with influencers and organizations:** Connect with influencers, organizations, and other advocates who are working on the same issue. Retweet their content, amplify their message, and collaborate on campaigns.

- **Track your progress:** Monitor the reach and engagement of your tweets to see how your activism or advocacy efforts are performing. Use Twitter Analytics to track your impressions, retweets, and mentions.

- **Take your activism offline:** Tweeting is just one piece of the puzzle. Take your activism offline by volunteering your time, donating to organizations, contacting your elected officials, or participating in protests or demonstrations.

Examples of Tweets for Activism and Advocacy:

- **Raising Awareness:** "Did you know that [Statistic/Fact] about [Issue]? We need to take action to address this problem. Learn more and get involved: [Link to Organization/Website] #[Issue] #Awareness #TakeAction"

- **Mobilizing Support:** "Join me in supporting [Organization/Campaign] that is working to [Goal]. Donate, volunteer, or spread the word to make a difference! #[Organization/Campaign] #Support #GetInvolved"

- **Pressuring Decision-Makers:** "Hey @[ElectedOfficial], I urge you to support [Policy/Legislation] that addresses [Issue]. Your constituents are counting on you to take action. #[Policy/Legislation] #[Issue] #HoldThemAccountable"

- **Amplifying Marginalized Voices:** "Amplifying the voices of [Marginalized Group] who are fighting for [Goal]. Listen to their stories, learn from their experiences, and support their movement. #[SocialJusticeIssue] #Amplify #Solidarity"

- **Celebrating a Victory:** "We did it! [Policy/Legislation] passed! Thank you to everyone who fought for this important change. #Victory #[Issue] #Progress"

Covering Sensitive Events: Tweeting with Respect and Compassion

Sensitive events, such as natural disasters, acts of violence, or tragedies, often dominate the news cycle and generate a lot of discussion on Twitter. While it's important to stay informed about these events and to express your support for those affected, it's crucial to do so with sensitivity, respect, and compassion.

Tips for Tweeting About Sensitive Events:

- **Avoid sharing graphic images or videos:** Don't share graphic images or videos that could be upsetting or traumatic to viewers, especially if they involve violence, death, or suffering.

- **Be mindful of the victims and their families:** Remember that real people are affected by these events. Avoid making insensitive or disrespectful comments that could add to their pain or grief.

- **Focus on providing support and resources:** Instead of sensationalizing the event or focusing on the negative, share information about how people can help, such as donating to relief organizations, volunteering their time, or offering emotional support.

- **Use trigger warnings:** If your tweet contains content that could be triggering for some viewers, such as discussions of violence, trauma, or mental health issues, use a trigger warning to alert them to the sensitive nature of the content.

- **Promote healing and unity:** Encourage empathy, compassion, and understanding in your tweets. Promote messages of hope, resilience, and community support.

Examples of Tweets About Sensitive Events:

- **Avoiding Graphic Content:** "My heart goes out to those affected by [Sensitive Event]. Please be mindful of the victims and their families and avoid sharing graphic images or videos. #[SensitiveEvent] #Support #Respect"

- **Providing Support and Resources:** "If you're looking for ways to help those affected by [Sensitive Event], here are some organizations providing relief efforts: [List of Organizations with Links] #[SensitiveEvent] #Donate #Volunteer"

- **Trigger Warning:** "Trigger Warning: This tweet discusses the topic of [Sensitive Topic]. Please be aware that this

content may be triggering for some viewers.
#TriggerWarning #[SensitiveTopic] #MentalHealth"

- **Promoting Healing and Unity:** "In the wake of [Sensitive Event], let's come together as a community to support each other, promote healing, and spread messages of hope and resilience. #[SensitiveEvent] #Community #Hope"

Tweeting About Global Issues: Broadening Your Perspective

Twitter connects us to a global community, allowing us to stay informed about events and issues happening around the world. From climate change and international conflicts to human rights violations and humanitarian crises, tweeting about global issues can help raise awareness, promote understanding, and encourage action.

Tips for Tweeting About Global Issues:

- **Seek out diverse perspectives:** Don't just rely on Western media sources for your information. Follow international news organizations, activists, and experts from different regions of the world to get a more balanced and nuanced understanding of global issues.

- **Be aware of your own biases:** Recognize that you may have biases or blind spots based on your own background and experiences. Be open to learning from others and challenging your own assumptions.

- **Use inclusive language:** Be mindful of cultural differences and use language that is inclusive and respectful of all people, regardless of their nationality, ethnicity, religion, or background.

- **Focus on solutions:** While it's important to highlight problems and injustices, also focus on potential solutions, positive initiatives, and organizations that are working to make a difference.

- **Connect with global communities:** Use Twitter to connect with people from different countries and cultures. Engage in conversations, share your perspectives, and learn from each other's experiences.

Examples of Tweets About Global Issues:

- **Seeking Diverse Perspectives:** "Following international news sources and activists from [Region/Country] to get a broader understanding of [Global Issue]. It's important to see the world through different lenses. #[GlobalIssue] #InternationalPerspectives #GlobalCitizenship"

- **Acknowledging Biases:** "I'm trying to be more aware of my own biases when it comes to understanding [Global Issue]. I'm committed to learning from others and challenging my own assumptions. #SelfReflection #BiasAwareness #OpenToLearning"

- **Focus on Solutions:** "While [Global Issue] is a complex and challenging problem, there are organizations and individuals working tirelessly to find solutions. Here are a few examples: [List of Organizations/Initiatives with Links] #[GlobalIssue] #Solutions #Hope"

- **Connecting with Global Communities:** "Interested in connecting with people from [Region/Country] to learn more about their perspectives on [Global Issue]. Please DM me if you're open to a conversation. #GlobalConnections #CrossCulturalCommunication #[GlobalIssue]"

Tweeting About Cultural Moments: Sharing the Zeitgeist

Twitter is often a reflection of the cultural zeitgeist, capturing the trends, the conversations, and the shared experiences that are shaping society. From viral memes and trending hashtags to award shows and sporting events, tweeting about cultural moments can be a fun and engaging way to connect with others, share your thoughts, and participate in the collective conversation.

Tips for Tweeting About Cultural Moments:

- **Embrace the humor:** Cultural moments are often ripe for humor. Share funny memes, witty observations, or clever takes on the latest trends.

- **Join the conversation:** Use relevant hashtags to join the conversation and engage with others who are discussing the same cultural moment.

- **Share your unique perspective:** Don't just echo what everyone else is saying. Share your own unique perspective, insights, or experiences related to the cultural moment.

- **Be respectful of different opinions:** Not everyone will share your enthusiasm for a particular cultural moment. Be respectful of different opinions and avoid getting into heated arguments.

- **Don't take it too seriously:** Cultural moments are often fleeting and ephemeral. Enjoy the ride, engage with the conversation, and don't be afraid to have a little fun.

Examples of Tweets About Cultural Moments:

- **Humorous Observation:** "The internet is obsessed with [Viral Trend] this week. I'm not sure if I should be amused or concerned. #[ViralTrend] #MemeCulture #InternetObsessed"

- **Joining the Conversation:** "Watching the #[AwardShow] tonight! Who are you rooting for? #[AwardShow] #RedCarpet #Predictions"

- **Sharing Your Perspective:** "[Cultural Moment] is a reminder that [Insight/Reflection]. It's important to [Action/Change]. #[CulturalMoment] #Perspective #CallToAction"

- **Respecting Different Opinions:** "I understand that not everyone is a fan of [Cultural Moment], but I'm enjoying it. To each their own! #[CulturalMoment] #RespectfulDisagreement #DiversityofTastes"

Tweeting as a Force for Good: Promoting Positivity and Change

Despite the potential for negativity and toxicity, Twitter can also be a force for good. By using your platform to promote positivity, empathy, and constructive dialogue, you can contribute to a more informed, engaged, and compassionate online community.

Tips for Tweeting as a Force for Good:

- **Focus on solutions, not just problems:** While it's important to acknowledge problems and injustices, also focus on potential solutions, positive initiatives, and organizations that are working to make a difference.

- **Celebrate the good in the world:** Highlight inspiring stories, acts of kindness, and examples of people making a positive impact on their communities and the world.

- **Promote empathy and understanding:** Encourage empathy, compassion, and understanding in your tweets. Challenge stereotypes, promote diversity, and advocate for inclusion.

- **Use your platform to amplify marginalized voices:** Give a platform to those who are often silenced or ignored. Retweet their stories, share their perspectives, and help them to reach a wider audience.

- **Be the change you want to see:** Don't just talk about making the world a better place – take action. Volunteer your time, donate to causes you care about, contact your elected officials, or participate in protests or demonstrations.

Examples of Tweets Promoting Positivity and Change:

- **Focusing on Solutions:** "Instead of dwelling on the problems, let's focus on the solutions. Here are some organizations working to address [Issue]: [List of Organizations with Links] #[Issue] #Solutions #Hope"

- **Celebrating the Good:** "This story about [Person/Organization] making a difference in their community is truly inspiring. Let's celebrate the good happening in the world! #[GoodNews] #PositiveImpact #MakingADifference"

- **Promoting Empathy:** "Let's remember to treat each other with kindness and understanding, especially during challenging times. Empathy is the key to building a more compassionate and just world. #Empathy #Compassion #KindnessMatters"

- **Amplifying Marginalized Voices:** "Giving a platform to [Marginalized Group] to share their perspectives on [Issue]. Their voices deserve to be heard. #[Issue] #Amplify #RepresentationMatters"

- **Call to Action:** "We can all make a difference in the world. Choose one cause you care about and take action. Donate, volunteer, or spread the word to make a positive

impact. #GetInvolved #MakeADifference
#ChangeTheWorld"

Tweeting with Impact: A Few Final Thoughts

Tweeting about current events can be a powerful way to stay informed, share your thoughts, engage in discussions, and even advocate for change. But it's essential to approach this responsibility with thoughtfulness, respect, and a commitment to accuracy and constructive dialogue.

Remember that Twitter is a public platform, and your tweets can have a real impact on others. Use your platform wisely, be mindful of your words, and strive to be a positive and constructive force in the online conversation.

By following these tips and examples, you can navigate the complex world of tweeting about current events and become a more informed, engaged, and responsible digital citizen.

CHAPTER EIGHTEEN: Holiday Cheer: Tweeting Festive Greetings

The holidays. A time for family, friends, good cheer, and, of course, an avalanche of themed content on Twitter (or X). From Thanksgiving feasts and spooky Halloween costumes to sparkly New Year's Eve celebrations, the holiday season provides a wealth of opportunities to connect with your followers, share festive greetings, and spread a little holiday cheer across the digital landscape.

This chapter will equip you with a sleigh full of tweet ideas to navigate the merriest time of the year. We'll explore different holidays, offering examples and tips to help you craft tweets that are both festive and engaging, whether you're celebrating with loved ones, sharing your holiday traditions, or simply spreading good vibes.

Halloween: Tweeting Spooktacular Greetings

Halloween. The one day a year when it's socially acceptable to dress up as your favorite superhero, villain, or pop culture icon (or, you know, a giant pumpkin). Twitter becomes a virtual costume parade, filled with spooky selfies, hilarious memes, and playful banter about candy corn and pumpkin spice everything.

Tweet Examples:

- **Costume Reveal:** "My Halloween costume this year is... [Costume]! Wish me luck on the candy haul! #HalloweenCostume #TrickOrTreat #[Character/Theme]" (Include a photo of your costume)

- **Spooky Selfie:** "Feeling spooky! 😈 Happy Halloween, everyone! #HalloweenSelfie #FangsOut #HalloweenVibes"

- **Candy Corn Debate:** "Let's settle this once and for all: candy corn – yay or nay? #CandyCornDebate #HalloweenTreats #TrickOrTreat"

- **Pumpkin Spice Overload:** "I think I've reached my pumpkin spice limit for the year. Pumpkin spice lattes, pumpkin spice cookies, pumpkin spice air freshener... enough already! #PumpkinSpiceEverything #HalloweenSeason #BasicButProud"

- **Movie Marathon:** "Having a Halloween movie marathon tonight! What are your favorite spooky flicks? #HalloweenMovies #MovieNight #HorrorFan"

Pro-Tip: Use Halloween-themed emojis like ghosts (👻), pumpkins (🎃), bats (🦇), spiders (🕷️), and skulls (💀) to add a touch of spookiness to your tweets.

Thanksgiving: Tweeting Turkey Day Gratitude

Thanksgiving. A time for family gatherings, delicious feasts, and, of course, reflecting on the things we're grateful for (even if it's just the fact that we survived another year). Twitter becomes a virtual gratitude journal, filled with heartfelt messages, funny family anecdotes, and the inevitable debates about stuffing versus dressing.

Tweet Examples:

- **Gratitude Post:** "Happy Thanksgiving! Grateful for family, friends, good food, and all the blessings in my life. What are you thankful for today? #Thanksgiving #Gratitude #Thankful"

- **Food Coma:** "Officially in a food coma after that Thanksgiving feast! 🦃🍽️ #ThanksgivingDinner #FoodComa #WorthIt"

- **Family Fun:** "Thanksgiving with my family is always an adventure. Lots of laughter, some questionable dance moves, and enough food to feed a small army. #ThanksgivingMemories #FamilyFun #GobbleTilYouWobble"

- **Travel Woes:** "Traveling for Thanksgiving is like running an obstacle course. Delayed flights, crowded airports, and traffic jams galore. But hey, at least I'm going to see my loved ones! #ThanksgivingTravel #WorthTheHassle #FamilyTime"

- **Stuffing vs. Dressing Debate:** "Let's settle this: stuffing or dressing? I'm firmly in the [Your Preference] camp. #ThanksgivingDebate #FoodFight #CulinaryControversy"

Pro-Tip: Use Thanksgiving-themed emojis like turkeys (□), cornucopias (🍂), and pie slices (□) to add a festive touch to your tweets.

Hanukkah: Tweeting Festival of Lights Greetings

Hanukkah. A joyous eight-day celebration filled with candle lighting, delicious foods like latkes and sufganiyot, and the exchange of gifts. Twitter becomes a platform for sharing Hanukkah traditions, spreading messages of hope and light, and perhaps even sparking a few friendly debates about the best way to make latkes.

Tweet Examples:

- **Candle Lighting:** "Lighting the first candle of the menorah tonight! Happy Hanukkah, everyone! #Hanukkah #FestivalOfLights #Shalom" (Include a photo of your menorah)

- **Latke Love:** "Can't get enough of those crispy, golden latkes! What's your secret ingredient for the perfect latke? #LatkeLife #HanukkahFood #Foodie"

- **Dreidel Games:** "Spinning the dreidel and hoping for a gimmel! Who else loves a good dreidel game? #Dreidel #HanukkahFun #GamesNight"

- **Gift Giving:** "Giving thanks for the gift of family, friends, and the miracle of Hanukkah. Happy holidays to all who celebrate! #HanukkahGifts #Gratitude #HolidayCheer"

- **Miracles and Traditions:** "Hanukkah is a reminder that even in the darkest of times, there is always hope and light. Wishing everyone a joyous and meaningful celebration. #HanukkahMiracle #JewishTraditions #HappyHanukkah"

Pro-Tip: Use Hanukkah-themed emojis like the menorah (□), the dreidel (✡□), and the Star of David (✡) to add a festive touch to your tweets.

Christmas: Tweeting Merry Christmas Greetings

Christmas. A time for twinkling lights, decorated trees, festive music, and gathering with loved ones to celebrate the holiday season. Twitter becomes a virtual winter wonderland, filled with Christmas cheer, gift-giving excitement, and perhaps even a few good-natured complaints about fruitcake.

Tweet Examples:

- **Christmas Countdown:** "Only [Number] days until Christmas! 🎄🎅☃ Can't wait to celebrate with family and friends. #ChristmasCountdown #HolidayExcitement #ChristmasCheer"

- **Festive Decor:** "My Christmas tree is finally up and decorated! Loving the twinkling lights and festive vibes. #ChristmasDecor #HolidaySpirit #WinterWonderland" (Include a photo of your decorated tree)

- **Gift Giving:** "Finished all my Christmas shopping! Now the hard part: wrapping all those presents!

#ChristmasShopping #GiftWrappingProcrastination #HolidayStress"

- **Ugly Christmas Sweater Party:** "Rocking my ugliest Christmas sweater at tonight's party! Wish me luck in the ugly sweater contest. #UglyChristmasSweater #HolidayParty #FestiveFashion" (Include a photo of your sweater)

- **Christmas Movie Marathon:** "Having a Christmas movie marathon tonight! What are your favorite holiday classics? #ChristmasMovies #MovieNight #HolidayCheer"

Pro-Tip: Use Christmas-themed emojis like Christmas trees (🎄), Santa Claus (🎅), gifts (🎁), reindeer (□), and snowmen (⛄) to add a festive touch to your tweets.

Kwanzaa: Tweeting Kwanzaa Greetings

Kwanzaa. A seven-day celebration of African-American heritage and culture, observed from December 26th to January 1st. Twitter becomes a platform for sharing Kwanzaa traditions, promoting cultural awareness, and celebrating community and unity.

Tweet Examples:

- **Kwanzaa Principles:** "Celebrating the seven principles of Kwanzaa: Umoja (Unity), Kujichagulia (Self-Determination), Ujima (Collective Work and Responsibility), Ujamaa (Cooperative Economics), Nia (Purpose), Kuumba (Creativity), and Imani (Faith). #Kwanzaa #SevenPrinciples #BlackCulture"

- **Candle Lighting:** "Lighting the Kinara tonight in honor of [Kwanzaa Principle]. #Kwanzaa #Kinara #BlackHeritage"

- **Community Celebration:** "Kwanzaa is a time to celebrate community, unity, and cultural heritage. Wishing everyone

273

a joyous and meaningful celebration. #Kwanzaa #BlackCommunity #Togetherness"

- **Cultural Awareness:** "Learning more about Kwanzaa traditions and the rich history of African-American culture. #Kwanzaa #Education #CulturalAppreciation"

- **Joyous Greetings:** "Happy Kwanzaa to all who celebrate! Wishing you a week filled with joy, peace, and unity. #Kwanzaa #HappyHolidays #PeaceAndLove"

Pro-Tip: Use Kwanzaa-themed emojis like the Kinara (□□) and the colors of the Pan-African flag (red, black, and green) to add a festive touch to your tweets.

New Year's Eve: Tweeting Sparkling Greetings

New Year's Eve. A time for reflection, celebration, and looking ahead to the possibilities of a new year. Twitter becomes a virtual countdown party, filled with New Year's resolutions, celebratory photos, and perhaps a few too many champagne emojis.

Tweet Examples:

- **New Year's Resolutions:** "My New Year's resolution is to [Your Resolution]. What are your goals for the new year? #NewYearsResolutions #Goals #NewBeginnings"

- **Countdown to Midnight:** "Counting down the hours until midnight! 🎊□ #NewYearsEve #Countdown #PartyTime"

- **Cheers to the New Year:** "Cheers to a new year filled with happiness, health, and adventure! □ #HappyNewYear #Cheers #2024"

- **Reflecting on the Past Year:** "Looking back on the past year with gratitude for the highs and lessons learned from the lows. Here's to a brighter future! #YearInReview #NewYearReflections #Growth"

- **Party Time:** "Ringing in the new year with friends and good vibes! Happy New Year, everyone! #NewYearsParty #Celebration #LetsGo2024" (Include a photo of your celebration)

Pro-Tip: Use New Year's Eve-themed emojis like champagne bottles (□), party poppers (🎉), confetti (🎊), and fireworks (🎆) to add a celebratory touch to your tweets.

General Holiday Cheer: Spreading Festive Vibes

Beyond specific holidays, the entire holiday season is a time for spreading good cheer, generosity, and festive vibes. Use your Twitter platform to share heartwarming stories, promote acts of kindness, and simply remind people to enjoy the magic of the holidays.

Tweet Examples:

- **Random Act of Kindness:** "Just paid for the coffee of the person behind me in line. Spreading a little holiday cheer! #RandomActOfKindness #HolidaySpirit #PayItForward"

- **Giving Back:** "Donated to [Charity/Cause] this holiday season. It's important to give back to those in need, especially during the holidays. #GivingBack #Charity #HolidayGiving"

- **Holiday Spirit:** "Loving all the holiday decorations, festive music, and twinkling lights! The holiday spirit is contagious. #HolidayVibes #WinterWonderland #TisTheSeason"

- **Appreciating Loved Ones:** "Taking a moment to appreciate all the wonderful people in my life. The holidays are a reminder of how lucky I am. #FamilyAndFriends #HolidayLove #Gratitude"

- **Spreading Joy:** "Wishing everyone a happy and healthy holiday season filled with joy, peace, and love! #HappyHolidays #SeasonGreetings #SpreadTheLove"

Pro-Tip: Use general holiday-themed emojis like snowflakes (❄️), stars (✹), hearts (♥️), and smiling faces (☺) to add a touch of festive cheer to your tweets.

A Few Final Tips for Tweeting Holiday Cheer

- **Be authentic and genuine:** Your holiday tweets should reflect your own personal style and sentiments. Don't force it or try to be someone you're not.

- **Use humor and wit:** Humor can be a great way to add personality to your tweets and make them more engaging. But be mindful of the context and avoid offensive or insensitive jokes.

- **Be inclusive:** Remember that not everyone celebrates the same holidays or has the same traditions. Be inclusive and respectful of different cultures and beliefs.

- **Spread positivity:** The holidays can be a stressful time for some people. Use your platform to spread positivity, encouragement, and good vibes.

- **Engage with your followers:** Respond to comments and questions, participate in discussions, and create a sense of community with your followers.

- **Have fun!** The holidays are a time for joy and celebration. Let your festive spirit shine through in your tweets and spread a little holiday cheer across the Twitterverse.

CHAPTER NINETEEN: Supporting Causes You Care About

We live in a world facing complex challenges, from climate change and poverty to social injustice and humanitarian crises. But amidst these challenges, there's a growing movement of individuals and organizations dedicated to making a difference. And in the age of social media, platforms like Twitter (or X) provide powerful tools for amplifying these efforts, connecting with like-minded individuals, and mobilizing support for causes that matter.

This chapter is your guide to using Twitter for good. We'll explore various strategies for supporting causes you care about, from raising awareness and fundraising to advocating for change and inspiring action. Get ready to unleash your inner activist and transform your Twitter presence into a force for positive impact.

Finding Your Cause: Identifying Issues That Resonate with You

The first step to supporting causes you care about on Twitter is to identify the issues that resonate with you. What are you passionate about? What problems in the world do you want to help solve? What injustices do you want to fight against?

Your cause doesn't have to be something grand or global. It could be a local issue, a specific community need, or a cause that's close to your heart for personal reasons. The most important thing is that you're genuinely passionate about it, as this will fuel your commitment and inspire others to join your efforts.

Tips for Finding Your Cause:

- **Reflect on your values:** What are your core values? What do you believe in? What kind of world do you want to live in? Your values can guide you towards causes that align with your beliefs and aspirations.

- **Consider your experiences:** Have you personally been affected by a particular issue? Have you witnessed injustice or hardship that you want to address? Your experiences can provide a powerful motivation for supporting a cause.

- **Research different organizations and initiatives:** Explore the work of different organizations and initiatives that are addressing issues you care about. Learn about their missions, their impact, and their approaches to solving problems.

- **Follow hashtags and accounts related to your interests:** Follow hashtags and accounts on Twitter that are related to your areas of interest or concern. This can help you to discover new organizations, campaigns, and perspectives.

- **Talk to people who are involved in causes you care about:** Connect with people who are already actively supporting causes you're interested in. Ask them about their experiences, their challenges, and their motivations.

Raising Awareness: Tweeting to Educate and Inform

One of the most effective ways to support a cause on Twitter is by raising awareness. By sharing information, statistics, stories, and resources, you can educate your followers about the issue, its impact, and the ways they can get involved.

Tips for Tweeting to Raise Awareness:

- **Share facts and statistics:** Use data and research to provide a compelling and credible case for the importance of the cause. Source your information from reputable organizations and publications.

- **Tell personal stories:** Personal stories can be incredibly powerful for connecting with people on an emotional level and inspiring empathy and action. Share your own experiences or the stories of others who have been affected by the issue.

- **Use visuals:** Visuals, such as photos, infographics, and videos, can be highly effective for grabbing attention and conveying information in a memorable way.

- **Create Twitter threads:** Twitter threads allow you to share more in-depth information and create a narrative around the issue. Break down complex topics into a series of tweets, using visuals and links to support your points.

- **Use relevant hashtags:** Hashtags can help increase the visibility of your tweets and connect you with a wider audience who are interested in the same cause. Research relevant hashtags and use a mix of general and specific tags.

- **Tag relevant organizations and influencers:** Tag organizations, influencers, and other individuals who are working on the cause to amplify their reach and encourage collaboration.

- **Use Twitter's features:** Take advantage of Twitter's features, such as polls, quizzes, and live Q&A sessions, to engage your followers and create interactive experiences that educate and inform.

Examples of Tweets Raising Awareness:

- **Facts and Statistics:** "Did you know that [Statistic/Fact] about [Issue]? This is a serious problem that affects [Impact]. Learn more from [Organization/Source]: [Link] #[Issue] #Awareness #FactsMatter"

- **Personal Story:** "My personal experience with [Issue] has shown me the importance of [Solution/Action]. Here's my story: [Tweet Thread] #[Issue] #MyStory #MakingADifference"

- **Visual Awareness:** "This infographic from [Organization/Source] illustrates the impact of [Issue] on [Affected Group/Community]. #[Issue] #Infographic #VisualAwareness" (Include the infographic in the tweet)

- **Twitter Thread:** "Breaking down the complex issue of [Issue] in this tweet thread. Follow along to learn about the problem, its causes, and potential solutions. #[Issue] #TweetThread #Education"

- **Interactive Engagement:** "What do you know about [Issue]? Take this quiz to test your knowledge and learn more about the cause. #[Issue] #Quiz #InteractiveLearning" (Include a link to the quiz)

Amplifying Voices: Retweeting and Sharing Content from Others

One of the easiest yet most impactful ways to support a cause on Twitter is by amplifying the voices of others who are working on the issue. Retweeting and sharing content from organizations, activists, experts, and individuals who are directly affected by the cause can help to expand their reach, increase their visibility, and validate their experiences.

Tips for Amplifying Voices:

- **Follow accounts that align with your cause:** Seek out and follow Twitter accounts of organizations, activists, experts, and individuals who are working on the cause you care about.

- **Retweet valuable content:** Retweet tweets that share important information, personal stories, calls to action, or other valuable content related to the cause.

- **Add your own commentary:** When retweeting, consider adding your own commentary to provide context, express your support, or encourage your followers to take action.

- **Quote tweet with your thoughts:** Use the quote tweet feature to share your thoughts and reactions to the original tweet, adding your own perspective and amplifying the message to your followers.

- **Create Twitter lists:** Create Twitter lists of accounts that focus on the cause you're supporting. This can make it easier for you to find and share relevant content and to connect with other supporters.

Examples of Tweets Amplifying Voices:

- **Retweet with Commentary:** "Retweeting this important message from @[Organization/Individual] about [Issue]. We need to do more to support [Solution/Action]. #[Issue] #Amplify #TakeAction"

- **Quote Tweet with Thoughts:** "[Quote Tweet] This is a powerful story that highlights the impact of [Issue] on [Affected Group/Community]. We must work together to create a more just and equitable world. #[Issue] #Empathy #Solidarity"

- **Sharing a Twitter List:** "I've created a Twitter list of organizations and individuals working to address [Issue]. Follow this list to stay informed and get involved: [Link to List] #[Issue] #Resources #GetInvolved"

Fundraising and Donations: Tweeting to Support Financial Needs

Many causes and organizations rely on financial support to carry out their work. Twitter can be an effective platform for fundraising and encouraging donations, allowing you to reach a wider audience, share compelling stories, and connect people with opportunities to contribute financially.

Tips for Tweeting to Fundraise and Encourage Donations:

- **Partner with organizations:** Collaborate with organizations that are working on the cause you're supporting. Promote their fundraising campaigns, share their donation links, and encourage your followers to contribute.

- **Tell compelling stories:** Share stories of how donations have made a difference in the lives of individuals or communities affected by the issue. Use personal anecdotes, photos, or videos to illustrate the impact of financial support.

- **Offer incentives:** Consider offering incentives for donations, such as matching donations up to a certain amount, offering exclusive merchandise or experiences, or providing public recognition for donors.

- **Create a sense of urgency:** Communicate the urgency of the need and emphasize the impact that even small donations can have. Use time-sensitive language, such as "donate today" or "every dollar counts."

- **Use Twitter's fundraising features:** Twitter has built-in features for fundraising, allowing you to create donation stickers for your tweets or to launch a fundraising campaign directly on the platform.

- **Promote matching campaigns:** If an organization is running a matching campaign, where donations are matched by a sponsor, promote this opportunity to encourage people to give.

- **Share progress updates:** Keep your followers informed about the progress of the fundraising campaign, sharing milestones, achievements, and expressions of gratitude for the support received.

Examples of Tweets for Fundraising and Donations:

- **Promoting a Campaign:** "Support @[Organization]'s fundraising campaign to [Goal]. Every donation helps to make a difference in the lives of [Affected Group/Community]. Donate here: [Link] #[Issue] #Fundraising #MakeADifference"

- **Sharing an Impact Story:** "This is [Name], a [Beneficiary of Organization's Work]. Thanks to your generous donations, [Name] is now able to [Positive Outcome]. Your support is changing lives! #[Issue] #DonationImpact #Storytelling" (Include a photo or video of the beneficiary)

- **Offering Incentives:** "I'll be matching all donations to @[Organization] up to [Amount] today! Let's double our impact and support their work to [Goal]. #[Issue] #MatchingDonations #GivingTuesday"

- **Sense of Urgency:** "Every dollar counts! Help us reach our goal of [Amount] to [Goal] by [Deadline]. Donate today and make a difference! #[Issue] #Fundraising #TimeSensitive"

- **Sharing Progress Update:** "We've raised [Amount] so far for @[Organization]'s campaign to [Goal]! Thank you to everyone who has donated! We're getting closer to our goal, but we still need your support. Donate here: [Link] #[Issue] #FundraisingUpdate #Gratitude"

Advocating for Change: Tweeting to Influence Policy and Action

Twitter can be a powerful tool for advocating for change, whether it's influencing policy decisions, holding elected officials accountable, or mobilizing support for specific legislation or initiatives. By using your platform to raise awareness, engage with decision-makers, and mobilize your followers, you can contribute to creating a more just and equitable world.

Tips for Tweeting to Advocate for Change:

- **Research the issue and the relevant policies:** Before advocating for change, make sure you have a thorough understanding of the issue, the current policies, and the proposed solutions.

- **Identify the key decision-makers:** Determine who has the power to make the changes you're advocating for, such as elected officials, government agencies, or corporate leaders.

- **Tag decision-makers in your tweets:** Tag the relevant decision-makers in your tweets to bring the issue to their attention and to encourage them to take action.

- **Use strong and persuasive language:** Craft your tweets with strong and persuasive language that clearly articulates your position and your call to action.

- **Provide evidence to support your arguments:** Support your claims with data, research, and personal stories that illustrate the need for change.

- **Mobilize your followers:** Encourage your followers to take action by contacting their elected officials, signing petitions, attending protests, or donating to organizations that are working on the issue.

- **Share success stories:** When your advocacy efforts lead to positive change, celebrate those victories and share them with your followers to inspire further action.

Examples of Tweets Advocating for Change:

- **Tagging Decision-Makers:** "Hey @[ElectedOfficial], I urge you to support [Policy/Legislation] that addresses [Issue]. Your constituents are counting on you to take a stand. #[Policy/Legislation] #[Issue] #HoldThemAccountable"

- **Persuasive Language:** "We need to demand action on [Issue]. The current situation is unacceptable, and we must work together to create a more just and equitable future. #[Issue] #DemandChange #EnoughIsEnough"

- **Evidence-Based Advocacy:** "Studies have shown that [Policy/Action] would have a positive impact on [Outcome]. We need to implement these solutions to address [Issue]. #[Issue] #EvidenceBasedPolicy #Solutions"

- **Mobilizing Followers:** "Call your elected officials today and demand action on [Issue]. Your voice matters! Here's how to contact them: [Link to Contact Information] #[Issue] #MakeYourVoiceHeard #CivicEngagement"

- **Celebrating a Victory:** "We did it! After months of advocacy, [Policy/Legislation] has been passed! This is a major victory for [Cause] and a step towards a better future. #[Issue] #Victory #Progress"

Inspiring Action: Tweeting to Motivate and Mobilize

Tweeting about causes you care about can be more than just sharing information or expressing opinions. It can also be a powerful way to inspire action and mobilize your followers to get involved and make a difference.

Tips for Tweeting to Inspire Action:

- **Use strong calls to action:** Clearly state what you want your followers to do, using action verbs and specific instructions.

- **Highlight the impact of their actions:** Explain how their actions can contribute to a solution or make a positive impact on the issue.

- **Make it easy to take action:** Provide links to petitions, donation pages, volunteer opportunities, or other resources that make it easy for your followers to get involved.

- **Share stories of success:** Share stories of individuals or groups who have taken action and made a difference. These stories can inspire others to get involved and show that their actions can have a real impact.

- **Use motivational language and imagery:** Use words and visuals that evoke emotions, inspire hope, and create a sense of urgency.

- **Create a sense of community:** Foster a sense of community by connecting with other supporters, sharing your experiences, and celebrating your collective achievements.

Examples of Tweets Inspiring Action:

- **Strong Call to Action:** "Sign this petition to demand action on [Issue]: [Link to Petition] Every signature counts! #[Issue] #Petition #MakeYourVoiceHeard"

- **Highlighting Impact:** "Even a small donation can make a big difference in the lives of [Affected Group/Community]. Donate to [Organization] today and help to [Goal]: [Link to Donation Page] #[Issue] #DonationImpact #EveryDollarCounts"

- **Easy Action Steps:** "Here are three simple ways you can support [Cause] today: 1) [Action Step 1] 2) [Action Step 2] 3) [Action Step 3] #[Cause] #TakeAction #MakeADifference"

- **Sharing a Success Story:** "Inspired by [Person/Group] who took action and made a difference on [Issue]. Their story shows that we can all make a positive impact. Read more about their efforts here: [Link] #[Issue] #Inspiration #Changemakers"

- **Motivational Language:** "Together, we can create a better world. Let's stand up for what we believe in, fight for justice, and make our voices heard. #[Issue] #UnitedWeStand #NeverGiveUp"

Measuring Your Impact: Tracking Your Twitter Activism

While the impact of social media activism can be difficult to quantify, there are ways to track your progress and measure the effectiveness of your efforts on Twitter. By monitoring your engagement, reach, and the actions taken by your followers, you can gain insights into the impact of your tweets and make adjustments to your strategy as needed.

Tips for Measuring Your Twitter Activism:

- **Track your engagement:** Monitor the number of likes, retweets, replies, and mentions you receive on your tweets related to the cause. This can give you an indication of how many people are engaging with your content.

- **Use Twitter Analytics:** Twitter Analytics provides insights into the reach and impressions of your tweets, as well as the demographics of your audience. This data can help you to understand who is seeing your messages and how they're responding.

- **Track link clicks:** If you include links to petitions, donation pages, or other resources in your tweets, use link shortening services like Bitly to track the number of clicks on those links. This can give you an indication of how many people are taking action based on your tweets.

- **Ask for feedback from your followers:** Consider asking your followers for feedback on your tweets related to the cause. You could create a poll asking them how your messages make them feel, what actions they've taken, or what kind of content they find most helpful or inspiring.

- **Monitor the conversation around the issue:** Use Twitter's search function to monitor the conversation around the issue you're supporting. Pay attention to the hashtags being used, the key influencers involved, and the overall sentiment of the discussion.

- **Focus on quality over quantity:** The number of followers or likes you have is less important than the quality of your engagement and the impact of your actions. Focus on creating meaningful conversations, inspiring action, and making a real difference, even if it's on a smaller scale.

Examples of Tweets Measuring Your Impact:

- **Tracking Engagement:** "I'm seeing a lot of engagement on my tweets about [Issue]. It's encouraging to know that people are interested in learning more and taking action. #[Issue] #TwitterActivism #MakingADifference"

- **Using Twitter Analytics:** "Just checked my Twitter Analytics and my tweets about [Issue] reached over [Number] people this week! I'm using this data to refine my strategy and make sure my message is reaching the right audience. #[Issue] #DataDrivenActivism #TwitterAnalytics"

- **Tracking Link Clicks:** "Over [Number] people clicked on the link to the [Petition/Donation Page] in my tweet about [Issue]! It's amazing to see people taking action based on my tweets. #[Issue] #TwitterImpact #CallToAction"

- **Asking for Feedback:** "I'm curious to know how my tweets about [Issue] have inspired you to take action. Have you donated to an organization, contacted your elected officials, or volunteered your time? Share your experiences in the comments! #[Issue] #Feedback #ImpactAssessment"

- **Monitoring the Conversation:** "I'm monitoring the conversation around [Issue] on Twitter to see what people are saying, what hashtags are trending, and what actions are being taken. #[Issue] #SocialListening #StayInformed"

Ethics and Responsibility: Tweeting with Integrity

Using Twitter for activism and advocacy carries a certain level of responsibility. It's important to approach your efforts with integrity, honesty, and a commitment to ethical practices.

Tips for Tweeting with Integrity:

- **Be transparent about your affiliations:** If you're affiliated with an organization or campaign, be transparent about your involvement. Disclose your connections and avoid any conflicts of interest.

- **Don't spread misinformation:** Double-check your facts and sources before sharing information. Avoid spreading rumors, conspiracy theories, or unsubstantiated claims.

- **Don't manipulate or exploit emotions:** While it's important to connect with people on an emotional level, avoid manipulating or exploiting their emotions for personal gain or to advance your agenda.

- **Respect privacy:** Don't share personal information about others without their consent. Be mindful of the privacy of individuals who are involved in the cause, especially if they are vulnerable or at risk.

- **Be accountable for your actions:** Be prepared to be held accountable for your tweets and your actions. Acknowledge your mistakes, apologize for any harm caused, and learn from your experiences.

Examples of Tweets Demonstrating Ethical Practices:

- **Transparency:** "Full disclosure: I'm a volunteer for @[Organization] and I'm passionate about their work on [Issue]. I'm tweeting in support of their campaign to [Goal]. #[Issue] #Transparency #Volunteer"

- **Fact-Checking:** "Before sharing information about [Issue] on social media, please take a moment to verify it from multiple sources. It's important to be accurate and to avoid spreading misinformation. #[Issue] #FactCheck #ReliableSources"

- **Respecting Privacy:** "I'm sharing stories about the impact of [Issue] on individuals, but I'm being mindful of their privacy and avoiding sharing any identifying information without their consent. #[Issue] #RespectPrivacy #EthicalStorytelling"

- **Accountability:** "I made a mistake in my previous tweet about [Issue]. I apologize for any confusion or misinformation I may have caused. I've corrected the information here: [Link to Corrected Tweet] #Accountability #LearningFromMistakes"

Self-Care for Activists: Tweeting with Balance

Using Twitter for activism and advocacy can be emotionally draining, especially when dealing with sensitive or challenging issues. It's important to prioritize your own mental health and well-being and to find ways to balance your online activism with self-care practices.

Tips for Self-Care for Activists on Twitter:

- **Set boundaries:** Limit your time on Twitter and schedule regular breaks. Don't feel obligated to engage with every tweet or to be constantly online.

- **Curate your feed:** Mute or block accounts or hashtags that are consistently negative or triggering. Follow accounts that inspire you, uplift you, and provide a positive counterbalance to the negativity.

- **Connect with supportive communities:** Find online or offline communities of like-minded individuals who are passionate about the same causes. Share your experiences, offer support to each other, and celebrate your collective achievements.

- **Engage in offline activities:** Balance your online activism with offline activities that bring you joy, such as spending time in nature, pursuing hobbies, connecting with loved ones, or engaging in physical activity.

- **Seek professional help if needed:** If you're feeling overwhelmed, stressed, or anxious, don't hesitate to seek professional help from a therapist or counselor.

Examples of Tweets Promoting Self-Care for Activists:

- **Setting Boundaries:** "Taking a break from Twitter today to recharge and reconnect with myself. It's important to step away from the digital world sometimes and focus on self-care. #[SelfCare] #DigitalDetox #MentalHealth"

- **Curating Your Feed:** "I'm unfollowing accounts that are consistently negative or triggering and following more accounts that share positive news, inspiring stories, and uplifting messages. #CuratingMyFeed #Positivity #MindfulScrolling"

- **Connecting with Supportive Communities:** "Grateful for the supportive community of activists I've found on Twitter. It's inspiring to connect with others who are passionate about the same causes and to work together to make a difference. #[Cause] #Community #SupportSystem"

- **Engaging in Offline Activities:** "Balancing my online activism with offline activities that bring me joy, such as hiking, reading, and spending time with loved ones. It's important to find balance and to take care of myself. #[SelfCare] #OfflineLife #Balance"

Sustaining Your Activism: Tweeting for the Long Haul

Social change is a marathon, not a sprint. Sustaining your activism over the long haul requires commitment, resilience, and a willingness to adapt your strategies as needed.

Tips for Sustaining Your Twitter Activism:

- **Pace yourself:** Don't burn yourself out by trying to do too much too soon. Set realistic goals, prioritize your efforts, and take breaks when needed.

- **Stay informed:** Keep up-to-date on the latest developments related to the cause you're supporting. Follow relevant news sources, experts, and organizations to stay informed about new research, policy changes, and opportunities for action.

- **Be adaptable:** The social media landscape is constantly changing, and the strategies that work today might not be effective tomorrow. Be willing to experiment with new approaches, adapt your tactics, and learn from your experiences.

- **Celebrate small victories:** Social change can be a slow and incremental process. Celebrate the small victories along the way to stay motivated and inspired.

- **Don't give up:** There will be setbacks, challenges, and moments of discouragement. But don't give up on the causes you care about. Keep fighting for a better world, one tweet at a time.

Examples of Tweets Promoting Sustainable Activism:

- **Pacing Yourself:** "I'm committed to supporting [Cause] for the long haul, but I'm also mindful of the need for self-care and balance. I'm pacing myself, setting realistic goals, and taking breaks when needed. #SustainableActivism #[Cause] #LongTermCommitment"

- **Staying Informed:** "Staying up-to-date on the latest news and research related to [Issue] by following [News Sources/Experts/Organizations]. Knowledge is power, and staying informed is essential for effective activism. #[Issue] #StayInformed #KnowledgeIsPower"

- **Adapting to Change:** "The social media landscape is constantly evolving, so I'm always experimenting with new approaches to my Twitter activism. It's important to be adaptable and to find what works best for me and the cause I'm supporting. #[Cause] #SocialMediaStrategy #Adaptability"

- **Celebrating Small Victories:** "Celebrating a small victory today! [Achievement/Milestone]. Even small steps forward can make a big difference in the long run. #[Cause] #SmallVictories #Progress"

- **Persistence and Resilience:** "There will be setbacks and challenges along the way, but I'm committed to fighting for [Cause] no matter what. Never give up on the things you believe in. #[Cause] #Persistence #Resilience"

A Few Final Tips for Tweeting About Causes

- **Be authentic and passionate:** Let your genuine passion for the cause shine through in your tweets. Your enthusiasm will be contagious and inspire others to get involved.

- **Be respectful and inclusive:** Remember that people come from diverse backgrounds and hold different perspectives. Be respectful of those who disagree with you, and avoid using language that could be offensive or alienating.

- **Don't be afraid to be vulnerable:** Sharing your personal experiences, your struggles, and your triumphs can make your tweets more relatable and inspire others to connect with the cause on a deeper level.

- **Collaborate and build community:** Connect with other supporters, organizations, and influencers who are working on the same cause. Collaboration amplifies your impact and creates a sense of collective effort.

- **Be patient and persistent:** Social change takes time and effort. Don't get discouraged if you don't see immediate results. Keep tweeting, keep advocating, and keep believing in the power of collective action.

By using Twitter thoughtfully and strategically, you can contribute to making the world a better place. Your tweets can raise awareness, inspire action, and mobilize support for causes that matter. So go forth, find your cause, and unleash the power of your Twitter voice for good.

CHAPTER TWENTY: Building Your Personal Brand on Twitter

So, you've mastered the art of crafting witty tweets, engaging in thoughtful discussions, and even using emojis like a pro. But are you using Twitter (or X) to its full potential? Are you building a personal brand that reflects your unique personality, expertise, and aspirations?

This chapter dives into the world of personal branding on Twitter. We'll explore why a strong personal brand is crucial in today's digital landscape, how to define your unique value proposition, and the steps you can take to cultivate a compelling online presence that attracts followers, builds credibility, and opens doors to new opportunities.

Why Personal Branding Matters: Standing Out in the Digital Crowd

In the vast, ever-expanding universe of Twitter, it's easy to get lost in the noise. With millions of users vying for attention, a strong personal brand is no longer a luxury – it's a necessity. It's the key to differentiating yourself, establishing your credibility, and attracting the right audience.

Think of your personal brand as your digital reputation, the online persona that reflects your values, your expertise, and your unique contribution to the world. A strong personal brand helps you to:

- **Stand out from the crowd:** In a sea of profiles, a well-defined personal brand helps you to stand out, attracting the attention of potential followers, collaborators, employers, or clients.

- **Establish your credibility:** A consistent and authentic personal brand builds trust and credibility, showcasing your expertise and making you a go-to resource in your field.

- **Attract your ideal audience:** By clearly communicating your interests, expertise, and values, you attract followers who are genuinely interested in what you have to say and who are more likely to engage with your content.

- **Open doors to opportunities:** A strong personal brand can lead to new opportunities, such as speaking engagements, collaborations, job offers, or even business ventures.

- **Control your narrative:** Building your own personal brand allows you to control the narrative around your online presence, shaping how others perceive you and your work.

Defining Your Brand: What Makes You Unique?

Before you start crafting your Twitter bio and tweeting your heart out, take some time to define your personal brand. What makes you unique? What are your passions, your skills, your experiences, and your values? What do you want to be known for?

This introspection is crucial for creating a brand that is both authentic and compelling. Consider these questions:

- **What are your passions and interests?:** What topics do you love to talk about? What are you naturally drawn to? Your passions will fuel your enthusiasm and make your tweets more engaging.

- **What are your skills and expertise?:** What are you good at? What knowledge or skills do you possess that others might find valuable? Your expertise can be a source of credibility and make you a go-to resource in your field.

- **What are your unique experiences?:** What life experiences, professional accomplishments, or personal challenges have shaped your perspective and your worldview? Your experiences can add depth and authenticity to your brand.

- **What are your core values?:** What principles guide your actions and decisions? What do you stand for? Your values can shape your brand's messaging and attract followers who share similar beliefs.

- **What do you want to achieve with your personal brand?:** What are your goals? Are you hoping to build a following, connect with potential employers, promote your business, or simply share your passions with the world? Your goals will influence your content strategy and your approach to building your brand.

Crafting Your Twitter Profile: Your Digital First Impression

Your Twitter profile is your digital first impression. It's the first thing people see when they visit your page, and it's your opportunity to make a strong and lasting impact.

Tips for Crafting a Compelling Twitter Profile:

- **Choose a professional profile picture:** Use a high-quality photo of yourself that is both professional and approachable. Avoid using blurry photos, group photos, or images that are unrelated to your personal brand.

- **Write a concise and compelling bio:** Your bio is your elevator pitch, your chance to summarize your personal brand in a few short sentences. Highlight your expertise, your interests, your values, and your goals.

- **Use keywords strategically:** Incorporate relevant keywords into your bio that people might use to search for someone with your skills or expertise. This will help your profile show up in search results.

- **Include a call to action:** Encourage people to follow you, visit your website, or connect with you on other platforms.

- **Use your header image creatively:** Your header image is valuable real estate on your profile. Use it to showcase your personality, your work, or your brand's aesthetic.

- **Pin a relevant tweet:** Pin a tweet to the top of your profile that highlights your expertise, your latest project, or a piece of content that you want to promote.

- **Update your profile regularly:** Keep your profile updated with your latest accomplishments, projects, and interests. A stale profile can make you seem inactive or unengaged.

Examples of Compelling Twitter Bios:

- **Expert Bio:** "[Your Name] | [Your Expertise] | Helping [Target Audience] achieve [Goal] | [Call to Action] #[Keyword] #[Keyword]"

- **Passionate Bio:** "[Your Name] | Passionate about [Interest] | Sharing my thoughts on [Topic] | [Call to Action] #[Keyword] #[Keyword]"

- **Humorous Bio:** "[Your Name] | [Your Expertise] | Making [Industry] less boring, one tweet at a time | [Call to Action] #[Keyword] #[Keyword]"

Crafting Your Content Strategy: Tweeting with Purpose

Your content strategy is the foundation of your personal brand on Twitter. It's the blueprint for the types of tweets you'll share, the topics you'll cover, the tone you'll use, and the goals you'll pursue. A well-defined content strategy ensures that your tweets are consistent with your brand, engage your target audience, and contribute to your overall goals.

Tips for Crafting Your Content Strategy:

- **Identify your target audience:** Who are you trying to reach with your tweets? What are their interests, their needs, and their pain points? Understanding your target audience will help you to create content that resonates with them.

- **Choose relevant topics:** Focus on topics that are relevant to your expertise, your interests, and your brand's messaging. This will establish you as a credible and authoritative voice in your field.

- **Mix up your content formats:** Don't just tweet text-based updates. Incorporate a variety of content formats, such as photos, videos, GIFs, polls, quizzes, and Twitter threads, to keep your content engaging and fresh.

- **Use a consistent tone and voice:** Establish a consistent tone and voice for your tweets that reflects your brand's personality. Are you witty and humorous? Are you informative and analytical? Are you passionate and enthusiastic?

- **Share your unique perspective:** Don't just retweet or rehash content from others. Share your own unique insights, experiences, and opinions to differentiate yourself and provide value to your followers.

- **Be consistent:** Consistency is key to building a strong personal brand on Twitter. Tweet regularly, even if it's just a few times a day, to stay top of mind with your followers.

- **Track your results:** Use Twitter Analytics to track your engagement, reach, and the overall performance of your tweets. This data can help you to refine your content strategy and make adjustments as needed.

Building Your Network: Connecting with Others on Twitter

Twitter is a social platform, and building a strong network is crucial for growing your personal brand. Connecting with other users, engaging in conversations, and building relationships can help you to expand your reach, gain new followers, and establish yourself as a valuable member of the community.

Tips for Building Your Network on Twitter:

- **Follow relevant accounts:** Follow accounts that align with your interests, your expertise, and your target audience. Look for thought leaders, influencers, organizations, publications, and other individuals who are actively engaged in conversations related to your field.

- **Engage in conversations:** Don't just passively consume content. Respond to tweets, ask questions, share your opinions, and participate in discussions to make yourself visible and build connections.

- **Use relevant hashtags:** Hashtags can help you to discover new conversations, connect with people who share your interests, and increase the visibility of your tweets.

- **Participate in Twitter chats:** Twitter chats are organized conversations around specific topics, providing a focused space to engage with other users, share your insights, and build relationships.

- **Attend virtual events:** Many conferences, workshops, and meetups are now held virtually, providing opportunities to connect with other professionals, share your expertise, and expand your network.

- **Be generous and supportive:** Support other users by retweeting their content, amplifying their voices, and offering encouragement and feedback. Building a strong network is a two-way street, and generosity goes a long way.

- **Be authentic and genuine:** People can spot insincerity a mile away. Be authentic in your interactions, be yourself, and focus on building genuine relationships.

Promoting Your Work: Tweeting Your Accomplishments and Projects

Twitter can be a valuable platform for promoting your work, whether you're an entrepreneur, a freelancer, an artist, a writer, or a professional in any field. By sharing your accomplishments, your projects, your insights, and your expertise, you can build credibility, attract potential clients or collaborators, and establish yourself as a thought leader in your field.

Tips for Promoting Your Work on Twitter:

- **Share your achievements:** Don't be afraid to toot your own horn! Share your achievements, your milestones, and your successes to showcase your skills and expertise.

- **Promote your projects:** Tweet about your current projects, your upcoming events, or your latest creations to generate interest and attract potential collaborators or clients.

- **Share your insights and expertise:** Offer valuable insights, tips, and advice related to your field to establish yourself as a thought leader and a go-to resource.

- **Use visuals:** Incorporate photos, videos, and infographics to make your tweets more visually appealing and engaging.

- **Use a call to action:** Encourage people to visit your website, learn more about your services, or connect with you on other platforms.

- **Don't be too self-promotional:** Balance your self-promotional tweets with other types of content, such as engaging discussions, sharing interesting articles, or participating in relevant conversations.

- **Track your results:** Use Twitter Analytics to track the performance of your promotional tweets. This data can help you to refine your strategy and make adjustments as needed.

Engaging with Your Audience: Building Relationships and Trust

Building a strong personal brand on Twitter is not just about broadcasting your message – it's about building relationships with your followers. Engaging with your audience, responding to their comments and questions, and fostering a sense of community can help you to build trust, loyalty, and a stronger connection with your followers.

Tips for Engaging with Your Audience:

- **Respond to comments and questions:** Take the time to respond to comments and questions from your followers, even if it's just a simple "thank you" or a quick answer. This shows that you're listening and that you value their engagement.

- **Ask questions and start conversations:** Don't just talk at your followers – engage them in conversations. Ask questions, solicit their opinions, and create opportunities for dialogue.

- **Use polls and quizzes:** Polls and quizzes are a fun and interactive way to engage your followers and gather insights into their interests and opinions.

- **Host Twitter chats:** Twitter chats are organized conversations around specific topics, providing a focused space to engage with your followers, answer their questions, and share your expertise.

- **Run contests and giveaways:** Contests and giveaways can be a fun way to generate excitement, reward your followers, and attract new followers to your brand.

- **Be authentic and relatable:** People are more likely to connect with you if they feel like they know you and can relate to your experiences. Share personal anecdotes, behind-the-scenes glimpses, and your own unique perspective.

Dealing with Negativity: Protecting Your Brand Reputation

While Twitter can be a positive and supportive platform, you're bound to encounter negativity at some point. Whether it's a critical comment, a negative review, or a troll trying to stir up drama, it's important to handle these situations gracefully and professionally to protect your brand reputation.

Tips for Dealing with Negativity on Twitter:

- **Don't engage with trolls:** Trolls are individuals who deliberately provoke others online for their own amusement. Don't feed the trolls by engaging with them or giving them the attention they crave. Ignore them, block them, or report them to Twitter if their behavior violates the platform's rules.

- **Respond to legitimate criticism constructively:** If someone offers legitimate criticism, take the time to respond thoughtfully and constructively. Acknowledge their concerns, address their points, and offer solutions if possible. This shows that you're open to feedback and that you're committed to providing a positive experience for your followers.

- **Apologize if necessary:** If you make a mistake or if your actions inadvertently offend someone, don't be afraid to apologize. A sincere apology can go a long way in repairing damage and restoring trust.

- **Don't take it personally:** It's easy to take negative comments personally, but remember that not everyone will agree with you or appreciate your work. Don't let the negativity get you down. Focus on the positive feedback and the relationships you're building with your loyal followers.

- **Maintain a professional demeanor:** Even when dealing with difficult situations, maintain a professional demeanor. Avoid getting into heated arguments, using profanity, or making personal attacks. Your responses should reflect your brand's values and professionalism.

Consistency and Evolution: Maintaining Your Personal Brand

Building a strong personal brand on Twitter is not a one-time effort. It's an ongoing process that requires consistency, adaptability, and a willingness to evolve your brand as you grow and change.

Tips for Maintaining Your Personal Brand:

- **Stay true to your values:** Your personal brand should be an authentic reflection of your values, your expertise, and your passions. As you evolve, make sure that your brand continues to align with your core beliefs and aspirations.

- **Adapt to the changing landscape:** The social media landscape is constantly evolving. Be willing to experiment with new strategies, adapt your tactics, and stay informed about the latest trends and best practices.

- **Listen to your audience:** Pay attention to the feedback you receive from your followers. What kind of content resonates with them? What are their interests and needs? Use this feedback to refine your content strategy and make adjustments to your brand's messaging.

- **Don't be afraid to experiment:** Try new things, experiment with different content formats, and explore new ways to engage your audience. Don't be afraid to take risks and step outside of your comfort zone.

- **Stay passionate:** Your passion for your brand will shine through in your tweets and inspire others to connect with you. Keep learning, keep growing, and keep sharing your enthusiasm with the world.

Building a strong personal brand on Twitter is a journey, not a destination. It's an ongoing process of self-discovery, experimentation, and engagement. By following these tips and strategies, you can cultivate a compelling online presence that reflects your unique value, attracts your ideal audience, and opens doors to new opportunities. So, go forth, unleash your authentic self, and build a personal brand that makes you proud.

CHAPTER TWENTY-ONE: Engaging with Your Followers

You've crafted the perfect profile, honed your tweeting style, and maybe even gained a few followers. Now what? It's time to engage! Because a Twitter (or X) account with no engagement is like a party with no guests – a little sad and definitely missing the point.

This chapter is all about turning your followers into a vibrant, interactive community. We'll explore the why, the how, and the what of engaging on Twitter. From responding to comments and sparking conversations to mastering the art of the retweet and using polls like a pro, you'll learn how to transform your feed from a one-way broadcast into a dynamic dialogue.

Why Engagement Matters: It's Not Just About the Numbers

It's easy to get caught up in the follower count game on Twitter. More followers, more influence, right? Well, not exactly. While a large following can be impressive, it's meaningless if those followers are just passive observers, scrolling past your tweets without a second glance.

Engagement – that magical interaction between you and your followers – is the true measure of success on Twitter. Here's why:

- **Builds Relationships:** Engagement is the foundation of any meaningful connection. Responding to comments, answering questions, and participating in discussions shows your followers that you're not just broadcasting into the void – you're actively listening and valuing their input.

- **Increases Visibility:** Twitter's algorithm favors engagement. The more your tweets are liked, retweeted, commented on, and shared, the more likely they are to appear in other users' feeds, even those who don't follow you.

- **Sparks Conversations:** Engagement isn't just about responding to others – it's also about starting conversations. Asking questions, sharing thought-provoking content, and encouraging dialogue can transform your feed into a hub of discussion and debate.

- **Humanizes Your Brand:** Whether you're building a personal or professional brand, engagement makes you more human. It allows your personality to shine through, showing your followers that you're not just a faceless entity – you're a real person with thoughts, opinions, and (gasp!) emotions.

- **Creates a Sense of Community:** A highly engaged Twitter account becomes more than just a collection of tweets – it transforms into a community, a space where people gather to share ideas, discuss their passions, and connect with like-minded individuals.

The Basics: Responding to Comments and Mentions

The most fundamental form of engagement on Twitter is responding to comments and mentions. It seems simple enough, but it's often overlooked. Don't be that person who tweets into the void and then disappears, leaving their followers' comments hanging in digital limbo.

Tips for Responding to Comments and Mentions:

- **Be Timely:** No one likes to be ignored. Respond to comments and mentions as promptly as possible, ideally within a few hours. The faster you respond, the more likely the conversation will continue.

- **Be Personable:** Even if it's just a simple "Thanks!", add a personal touch to your responses. Use the person's Twitter handle, acknowledge their comment specifically, and show that you're actually reading and appreciating their input.

- **Go Beyond the Basic Reply:** Don't just offer generic responses like "Great point!" or "Thanks for sharing." Add to the conversation by expanding on their point, asking a follow-up question, or sharing a related anecdote.

- **Use Humor and Wit (When Appropriate):** Humor can be a great way to make your responses more engaging and memorable. But be mindful of the context and avoid using humor that could be misconstrued as offensive or insensitive.

- **Know When to Disengage:** Not every comment warrants a response. If someone is being abusive, trolling, or simply trying to start an argument, it's best to ignore them, block them, or report them to Twitter if their behavior violates the platform's rules.

Examples of Engaging Responses:

Comment: "Great article! I completely agree with your points about [Topic]."

Engaging Response: "Thanks, @[TwitterUser]! I'm glad you found the article insightful. What are your thoughts on [Specific Point from the Article]?"

Mention: "@[YourTwitterHandle] What's your favorite [Type of Food/Movie/Book/Music]?"

Engaging Response: "Hey @[TwitterUser], that's a great question! My all-time favorite [Type of Food/Movie/Book/Music] is definitely [Your Choice]. What about you?"

Comment: "This is a terrible article. You're completely wrong about everything."

Non-Engaging Response: "You're wrong."

Engaging Response (If You Choose to Engage): "I understand that you disagree with my perspective, @[TwitterUser]. I'm curious to hear more about your viewpoint. What specific points did you disagree with, and why?"

Beyond the Basics: Sparking Conversations and Building Engagement

Responding to comments and mentions is just the first step. To truly level up your engagement game, you need to proactively spark conversations, create opportunities for interaction, and foster a sense of community around your tweets.

Tips for Sparking Conversations and Building Engagement:

- **Ask Questions:** Questions are conversation starters. Ask your followers about their opinions, their experiences, their recommendations, or anything else that might spark a dialogue.

- **Share Thought-Provoking Content:** Tweets that provoke thought, challenge assumptions, or spark debate are more likely to generate comments and discussions.

- **Use Polls and Quizzes:** Polls and quizzes are a fun and interactive way to engage your followers, gather insights, and spark conversations.

- **Run Contests and Giveaways:** Contests and giveaways can generate excitement, increase engagement, and attract new followers.

- **Host Twitter Chats:** Twitter chats are organized conversations around specific topics, providing a focused space for discussion and interaction.

- **Live-Tweet Events:** Live-tweeting events, such as conferences, award shows, or sporting events, can create a sense of community and shared experience.

- **Use Humor and Wit:** Humor is a universal language that can connect people and make your tweets more memorable. But be mindful of the context and avoid offensive or insensitive humor.

- **Be Authentic and Vulnerable:** Sharing personal stories, challenges, or triumphs can make you more relatable and humanize your brand.

Examples of Tweets Sparking Conversations:

- **Question:** "What's the best book you've read this year? #BookRecommendations #ReadingCommunity"

- **Thought-Provoking Statement:** "I think [Controversial Opinion]. What are your thoughts? #[Topic] #Debate #DifferentPerspectives"

- **Poll:** "Which [Movie/TV Show/Music Album] are you most excited about this year? #Poll #[Topic] #Entertainment"

- **Contest:** "Retweet this tweet and follow me to enter to win a [Prize]! Winner will be announced on [Date]. #Contest #Giveaway #[Topic]"

- **Twitter Chat Announcement:** "Join me for the #[ChatHashtag] Twitter chat on [Date] at [Time] to discuss [Topic]. #TwitterChat #[Topic] #Discussion"

- **Live-Tweet:** "Live-tweeting the #[EventName] tonight! Follow along for updates, commentary, and behind-the-scenes insights. #[EventName] #LiveTweet #EventCoverage"

- **Humorous Tweet:** "[Relatable Joke About Everyday Life] #Humor #Relatable #Life"

- **Vulnerable Tweet:** "Sharing a personal story about [Challenge/Triumph]. It's important to be vulnerable and to connect with others who might be going through similar experiences. #[Topic] #Vulnerability #SharingMyStory"

The Art of the Retweet: Sharing and Amplifying Content

Retweeting is a simple yet powerful way to engage with other users, share valuable content, and expand your reach on Twitter. It's also an effective way to show your support for others, amplify their voices, and contribute to the conversation.

Tips for Mastering the Art of the Retweet:

- **Be Selective:** Don't retweet everything you see. Be selective about the content you share, choosing tweets that are relevant to your interests, your brand, and your target audience.

- **Add Commentary:** When retweeting, consider adding your own commentary to provide context, express your opinion, or encourage engagement from your followers.

- **Use Quote Tweets:** Quote tweets allow you to share the original tweet along with your own commentary, providing more space for your thoughts and reactions.

- **Retweet Different Types of Content:** Don't just retweet text-based updates. Share articles, videos, infographics, photos, and other types of content that you find valuable or interesting.

- **Retweet from Diverse Sources:** Amplify the voices of underrepresented groups, diverse perspectives, and individuals or organizations that are working to make a difference.

- **Be Mindful of the Source:** Before retweeting, consider the source of the information. Is it a credible source? Is the information accurate? Avoid retweeting content from sources that are known to spread misinformation or to engage in unethical practices.

Examples of Effective Retweets:

- **Retweet with Commentary:** "RT @[TwitterUser] This is a great article about [Topic]. I especially agree with the point about [Specific Point]. #[Topic] #MustRead"

- **Quote Tweet with Opinion:** "[Quote Tweet] I completely disagree with this statement. Here's why: [Your Reasoning] #[Topic] #DifferentPerspective"

- **Retweet with Call to Action:** "RT @[Organization] Please consider donating to this worthy cause. Every little bit helps! #[Cause] #Fundraising #MakeADifference"

- **Retweet from a Diverse Source:** "RT @[UnderrepresentedVoice] This is a powerful story that needs to be heard. #[Issue] #Amplify #RepresentationMatters"

Poll Power: Engaging Your Followers with Interactive Content

Polls are a fun, easy, and effective way to engage your followers, gather insights, and spark conversations. Whether you're asking for opinions, testing your followers' knowledge, or simply having a bit of fun, polls can be a great tool for boosting your engagement and creating a more interactive experience on Twitter.

Tips for Creating Engaging Polls:

- **Ask Clear and Concise Questions:** Keep your poll questions clear, concise, and easy to understand. Avoid

using jargon or complex language that might confuse your
followers.

- **Offer Compelling Choices:** Provide answer choices that
  are interesting, relevant, and likely to spark debate or
  discussion.

- **Use a Variety of Poll Formats:** Twitter allows you to
  create polls with multiple choice answers, yes/no answers,
  or even emoji-based answers. Experiment with different
  formats to keep your polls fresh and engaging.

- **Use Relevant Hashtags:** Hashtags can help increase the
  visibility of your polls and connect them to relevant
  conversations.

- **Promote Your Polls:** Share your polls with your followers
  and encourage them to participate. You can also promote
  your polls in other online communities or on other social
  media platforms.

- **Share the Results:** Once the poll has ended, share the
  results with your followers and discuss the findings. This
  can provide valuable insights into your audience's
  preferences and opinions.

Examples of Engaging Polls:

- **Opinion Poll:** "What's your favorite [Type of
  Food/Movie/Book/Music]? #Poll #[Topic]" (Offer a choice
  of four or five popular options)

- **Knowledge-Based Poll:** "Can you guess the [Trivia
  Question]? #[Topic] #Trivia #TestYourKnowledge" (Offer
  a choice of four possible answers)

- **Emoji Poll:** "How are you feeling today? #Mood
  #EmojiPoll" (Offer a choice of four or five emojis that
  represent different moods)

- **Decision-Making Poll:** "I'm trying to decide between [Option A] and [Option B]. Which one should I choose? #Poll #DecisionMaking #HelpMeDecide"

- **Fun Poll:** "Would you rather [Humorous Scenario A] or [Humorous Scenario B]? #WouldYouRather #FunPoll #SillyQuestions"

Measuring Engagement: Tracking Your Success

Tracking your engagement on Twitter is crucial for understanding what's working, what's not, and how you can improve your strategy. Twitter Analytics provides a wealth of data that can help you to measure your progress and make data-driven decisions about your engagement efforts.

Key Metrics to Track:

- **Impressions:** Impressions are the number of times your tweets have been seen by users. This metric indicates the potential reach of your content.

- **Engagement Rate:** Engagement rate is the percentage of users who interacted with your tweets (likes, retweets, replies, clicks, etc.) out of the total number of impressions. A higher engagement rate indicates that your content is resonating with your audience.

- **Likes:** Likes are a simple way for users to show their appreciation for your tweets. While likes are a relatively passive form of engagement, they can still be a useful indicator of the popularity of your content.

- **Retweets:** Retweets indicate that users found your content valuable enough to share with their own followers. Retweets are a powerful way to expand your reach and amplify your message.

- **Replies:** Replies indicate that users want to engage with you directly, either to share their thoughts, ask questions, or continue the conversation.

- **Link Clicks:** If you include links in your tweets, track the number of clicks on those links to see how many users are taking action based on your content.

- **Profile Visits:** Track the number of visits to your profile to see how many users are interested in learning more about you or your brand.

- **Follower Growth:** Monitor your follower growth to see if your engagement efforts are attracting new followers to your account.

A Few Final Tips for Engaging with Your Followers

- **Be authentic and genuine:** People can spot insincerity a mile away. Be yourself, share your passions, and engage with your followers in a way that feels natural and authentic.

- **Be consistent:** Consistency is key to building a strong and engaged following. Tweet regularly, participate in conversations, and make engagement a part of your daily Twitter routine.

- **Be patient:** Building a highly engaged following takes time and effort. Don't get discouraged if you don't see immediate results. Keep engaging, keep experimenting, and keep building relationships, and your efforts will eventually pay off.

- **Don't be afraid to ask for help:** If you're struggling to engage your followers or if you're not sure how to improve your strategy, don't be afraid to ask for help from other Twitter users, social media experts, or online resources.

- **Have fun!** Engaging with your followers should be an enjoyable experience. Let your personality shine through, connect with others who share your interests, and enjoy the journey of building a vibrant and interactive Twitter community.

CHAPTER TWENTY-TWO: Handling Negativity and Trolls

Ah, the dark side of Twitter (or X). While the platform can be a source of connection, humor, and inspiration, it also has a shadow side – a breeding ground for negativity, trolls, and all sorts of online unpleasantness. It's the internet equivalent of that one relative who always seems to bring a raincloud to every family gathering.

But fear not, intrepid tweeter! This chapter will equip you with the tools and strategies to navigate the murky waters of negativity and emerge unscathed (or at least with your sanity intact). We'll explore how to identify trolls, deal with negativity effectively, protect your mental health, and ultimately, maintain your sanity in the sometimes chaotic world of social media.

Identifying the Troublemakers: Spotting Trolls and Negative Nancies

Before you can tackle negativity, you need to know what you're dealing with. Not all negative comments are created equal. Some might be genuine criticisms, while others might be the work of trolls or individuals who simply enjoy stirring up trouble.

Here are a few telltale signs that you might be dealing with a troll or a Negative Nancy:

- **They're deliberately provocative:** Trolls often post inflammatory or offensive comments solely for the purpose of provoking a reaction. They thrive on drama and attention, and they're not interested in engaging in meaningful conversations.

- **They're anonymous or use fake accounts:** Many trolls hide behind anonymity, using fake accounts or pseudonyms to avoid accountability for their actions.

- **They engage in personal attacks:** Trolls often resort to personal attacks, insults, and name-calling, rather than addressing the issue at hand.

- **They derail conversations:** Trolls will often derail conversations by introducing irrelevant topics, spreading misinformation, or simply trying to stir up chaos.

- **They're persistent and relentless:** Trolls are notoriously persistent and relentless. They might bombard you with multiple comments, replies, or direct messages, even after you've asked them to stop.

- **They lack empathy and compassion:** Trolls generally lack empathy and compassion for others. They're often indifferent to the harm they cause, and they might even take pleasure in upsetting or angering others.

Negative Nancies, on the other hand, might not be deliberately malicious, but their constant negativity can still be draining and disheartening. They might:

- **Complain constantly:** Negative Nancies seem to find fault with everything, always focusing on the negative aspects of any situation.

- **Criticize without offering solutions:** They might criticize your opinions, your work, or even your personality, without offering any constructive feedback or solutions.

- **Dwell on the negative:** They tend to dwell on negative news, events, or trends, often amplifying fear, anxiety, or pessimism.

- **Drain your energy:** Interacting with Negative Nancies can be emotionally draining and leave you feeling depleted.

Don't Feed the Trolls: The Power of Ignoring

One of the most effective ways to deal with trolls is to simply ignore them. Trolls thrive on attention, and by responding to their provocations, you're essentially giving them what they want – a reaction.

Ignoring a troll can be incredibly difficult, especially when their comments are hurtful or offensive. But remember, trolls are often looking for a rise out of you, and by refusing to engage, you're taking away their power.

Here's why ignoring trolls is often the best strategy:

- **It denies them the attention they crave:** Trolls are attention-seekers. By ignoring them, you're depriving them of the satisfaction of getting a reaction from you.

- **It prevents the situation from escalating:** Responding to a troll often just escalates the situation, leading to a back-and-forth exchange of insults and negativity. Ignoring them prevents the drama from spiraling out of control.

- **It protects your mental health:** Engaging with trolls can be emotionally draining and stressful. Ignoring them protects your mental health and prevents them from ruining your day.

- **It sends a message:** Ignoring a troll sends a powerful message – that their words don't have power over you and that you're not going to waste your time or energy on their negativity.

Of course, ignoring trolls isn't always easy. It can be tempting to fire back a witty comeback or to try to reason with them. But in most cases, ignoring is the most effective way to deal with these digital pests.

Beyond Ignoring: Additional Strategies for Dealing with Trolls

While ignoring is often the best strategy for dealing with trolls, there are situations where other tactics might be necessary.

Here are a few additional strategies:

- **Mute or block the troll:** Twitter allows you to mute or block accounts that you don't want to interact with. Muting an account hides their tweets from your feed, while blocking an account prevents them from following you, seeing your tweets, or sending you direct messages.

- **Report the troll to Twitter:** If a troll's behavior violates Twitter's rules, such as engaging in harassment, abuse, or hate speech, you can report their account to Twitter.

- **Expose the troll's behavior (with caution):** In some cases, it might be appropriate to expose the troll's behavior by publicly calling them out or by retweeting their offensive comments with your own commentary. However, be cautious with this approach, as it can sometimes backfire and give the troll more attention.

- **Use humor to deflect the negativity:** If a troll's comments are particularly absurd or ridiculous, you can sometimes use humor to deflect their negativity and turn the situation around.

- **Engage with a constructive counter-argument:** If a troll is spreading misinformation or making false claims, you can sometimes engage with them by providing evidence-based counter-arguments. However, be prepared for resistance and don't expect to change their mind.

Handling Negativity: Strategies for Dealing with Difficult Comments

Not all negativity on Twitter comes from trolls. Sometimes, you'll encounter genuine criticism, complaints, or negative feedback from real people who have legitimate concerns. It's important to address these situations thoughtfully and professionally to maintain your reputation and to foster a positive online environment.

Tips for Handling Negativity from Real People:

- **Listen actively:** Before responding to a negative comment, take the time to read it carefully and try to understand the person's perspective. Acknowledge their feelings and show empathy, even if you disagree with their opinion.

- **Respond calmly and professionally:** Avoid getting defensive or emotional in your response. Maintain a calm and professional tone, even if you're feeling frustrated or angry.

- **Address the specific concerns:** Don't offer generic or dismissive responses. Address the specific concerns raised in the comment and provide clear and concise answers or explanations.

- **Offer solutions or alternatives:** If the person has a legitimate complaint or concern, try to offer solutions or alternatives. This shows that you're taking their feedback seriously and that you're committed to improving their experience.

- **Take the conversation offline if necessary:** If the conversation becomes heated or unproductive, it might be appropriate to take it offline by suggesting that the person contact you via email or direct message.

- **Know when to disengage:** If someone is being unreasonable, abusive, or simply unwilling to engage in a constructive conversation, it's okay to disengage. You don't have to respond to every negative comment.

Examples of Responses to Negative Comments:

Negative Comment: "I'm really disappointed with [Your Product/Service]. It doesn't work as advertised."

Professional Response: "I'm sorry to hear that you're having trouble with [Your Product/Service], @[TwitterUser]. Can you please provide more details about the issue you're experiencing so that I can assist you? We're committed to resolving any problems and ensuring that our customers are satisfied."

Negative Comment: "Your recent article on [Topic] was terrible. You clearly don't understand the issue."

Constructive Response: "I appreciate your feedback, @[TwitterUser]. I'm always open to hearing different perspectives. Can you please elaborate on what you found problematic about the article? I'm committed to learning and improving my understanding of the issue."

Negative Comment: "You're a terrible writer. Your tweets are boring and uninformative."

Disengagement Response: (Ignore the comment or block the user if their behavior is consistently negative or abusive.)

Protecting Your Mental Health: Staying Sane in the Face of Negativity

It's easy to get caught up in the negativity of Twitter, especially if you're dealing with trolls, hateful comments, or a constant barrage of criticism. It's important to remember that you don't have to subject yourself to this toxicity. You have the power to control your online experience and to protect your mental health.

Tips for Protecting Your Mental Health on Twitter:

- **Be mindful of your emotional state:** Pay attention to how Twitter makes you feel. If you find yourself feeling stressed, anxious, or overwhelmed after using the platform, it might be a sign that you need to take a break or to make some changes to your usage habits.

- **Curate your feed:** Unfollow, mute, or block accounts that consistently post negative or triggering content. Follow accounts that inspire you, uplift you, and make you feel good.

- **Limit your time on Twitter:** Set limits on your Twitter usage and schedule regular breaks. Don't feel obligated to be constantly online or to respond to every notification.

- **Focus on the positive:** Make a conscious effort to engage with positive content, such as inspiring stories, uplifting messages, or humorous observations. This can help to counterbalance the negativity and create a more enjoyable Twitter experience.

- **Don't take it personally:** Remember that the negativity you encounter on Twitter is often a reflection of the person posting it, not of you. Don't let the negativity of others affect your self-worth or your sense of purpose.

- **Connect with supportive communities:** Find online or offline communities of like-minded individuals who share your interests and values. These communities can provide a sense of belonging, support, and encouragement.

- **Engage in self-care practices:** Prioritize your mental health and well-being by engaging in self-care practices that work for you, such as exercise, meditation, spending time in nature, or connecting with loved ones.

- **Seek professional help if needed:** If you're struggling with anxiety, depression, or other mental health issues, don't hesitate to seek professional help from a therapist or counselor.

Examples of Tweets Promoting Mental Health and Well-Being:

- **Mindful Usage:** "I'm taking a break from Twitter today to focus on my mental health and well-being. It's important to step away from the digital world sometimes and recharge. #SelfCare #DigitalDetox #MentalHealthMatters"

- **Curating Your Feed:** "I'm unfollowing accounts that consistently post negative or triggering content. I'm choosing to focus on more positive and uplifting voices. #CuratingMyFeed #Positivity #MentalWellbeing"

- **Connecting with Support:** "Grateful for the supportive community I've found on Twitter. It's a reminder that we're not alone in our struggles and that there are people who care. #Community #SupportSystem #MentalHealth"

- **Offline Activities:** "Balancing my time on Twitter with offline activities that bring me joy, such as hiking, reading, and spending time with loved ones. It's important to find a healthy balance. #OfflineLife #SelfCare #Wellbeing"

Reporting and Blocking: When to Take Action

Twitter has clear rules and guidelines to protect its users from harassment, abuse, and other forms of harmful behavior. If you encounter negativity or abuse that violates these rules, don't hesitate to report it to Twitter.

When to Report or Block:

- **Harassment:** If someone is repeatedly targeting you with unwanted attention, insults, threats, or other forms of harassment, report them to Twitter.

- **Abuse:** If someone is using abusive language, engaging in personal attacks, or making threats of violence, report them to Twitter.

- **Hate speech:** If someone is promoting violence or hatred against a particular group of people based on their race, ethnicity, religion, gender, sexual orientation, or other protected characteristics, report them to Twitter.

- **Spam:** If an account is repeatedly sending you unsolicited messages, promoting products or services, or engaging in other forms of spam, report them to Twitter.

- **Impersonation:** If someone is impersonating you or another user, report them to Twitter.

- **Copyright infringement:** If someone is using your copyrighted material without permission, report them to Twitter.

How to Report or Block:

- **To report a tweet:** Click on the three dots icon in the upper right corner of the tweet and select "Report Tweet."

- **To report an account:** Go to the account's profile, click on the three dots icon, and select "Report."

- **To block an account:** Go to the account's profile, click on the three dots icon, and select "Block @[Account Name]."

A Few Final Tips for Handling Negativity and Trolls

- **Don't take it personally:** The negativity you encounter on Twitter is often a reflection of the person posting it, not of you. Don't let their words define you or your worth.

- **Don't engage in arguments:** Arguing with trolls or negative individuals rarely leads to a productive outcome. It's usually best to ignore them or disengage from the conversation.

- **Focus on building a positive community:** Surround yourself with supportive followers who share your interests and values. Create a positive and engaging online environment where negativity is not tolerated.

- **Remember your purpose:** Why are you on Twitter? What are you hoping to achieve? Focus on your goals and don't let the negativity distract you from your purpose.

- **Take care of yourself:** Protecting your mental health and well-being is paramount. Take breaks when needed, engage in self-care practices, and seek professional help if you're struggling to cope with the negativity.

Twitter can be a wonderful platform for connecting with others, sharing your passions, and building a community. But like any online space, it has its share of negativity and trolls. By following these tips and strategies, you can navigate the dark side of Twitter with grace, resilience, and a healthy dose of humor.

CHAPTER TWENTY-THREE: Mastering the Art of the Hashtag

Hashtags. Those little pound signs (#) followed by a word or phrase that have become ubiquitous on social media. They're more than just a quirky symbol – they're the secret sauce of Twitter (or X, as it's now known), the key to unlocking a world of conversations, communities, and connections.

Think of hashtags as the digital equivalent of filing systems. They organize tweets into categories, making it easier for users to find content that interests them. When you use a hashtag in your tweet, it becomes discoverable by anyone who searches for that hashtag, even if they don't follow you.

This chapter will delve into the strategies and nuances of using hashtags effectively on Twitter. We'll explore the different types of hashtags, tips for choosing the right hashtags for your tweets, common hashtag mistakes to avoid, and how to use hashtags to expand your reach, build your brand, and become a more influential voice in the Twitterverse.

Hashtag Basics: Understanding the Fundamentals

Before we dive into the strategic depths of hashtag mastery, let's start with the fundamentals. A hashtag is simply a word or phrase preceded by a pound sign (#) that categorizes your tweet and makes it discoverable by other users who are interested in that topic.

How Hashtags Work:

- **Categorization:** When you use a hashtag in your tweet, it's automatically grouped with other tweets that use the same hashtag.

- **Discoverability:** Users can search for hashtags on Twitter to find tweets related to specific topics, even if they don't follow the accounts that posted those tweets.

- **Trending Topics:** Hashtags that are being used frequently often become trending topics, appearing in a dedicated section on Twitter's website and app. Trending topics reflect the conversations and events that are currently capturing the attention of the Twitter community.

Types of Hashtags:

- **Brand Hashtags:** Brand hashtags are unique to a specific brand or company, often incorporating their name or a slogan. They're used to promote the brand, track conversations about the brand, and encourage user-generated content.

- **Campaign Hashtags:** Campaign hashtags are used for specific marketing campaigns or events, often with a defined start and end date. They're used to generate buzz, track engagement, and measure the success of the campaign.

- **Event Hashtags:** Event hashtags are used for conferences, festivals, concerts, or other events, allowing attendees and organizers to share updates, photos, and experiences using a common hashtag.

- **Community Hashtags:** Community hashtags are used to connect people who share common interests or passions, creating a virtual space for discussions, sharing, and support.

- **Trending Hashtags:** Trending hashtags are those that are being used frequently at a particular moment, reflecting current events, conversations, or viral trends.

- **Content Hashtags:** Content hashtags are used to categorize tweets based on their content, such as #news, #sports, #music, #travel, or #food.

Choosing the Right Hashtags: A Strategic Approach

The key to using hashtags effectively is to choose the right hashtags for your tweets. The goal is to use hashtags that are relevant to your content, that will reach your target audience, and that will help you to achieve your desired outcomes, whether it's increasing visibility, building your brand, or sparking conversations.

Tips for Choosing the Right Hashtags:

- **Consider your content:** What is the main topic of your tweet? What keywords or phrases would someone use to search for content like yours?

- **Research relevant hashtags:** Use Twitter's search function to explore hashtags related to your topic. Look for hashtags that are being used frequently, that have a high level of engagement, and that align with your target audience.

- **Use a mix of general and specific hashtags:** General hashtags, such as #travel or #photography, cast a wide net, while specific hashtags, such as #solofemaletravel or #wildlifephotography, target a more niche audience. Use a mix of general and specific hashtags to reach both a broad and a targeted audience.

- **Check the hashtag's context:** Before using a hashtag, take a moment to browse the tweets that are already using that hashtag. Make sure that the hashtag is being used for the purpose you intend and that it's not associated with any negative or controversial content.

- **Don't overdo it:** Using too many hashtags can make your tweets look spammy and cluttered. Stick to a few relevant hashtags per tweet, ideally no more than three or four.

- **Use a hashtag tracking tool:** Several tools, such as Hashtagify.me or RiteTag, can help you to research hashtag popularity, track hashtag performance, and discover related hashtags.

Hashtag Best Practices: Tweeting Like a Pro

Once you've chosen the right hashtags, it's important to use them effectively to maximize their impact. Here are a few best practices to keep in mind:

- **Place hashtags at the end of your tweet:** Hashtags are most effective when placed at the end of your tweet, rather than interrupting the flow of your message.

- **Capitalize the first letter of each word in multi-word hashtags:** This improves readability and makes your hashtags easier to understand, especially for screen readers.

- **Use hashtags in a natural and conversational way:** Don't force hashtags into your tweets if they don't fit naturally into the flow of your message.

- **Use a consistent hashtag strategy:** If you're building a brand or promoting a campaign, use a consistent hashtag strategy across all of your tweets and social media platforms.

- **Track your hashtag performance:** Use Twitter Analytics or hashtag tracking tools to monitor the performance of your hashtags. See which hashtags are generating the most engagement and adjust your strategy accordingly.

Hashtag Mistakes: Avoiding Common Pitfalls

Even the most experienced tweeters can make mistakes with hashtags. Here are a few common hashtag blunders to avoid:

- **Using irrelevant hashtags:** Using hashtags that are unrelated to your content is a surefire way to annoy your followers and make your tweets look spammy.

- **Using too many hashtags:** As mentioned earlier, using too many hashtags can make your tweets look cluttered and unprofessional. Stick to a few relevant hashtags per tweet.

- **Using overly long or complicated hashtags:** Hashtags should be easy to read and understand. Avoid using overly long or complicated hashtags that are difficult to remember or type.

- **Using hashtags that are already associated with negative or controversial content:** Always check the context of a hashtag before using it to make sure that it's not associated with any unwanted baggage.

- **Using hashtags that are too broad or too niche:** Strike a balance between general hashtags that cast a wide net and specific hashtags that target a more niche audience.

- **Hijacking trending hashtags:** Don't use trending hashtags that are unrelated to your content just to try to get more visibility. This can be seen as opportunistic and can damage your reputation.

Beyond the Basics: Advanced Hashtag Strategies

Once you've mastered the fundamentals of hashtag usage, you can explore more advanced strategies to take your tweeting to the next level.

Advanced Hashtag Strategies:

- **Create a branded hashtag:** If you're building a brand or promoting a business, create a unique branded hashtag that you use consistently across all of your tweets and social media platforms. This will help to build brand awareness, track conversations about your brand, and encourage user-generated content.

- **Run hashtag contests and giveaways:** Engage your followers and attract new followers by running hashtag contests or giveaways. Ask your followers to tweet about a specific topic using your branded hashtag for a chance to win a prize.

- **Use hashtags to connect with influencers:** Research influencers in your niche who are using relevant hashtags. Engage with their tweets, share their content, and use the same hashtags to get on their radar and potentially build relationships.

- **Use hashtags to monitor industry trends:** Follow hashtags related to your industry or interests to stay informed about the latest trends, news, and conversations.

- **Use hashtags to participate in Twitter chats:** Twitter chats are organized conversations around specific topics, often using a dedicated hashtag. Participating in Twitter chats can help you to connect with other users, share your expertise, and build your network.

- **Use hashtags to support social causes:** Hashtags are often used to raise awareness and mobilize support for social causes. Use relevant hashtags to join the conversation, share your support, and amplify the voices of those working on the issue.

Hashtags and Branding: Building a Consistent Identity

If you're using Twitter to build a personal or professional brand, hashtags can be a powerful tool for creating a consistent brand identity, reinforcing your messaging, and connecting with your target audience.

Tips for Using Hashtags for Branding:

- **Create a branded hashtag:** As mentioned earlier, a branded hashtag is essential for any brand or business on Twitter. It provides a way to track conversations, promote your brand, and encourage user-generated content.

- **Use your branded hashtag consistently:** Incorporate your branded hashtag into all of your relevant tweets, as well as your bio, your header image, and your pinned tweet.

- **Encourage your followers to use your branded hashtag:** Run contests, giveaways, or other promotions to encourage your followers to use your branded hashtag. This will help to spread brand awareness and create a sense of community around your brand.

- **Monitor your branded hashtag:** Use Twitter's search function or a hashtag tracking tool to monitor the conversations happening around your branded hashtag. Engage with users who are using your hashtag, respond to their comments, and address any negative or misleading content.

- **Use other relevant hashtags strategically:** In addition to your branded hashtag, use other relevant hashtags that align with your brand's messaging, your target audience, and the specific content of your tweets.

Hashtags and Analytics: Tracking Your Performance

Twitter Analytics provides a wealth of data that can help you to track the performance of your hashtags and make data-driven decisions about your strategy.

Key Hashtag Metrics to Track:

- **Impressions:** Impressions indicate the number of times your tweets using a specific hashtag have been seen by users.

- **Engagement Rate:** Engagement rate measures the percentage of users who interacted with your tweets using a specific hashtag. A higher engagement rate suggests that the hashtag is effectively reaching your target audience and sparking interest.

- **Top Tweets:** Twitter Analytics shows you the top-performing tweets that used a specific hashtag, allowing you to see which types of content are resonating with your audience.

- **Hashtag Activity:** This metric shows you the volume of tweets using a specific hashtag over time, giving you an indication of the hashtag's popularity and relevance.

By tracking these metrics, you can gain insights into which hashtags are most effective for reaching your target audience, generating engagement, and achieving your desired outcomes. You can then use this data to refine your hashtag strategy, experiment with new hashtags, and optimize your content for maximum impact.

The Future of Hashtags: Evolving with the Platform

Hashtags have become an integral part of the Twitter experience, but as the platform continues to evolve, it's likely that the way we use hashtags will also change.

Potential Future Trends:

- **Increased focus on context and relevance:** As Twitter's algorithm becomes more sophisticated, it's likely that the platform will prioritize hashtags that are highly relevant to the content of the tweet and to the user's interests.

- **Integration with other features:** Hashtags might be integrated with other Twitter features, such as Twitter Spaces, Twitter Communities, or even Twitter's shopping features.

- **New hashtag formats:** Twitter might introduce new hashtag formats, such as interactive hashtags, visual hashtags, or even audio hashtags.

- **Personalization and recommendations:** Twitter might use machine learning to personalize hashtag recommendations based on a user's interests, past behavior, and social connections.

As Twitter continues to evolve, it's important to stay informed about the latest trends, best practices, and innovations related to hashtag usage. By adapting your strategy and experimenting with new approaches, you can ensure that your tweets continue to reach the right audience, generate engagement, and contribute to your overall goals.

CHAPTER TWENTY-FOUR: Using Twitter for Business and Marketing

Twitter (or X, as it's now called), with its fast-paced, real-time nature and massive user base, can be a powerful tool for businesses of all sizes. It's a platform for connecting with customers, building brand awareness, promoting products or services, and even driving sales. But it's not enough to simply create a profile and start tweeting randomly. To harness the true potential of Twitter for business and marketing, you need a strategic approach, a keen understanding of the platform's dynamics, and a commitment to engaging with your audience in a meaningful way.

This chapter will delve into the strategies and tactics that can transform your Twitter presence from a digital ghost town into a bustling hub of customer engagement and brand advocacy. We'll explore the key elements of a successful Twitter marketing strategy, from defining your target audience and crafting compelling content to using hashtags effectively and leveraging Twitter's advertising platform. Get ready to unleash the marketing power of Twitter and turn your followers into loyal customers and brand evangelists.

Defining Your Target Audience: Tweeting to the Right People

Before you start crafting your tweets, you need to know who you're talking to. Who is your target audience on Twitter? What are their interests, their needs, their pain points, and their online behaviors?

Understanding your target audience is crucial for creating content that resonates with them, for using the right hashtags to reach them, and for tailoring your messaging to their specific preferences.

Tips for Defining Your Target Audience:

- **Analyze your existing customer base:** If you have an existing customer base, start by analyzing their demographics, their interests, their online behavior, and their social media usage. What other brands do they follow on Twitter? What kind of content do they engage with?

- **Research your competitors:** Look at the Twitter accounts of your competitors. Who are they following? What kind of content are they posting? What hashtags are they using? This can give you insights into the audience that is already interested in your industry or niche.

- **Use Twitter Analytics:** Twitter Analytics provides valuable data about your followers, including their demographics, their interests, and their engagement patterns. Use this data to gain a deeper understanding of your existing audience and to identify potential new followers.

- **Create buyer personas:** Buyer personas are fictional representations of your ideal customers. Develop detailed profiles of your target audience, including their demographics, their psychographics, their online behaviors, and their motivations. These personas can help you to create more targeted and effective marketing campaigns.

- **Use Twitter's advanced search features:** Twitter's advanced search features allow you to search for users based on keywords, interests, locations, and other criteria. Use these features to identify potential followers who align with your target audience.

Crafting Compelling Content: Tweeting What Your Audience Wants

Content is king on Twitter, and if you want to attract and engage your target audience, you need to create content that is valuable, relevant, and shareable. But what constitutes compelling content for a business on Twitter?

It's not just about promoting your products or services – it's about providing value to your followers, building relationships, and establishing your brand as a trusted source of information, entertainment, or inspiration.

Tips for Crafting Compelling Content:

- **Focus on your audience's needs and interests:** What problems are they trying to solve? What information are they seeking? What kind of content do they find entertaining or inspiring?

- **Share industry insights and expertise:** Establish your brand as a thought leader by sharing your knowledge, insights, and expertise related to your industry or niche.

- **Provide helpful tips and advice:** Offer practical tips, advice, or solutions that your followers can use to improve their lives or their businesses.

- **Showcase your products or services in action:** Don't just tell people about your products or services – show them! Share photos, videos, or testimonials that demonstrate the value and benefits of what you offer.

- **Run contests and giveaways:** Contests and giveaways can generate excitement, increase engagement, and attract new followers.

- **Share behind-the-scenes content:** Give your followers a glimpse into your company culture, your team, or your creative process. This humanizes your brand and makes you more relatable.

- **Curate content from other sources:** Share interesting articles, videos, or tweets from other sources that are relevant to your audience. This shows that you're staying informed about industry trends and that you're a valuable resource for information.

- **Use a variety of content formats:** Don't just tweet text-based updates. Incorporate a variety of content formats, such as photos, videos, GIFs, polls, quizzes, and Twitter threads, to keep your content engaging and fresh.

- **Use a consistent brand voice:** Establish a consistent tone and voice for your tweets that reflects your brand's personality. Are you witty and humorous? Are you informative and analytical? Are you passionate and enthusiastic?

- **Be authentic and genuine:** People can spot insincerity a mile away. Be authentic in your interactions, be yourself, and focus on building genuine relationships.

Examples of Compelling Content for Businesses:

- **Industry Insights:** "The future of [Your Industry] is [Prediction]. Here are three trends to watch: [Tweet Thread] #[YourIndustry] #Trends #Futureof[YourIndustry]"

- **Helpful Tip:** "Struggling with [Common Problem]? Try this simple solution: [Tip/Advice] #[YourIndustry] #ProblemSolving #LifeHack"

- **Product Showcase:** "Our [Product Name] can help you to [Benefit]. See it in action here: [Link to Video] #[ProductName] #[YourIndustry] #Solution"

- **Contest:** "Retweet this tweet and follow us to enter to win a [Prize]! Winner will be announced on [Date]. #[Contest] #Giveaway #[YourBrand]"

- **Behind-the-Scenes Content:** "Meet our amazing team! [Photo of Team Members] We're passionate about [Your Mission] and dedicated to providing the best [Your Products/Services]. #[YourBrand] #CompanyCulture #Teamwork"

- **Curated Content:** "Interesting article from @[Publication] about the latest trends in [Your Industry]: [Link to Article] #[YourIndustry] #Trends #MustRead"

- **Poll:** "What's your biggest challenge in [Your Industry]? #Poll #[YourIndustry] #Challenges #Feedback"

Using Hashtags Effectively: Reaching Your Target Audience

Hashtags are essential for increasing the visibility of your tweets and connecting with a wider audience on Twitter. By using relevant hashtags, you can categorize your content, participate in conversations, and reach potential customers or clients who are interested in your industry or niche.

Tips for Using Hashtags Effectively:

- **Research relevant hashtags:** Use Twitter's search function to explore hashtags related to your industry, your products or services, and your target audience. Look for hashtags that are being used frequently, that have a high level of engagement, and that align with your brand's messaging.

- **Use a mix of general and specific hashtags:** General hashtags, such as #marketing or #technology, cast a wide net, while specific hashtags, such as #digitalmarketing or #artificialintelligence, target a more niche audience. Use a mix of general and specific hashtags to reach both a broad and a targeted audience.

- **Create a branded hashtag:** Develop a unique branded hashtag that you use consistently across all of your tweets and social media platforms. This will help to build brand awareness, track conversations about your brand, and encourage user-generated content.

- **Use campaign-specific hashtags:** If you're running a specific marketing campaign or promotion, create a unique hashtag for that campaign. This will help you to track engagement, measure the success of the campaign, and create a sense of community around the event.

- **Use event hashtags:** If you're attending or sponsoring a conference, trade show, or other event, use the event's official hashtag in your tweets to connect with other attendees and promote your presence at the event.

- **Monitor trending hashtags:** Keep an eye on trending hashtags that are relevant to your industry or niche. Participating in conversations around trending topics can help you to increase your visibility and reach a wider audience.

- **Don't overdo it:** Using too many hashtags can make your tweets look spammy and cluttered. Stick to a few relevant hashtags per tweet, ideally no more than three or four.

- **Use a hashtag tracking tool:** Several tools, such as Hashtagify.me or RiteTag, can help you to research hashtag popularity, track hashtag performance, and discover related hashtags.

Engaging with Your Followers: Building Relationships and Trust

Engaging with your followers on Twitter is crucial for building relationships, fostering loyalty, and turning casual followers into brand advocates. It's not enough to simply broadcast your message – you need to interact with your audience, respond to their comments, answer their questions, and create a sense of community around your brand.

Tips for Engaging with Your Followers:

- **Respond to comments and mentions:** Take the time to respond to comments and mentions from your followers, even if it's just a simple "thank you" or a quick answer. This shows that you're listening and that you value their engagement.

- **Ask questions and start conversations:** Don't just talk at your followers – engage them in conversations. Ask questions, solicit their opinions, and create opportunities for dialogue.

- **Use polls and quizzes:** Polls and quizzes are a fun and interactive way to engage your followers and gather insights into their interests and opinions.

- **Host Twitter chats:** Twitter chats are organized conversations around specific topics, providing a focused space to engage with your followers, answer their questions, and share your expertise.

- **Run contests and giveaways:** Contests and giveaways can generate excitement, increase engagement, and attract new followers.

- **Be authentic and relatable:** People are more likely to connect with you if they feel like they know you and can relate to your experiences. Share personal anecdotes, behind-the-scenes glimpses, and your own unique perspective.

- **Provide excellent customer service:** Use Twitter as a channel for providing excellent customer service. Respond to complaints promptly and professionally, offer solutions, and go the extra mile to resolve issues and make your customers happy.

- **Be a good listener:** Pay attention to what your followers are saying. Monitor your mentions, track relevant hashtags, and use social listening tools to gain insights into your audience's needs, interests, and concerns.

Running Twitter Contests and Giveaways: Boosting Engagement and Brand Awareness

Twitter contests and giveaways can be a fun and effective way to boost engagement, attract new followers, generate buzz around your brand, and even collect valuable user-generated content.

Tips for Running Successful Twitter Contests and Giveaways:

- **Set clear goals:** What do you want to achieve with your contest or giveaway? Are you trying to increase brand awareness, generate leads, collect user-generated content, or drive traffic to your website?

- **Choose a relevant prize:** The prize should be something that is relevant to your brand and that will appeal to your target audience. It could be a product or service you offer, a gift card, a discount code, or even an experience related to your brand.

- **Create simple and easy-to-follow rules:** Keep the rules of the contest or giveaway simple and easy to understand. Avoid complicated entry requirements that might deter people from participating.

- **Use a catchy hashtag:** Create a unique hashtag for your contest or giveaway to make it easy to track entries and to promote the event on Twitter.

- **Promote your contest or giveaway:** Spread the word about your contest or giveaway by tweeting about it regularly, using relevant hashtags, and promoting it on other social media platforms.

- **Choose a winner fairly:** Use a random selection process to choose a winner, ensuring that the contest or giveaway is fair and transparent.

- **Announce the winner publicly:** Announce the winner of the contest or giveaway on Twitter, tagging them in your tweet and congratulating them.

- **Follow up with the winner:** Contact the winner privately to arrange for prize delivery or fulfillment.

- **Track your results:** Use Twitter Analytics to track the performance of your contest or giveaway. Monitor the number of entries, the reach of your tweets, and the overall engagement generated by the event.

Examples of Twitter Contests and Giveaways:

- **Photo Contest:** "Share a photo of you using our [Product Name] with the hashtag #[ContestHashtag] for a chance to win a [Prize]! #Contest #Giveaway #[YourBrand]"

- **Caption Contest:** "Write a funny caption for this photo: [Link to Photo] and use the hashtag #[ContestHashtag] to enter to win a [Prize]! #[Contest] #CaptionContest #[YourBrand]"

- **Trivia Contest:** "Answer this trivia question correctly: [Trivia Question] and use the hashtag #[ContestHashtag] to enter to win a [Prize]! #[Contest] #Trivia #[YourBrand]"

- **Retweet to Win:** "Retweet this tweet and follow us to enter to win a [Prize]! #[Contest] #Giveaway #[YourBrand]"

Leveraging Twitter Ads: Reaching a Wider Audience

While organic reach on Twitter can be effective, Twitter's advertising platform provides a powerful way to reach a wider audience, target specific demographics or interests, and amplify your marketing message.

Types of Twitter Ads:

- **Promoted Tweets:** Promoted tweets are regular tweets that you pay to have displayed to a wider audience. They appear in users' timelines and search results, even if those users don't follow your account.

- **Promoted Accounts:** Promoted accounts are suggestions for accounts that users might want to follow. They appear in users' "Who to Follow" suggestions and in search results.

- **Promoted Trends:** Promoted trends are hashtags that you pay to have displayed in Twitter's trending topics list. This can significantly increase the visibility of your hashtag and generate buzz around a particular topic or campaign.

Tips for Using Twitter Ads Effectively:

- **Define your campaign goals:** What do you want to achieve with your Twitter ad campaign? Are you trying to increase brand awareness, generate leads, drive website traffic, or promote a specific product or service?

- **Target your audience:** Twitter's advertising platform allows you to target your ads based on a variety of criteria, including demographics, interests, behaviors, keywords, and even followers of specific accounts. Use this targeting capability to ensure that your ads are reaching the right people.

- **Create compelling ad copy:** Your ad copy should be concise, attention-grabbing, and relevant to your target audience. Highlight the key benefits of your product or service, use a strong call to action, and incorporate relevant hashtags.

- **Use high-quality visuals:** Visuals are crucial for grabbing attention on Twitter. Use high-quality images or videos that are relevant to your ad copy and that will appeal to your target audience.

- **Set a budget and track your results:** Determine your advertising budget and use Twitter Analytics to track the performance of your ads. Monitor your impressions, clicks, conversions, and other relevant metrics to measure the success of your campaign and make adjustments as needed.

Measuring Your Success: Tracking Your Twitter Marketing Results

Tracking your results is essential for any successful Twitter marketing strategy. By monitoring your key performance indicators (KPIs), you can measure the effectiveness of your efforts, identify areas for improvement, and make data-driven decisions to optimize your approach.

Key Metrics to Track:

- **Follower Growth:** Track the number of new followers you're gaining over time. A steady increase in followers indicates that your content is resonating with your target audience and that your brand is gaining traction.

- **Engagement Rate:** Engagement rate measures the percentage of users who interact with your tweets (likes, retweets, replies, clicks, etc.) out of the total number of impressions. A higher engagement rate suggests that your content is engaging and that your audience is finding value in what you're sharing.

- **Website Traffic:** If you're using Twitter to drive traffic to your website, use analytics tools like Google Analytics to track the number of visitors coming from Twitter.

- **Lead Generation:** If you're using Twitter to generate leads, track the number of sign-ups, inquiries, or other conversions that result from your Twitter marketing efforts.

- **Sales:** If you're selling products or services directly on Twitter or through your website, track the number of sales that can be attributed to your Twitter marketing efforts.

- **Brand Sentiment:** Monitor the overall sentiment towards your brand on Twitter. Use social listening tools to track mentions of your brand, identify positive and negative feedback, and address any issues or concerns that arise.

Twitter Marketing Tools: Enhancing Your Efforts

A variety of tools can help you to streamline your Twitter marketing efforts, from scheduling tweets and managing your followers to tracking your performance and analyzing your results.

Popular Twitter Marketing Tools:

- **TweetDeck:** TweetDeck is a free tool from Twitter that allows you to manage multiple Twitter accounts, schedule tweets, track hashtags, and monitor your mentions.

- **Hootsuite:** Hootsuite is a social media management platform that allows you to schedule tweets, track your performance, and manage multiple social media accounts from a single dashboard.

- **Buffer:** Buffer is a social media scheduling tool that allows you to plan and schedule your tweets in advance, ensuring that you're consistently posting content even when you're busy.

- **Sprout Social:** Sprout Social is a comprehensive social media management platform that offers a wide range of features, including social listening, analytics, engagement tools, and reporting.

- **BuzzSumo:** BuzzSumo is a content marketing tool that allows you to research popular content, identify influencers, and track your brand mentions on social media.

Twitter Marketing Best Practices: Tweeting for Success

Here are a few general best practices to keep in mind as you develop your Twitter marketing strategy:

- **Be consistent:** Consistency is key to building a strong and engaged following on Twitter. Tweet regularly, even if it's just a few times a day, to stay top of mind with your followers.

- **Be patient:** Building a successful Twitter marketing strategy takes time and effort. Don't expect to see results overnight. Be patient, experiment with different approaches, and learn from your experiences.

- **Be creative:** Don't be afraid to experiment with different content formats, try new strategies, and find creative ways to engage your audience.

- **Be authentic:** People are more likely to connect with a brand that feels genuine and authentic. Be yourself, share your passions, and let your brand's personality shine through in your tweets.

- **Be helpful:** Provide value to your followers by sharing helpful tips, advice, resources, or insights that can improve their lives or their businesses.

- **Be engaging:** Don't just broadcast your message – engage with your followers, respond to their comments, answer their questions, and create a sense of community around your brand.

- **Be analytical:** Use Twitter Analytics and other tracking tools to monitor your performance, identify what's working, and make data-driven decisions to optimize your strategy.

- **Be adaptable:** The social media landscape is constantly changing, and what works today might not work tomorrow. Be adaptable, experiment with new approaches, and stay informed about the latest trends and best practices.

Twitter Marketing Trends: Staying Ahead of the Curve

The world of social media is constantly evolving, and Twitter is no exception. To stay ahead of the curve and ensure that your Twitter marketing efforts are effective, it's important to stay informed about the latest trends and innovations.

Current Twitter Marketing Trends:

- **Short-Form Video:** Short-form video content, such as TikTok-style videos or Instagram Reels, is becoming increasingly popular on Twitter. Experiment with creating engaging video content to capture attention and tell your brand's story in a more visually compelling way.

- **Live Audio:** Twitter Spaces, Twitter's live audio feature, provides a new way to connect with your audience in real time, host discussions, answer questions, and build community.

- **Community Building:** Twitter is placing a greater emphasis on building communities around shared interests. Consider creating or joining Twitter Communities that align with your brand's target audience to engage with potential customers and foster a sense of belonging.

- **Social Commerce:** Twitter is making it easier for businesses to sell products or services directly on the platform. Explore Twitter's shopping features and consider integrating them into your marketing strategy.

- **Personalization:** Personalization is becoming increasingly important in marketing. Use Twitter's targeting capabilities to create more personalized experiences for your followers and to deliver the right message to the right people at the right time.

- **Data-Driven Decision-Making:** Twitter Analytics provides a wealth of data that can help you to make data-driven decisions about your marketing strategy. Use this data to track your performance, identify what's working, and optimize your approach for maximum impact.

By staying informed about the latest trends and innovations, experimenting with new approaches, and adapting your strategy to the evolving landscape of Twitter, you can ensure that your Twitter marketing efforts are effective and that your brand stays ahead of the curve.

CHAPTER TWENTY-FIVE: The Future of Twitter (or X)

Predicting the future is a fool's errand, especially when it comes to the ever-shifting landscape of social media. Remember MySpace? Friendster? Vine? Platforms rise and fall, trends come and go, and the next big thing is always lurking around the corner, ready to disrupt the status quo.

Twitter, or X as it's been rebranded, has already undergone significant transformations since its inception in 2006. From the introduction of the retweet button and the expansion from 140 to 280 characters to the rise of live video and the integration of audio spaces, the platform has continuously evolved to adapt to changing user behaviors and technological advancements.

As we peer into the crystal ball of social media, it's impossible to say with certainty what the future holds for Twitter/X. But by analyzing current trends, emerging technologies, and the platform's own stated ambitions, we can make some educated guesses about the potential directions it might take in the coming years.

The Elon Musk Effect: A New Vision for X?

Elon Musk's acquisition of Twitter in late 2022 sent shockwaves through the tech world and the social media landscape. Musk, a self-proclaimed "free speech absolutist," has expressed a vision for Twitter/X that is significantly different from its previous incarnation. He envisions a platform that prioritizes free speech, reduces censorship, and embraces decentralized technologies like blockchain.

Musk's vision for X includes:

- **Reduced Content Moderation:** Musk has criticized Twitter's previous content moderation policies, arguing that they stifle free speech and unfairly target conservative voices. He has suggested that X will adopt a more hands-off approach to content moderation, allowing a wider range of viewpoints to be expressed, even if they are controversial or offensive.

- **Decentralized Technology:** Musk has expressed interest in incorporating decentralized technologies, such as blockchain, into X. This could potentially give users more control over their data and content, and make the platform more resistant to censorship or manipulation.

- **Integration with Other Services:** Musk has suggested that X could become an "everything app," integrating a wide range of services, such as payments, messaging, and even ride-hailing, into a single platform. This would create a more comprehensive and interconnected digital ecosystem.

- **Focus on Creators:** Musk has emphasized the importance of supporting creators on X. He has suggested that the platform will offer new tools and features to help creators monetize their content and build a loyal following.

However, Musk's vision for X has also faced criticism and skepticism. Some argue that reducing content moderation will lead to a rise in hate speech, misinformation, and other forms of harmful content. Others question the feasibility of integrating decentralized technologies into a platform with such a large and diverse user base.

Only time will tell how Musk's vision for X will unfold and what impact his leadership will have on the platform's future.

The Rise of Short-Form Video: TikTok-ifying X?

Short-form video content, popularized by platforms like TikTok and Instagram Reels, has taken the social media world by storm. These bite-sized, highly engaging videos are designed to capture attention, entertain, and often go viral, spreading rapidly through social networks.

Twitter/X has already begun to embrace short-form video, integrating features like looping videos and allowing users to easily share videos from other platforms. It's likely that this trend will continue, with X potentially becoming more video-centric, offering new tools and features for creating, sharing, and discovering short-form video content.

Potential Features for Short-Form Video on X:

- **Enhanced Video Editing Tools:** X could offer more robust video editing tools, allowing users to create more polished and professional-looking videos directly within the app.

- **Video Filters and Effects:** X could introduce a library of video filters and effects, similar to those found on TikTok and Instagram, to make videos more visually engaging and creative.

- **Video Monetization Options:** X could offer new ways for creators to monetize their video content, such as through advertising revenue sharing, tipping features, or subscription models.

- **Dedicated Video Feed:** X could create a dedicated video feed, similar to TikTok's "For You" page, that curates and recommends videos based on user interests and engagement patterns.

The Power of Live Audio: Spaces as a Community Builder

Twitter Spaces, X's live audio feature, launched in late 2020, allows users to host and participate in real-time audio conversations. Spaces provide a new way to connect with followers, share ideas, host discussions, and build community on the platform.

While Spaces are still a relatively new feature, they have the potential to become a significant part of X's future, especially as audio content continues to gain popularity in the form of podcasts, audiobooks, and voice assistants.

Potential Developments for Twitter Spaces:

- **Enhanced Moderation Tools:** X could provide more robust moderation tools for Spaces hosts, allowing them to better control the conversation, mute or remove disruptive participants, and create a more positive and productive environment.

- **Recording and Archiving:** X could allow users to record and archive their Spaces, making them available for later listening or downloading. This would provide a way to create evergreen content and to reach a wider audience who might not have been able to participate in the live event.

- **Monetization Options:** X could offer ways for Spaces hosts to monetize their audio content, such as through ticket sales, subscriptions, or sponsorship opportunities.

- **Integration with Other Features:** Spaces could be integrated with other X features, such as polls, Q&A sessions, or even live video, creating a more interactive and engaging experience.

The Everything App: Integrating Services and Expanding Functionality

Elon Musk has expressed a vision for X to become an "everything app," a comprehensive digital platform that integrates a wide range of services and functionalities, going beyond the traditional realm of social media.

Potential Services and Functionalities:

- **Payments and Financial Services:** X could integrate payment processing capabilities, allowing users to send and receive money, make purchases, and even invest directly within the app. This could potentially disrupt traditional financial institutions and create a more seamless and accessible financial ecosystem.

- **E-Commerce and Shopping:** X could expand its existing shopping features, allowing businesses to showcase their products or services, process orders, and manage customer interactions directly within the platform. This could create a more integrated and streamlined shopping experience.

- **Messaging and Communication:** X could enhance its direct messaging capabilities, offering features like encrypted messaging, group chats, and even voice or video calls. This could potentially compete with existing messaging apps like WhatsApp or Telegram.

- **News and Information:** X could curate and aggregate news content from reputable sources, providing users with a personalized news feed based on their interests and preferences. This could potentially challenge traditional news outlets and create a more decentralized news ecosystem.

- **Entertainment and Gaming:** X could integrate streaming services for music, movies, and TV shows, as well as gaming platforms, creating a one-stop shop for entertainment.

- **Travel and Transportation:** X could integrate ride-hailing services, travel booking platforms, and other transportation-related functionalities, creating a more seamless travel experience.

While the concept of an "everything app" is ambitious and faces numerous technical, regulatory, and logistical challenges, it's a vision that aligns with the growing trend towards super-apps, particularly in Asia, where platforms like WeChat and Alipay have already achieved significant success in integrating a wide range of services into a single app.

Decentralization and Blockchain: A New Paradigm for Social Media?

Elon Musk has expressed interest in incorporating decentralized technologies, such as blockchain, into X. Blockchain, the technology underlying cryptocurrencies like Bitcoin, is a distributed ledger that records transactions in a secure and transparent way, making it resistant to censorship or manipulation.

Integrating blockchain into X could potentially:

- **Give users more control over their data:** Blockchain technology could allow users to own and control their data, rather than having it controlled by a centralized platform.

- **Reduce censorship:** A decentralized platform would be more difficult to censor, as there would be no single entity that could control the flow of information.

- **Create new monetization opportunities:** Blockchain technology could enable new monetization models for creators, such as tokenized rewards, micropayments, or decentralized marketplaces for digital content.

- **Enhance security and transparency:** Blockchain's secure and transparent nature could enhance the security of X and make it more resistant to hacking or data breaches.

However, integrating blockchain into X also presents significant challenges:

- **Scalability:** Blockchain technology can be slow and expensive to scale to a platform with millions of users.

- **User experience:** Using blockchain technology often requires technical knowledge and specialized tools, which could create a barrier to entry for mainstream users.

- **Regulatory uncertainty:** The regulatory landscape around blockchain technology is still evolving, and there are legal and compliance issues that would need to be addressed.

The Future of Tweeting: How X Might Change Our Communication

If X evolves in the directions outlined above, it could significantly impact the way we communicate and interact on the platform. Here are a few potential shifts:

- **From Text to Multimedia:** X could become less text-centric and more multimedia-focused, with a greater emphasis on short-form video, live audio, and interactive content.

- **From Broadcasting to Community:** X could shift from a platform primarily for broadcasting information to a platform that prioritizes community building, fostering connections, and facilitating discussions.

- **From Centralized to Decentralized:** X could move towards a more decentralized model, giving users more control over their data and content, and making the platform more resistant to censorship.

- **From Social Network to Super-App:** X could evolve from a social network into a more comprehensive "everything app," integrating a wide range of services and functionalities into a single platform.

The Uncertain Future: Challenges and Opportunities

The future of Twitter/X is uncertain, and the platform faces numerous challenges:

- **Competition:** X faces stiff competition from other social media platforms, such as TikTok, Instagram, Facebook, and YouTube, all of which are constantly evolving and innovating.

- **Misinformation and Disinformation:** X, like all social media platforms, struggles to combat the spread of misinformation and disinformation. Finding the right balance between free speech and responsible content moderation will continue to be a challenge.

- **Privacy and Security:** Protecting user data and privacy is a major concern for all social media platforms. X will need to address these concerns as it evolves and integrates new features and services.

- **Monetization:** Finding sustainable monetization models that both support creators and satisfy users is an ongoing challenge for social media platforms.

Despite these challenges, X also has significant opportunities:

- **Innovation:** X has a history of innovation and adaptation. By embracing emerging technologies, developing new features, and listening to user feedback, X can continue to evolve and stay ahead of the curve.

- **Community:** X has a large and passionate user base. By fostering a sense of community, creating engaging experiences, and providing valuable services, X can strengthen its position as a leading social media platform.

- **Global Reach:** X has a global reach, connecting people from all over the world. This global reach provides opportunities to build bridges, promote cross-cultural understanding, and address global issues.

A Platform in Transition: The Road Ahead

Twitter/X is a platform in transition. As it navigates the challenges and opportunities ahead, it's likely to undergo significant transformations, both in its technology and in its role in society. Whether it becomes a decentralized, blockchain-powered social network, an "everything app" that integrates a wide range of services, or a more video-centric platform that embraces the trends of the future, one thing is certain: Twitter/X will continue to be a dynamic and influential force in the ever-evolving world of social media.

As users, we have the power to shape the future of X by engaging in thoughtful conversations, demanding responsible practices, and supporting creators and communities that align with our values. The future of Twitter/X is not predetermined – it's a collaborative effort, and we all have a role to play in shaping its destiny.